This book is dedicated to my loving mother, Patricia Ann Forrest, who with her wonderful support has contributed to so many of my successes. I also thank W. Andrea Ziarno my editor, business partner, and friend for taking the time to edit this edition of The Meaning of Life. Enjoy the read and the powerful Truths that are shared in my book.

Contact information for ITZA Global Books–
www.itza.global

ISBN: 978-1-8384217-0-0 (print)
ISBN: 978-1-8384217-1-7 (ebook)

Ordering Information:
Special discounts are available on quantity purchases by
corporations, associations, and others. For details, contact
through www.itza.global.

The
MEANING
OF
LIFE

When the black dog is
barking up the right tree

M. H. FORREST

TO HEROES PAST AND PRESENT
WHO WERE BITTEN BY THE "BLACK DOG:"

(A non-exhaustive list which is a fraction of the famous who are/ were "bitten" and does not extend to the billions of equally precious souls who have not attained notoriety.)

GEORGE MICHAEL

ALAN TURING

CHARLES DARWIN

STEPHEN FRY

ROBIN WILLIAMS

ISAAC NEWTON

JIM CARREY

ELLEN DEGENERES

JOHNNY DEPP

EMINEM

HARRISON FORD

JOSEPH GORDON-LEVITT

ANNE HATHAWAY

ANGELINA JOLIE-PITT

LADY GAGA

HUGH LAURIE

GWYNETH PALTROW

DOLLY PARTON

MATTHEW PERRY

MICHAEL PHELPS

BRAD PITT

J. K. ROWLING

BROOKE SHIELDS

BRITNEY SPEARS

CHANNING TATUM

EMMA THOMPSON

OWEN WILSON

REESE WITHERSPOON

PRINCESS DIANA

ANDREW KOENIG

WINONA RYDER

ALEC BALDWIN

CHRISTIAN BALE

HALLE BERRY

MARILYN MONROE

SIR ANTHONY HOPKINS

BEYONCE

JANET JACKSON

BOB DYLAN

BILL HICKS

AVICII

CHARLES DICKENS

DEADMAU5

JOHNNY CASH

RAY CHARLES

CHEVVY CHASE

HEATH LEDGER

BILL MURRAY

JOHN LENNON

KYLIE MINOGUE

MOBY

LIL CHRIS

EWAN MCGREGOR

MICHAEL JACKSON

JULIAN ASSANGE

DAVID ARQUETTE

HANS CHRISTIAN AN-DERSEN

WINSTON CHURCHILL

ABRAHAM LINCOLN

ALAN ALDA

BUZZ ALDRIN

MICHELANGELO

SIDDHARTHA GAUTA-MA (BUDDHA)

SIGMUND FREUD

KANYE WEST

VINCENT VAN GOGH

UMA THURMAN

ROBBIE WILLIAMS

FRANK SINATRA

OPRAH WINFREY

ROBERT OPPENHEIMER

WOLFGANG AMADEUS
MOZART

FRIEDRICH NIETZSCHE

VIRGINIA WOOLF

LEO TOLSTOY

BRUCE SPRINGSTEEN

STING

DAVID WALLIAMS

BERTRAND RUSSELL

MARK TWAIN

MIKE TYSON

RUBY WAX

KATHRINE ZETA JONES

RONNIE O'SULLIVAN

JOHN D. ROCKEFELLER

MOTHER TERESA

The AUDIOBOOK edition begins with an excerpt
from the ITZA Global Records music

ITZA Stairway to Heaven

to enjoy the official video go to "ITZA Stairway" on YouTube
or go to: https://youtu.be/3xGfrJNyn3w

CONTENTS

FOREWORD

"I'm pleased to know Matthew as a friend and watched him operate around the globe as a successful entrepreneur and visionary. Having spent my entire career in the medical profession, it's both fun and refreshing to read a book that takes a radical stand against what is viewed as conventional wisdom. I couldn't put the book down from the first page. It has given me hours of material to reflect upon. What is unique about the book is that from beginning to end it is written in the language of logic. It is a religion-less book which means that those with a science-based background do not need to take a leap of faith. The messages are communicated clearly. I couldn't resist sending prepublication copies to my inner circle of friends and colleagues with Matthew's permission."

Dr. A. Singh, MRCGP

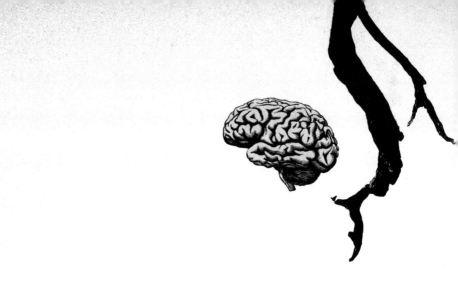

1

INTRODUCTION

"Do not believe in anything simply because you have heard it. Do not believe in anything simply because it is spoken and rumoured by many. Do not believe in anything simply because it is found written in your religious books. Do not believe in anything merely on the authority of your teachers and elders. Do not believe in traditions because they have been handed down for many generations. But after observation and analysis, when you find that anything agrees with reason and is conducive to the good and benefit of one and all, then accept it and live up to it."

Hindu Prince Gautama Siddhartha,

the founder of Buddhism, 563–483 B.C.

Although this book contains elements of self-help manuals, it is more an exploration of the human mind, our mental as well as perceived physical reality and, to a lesser extent, mood disorders and what their accounts and observations disclose of the nature of human experience. Yet, primarily, this book is much more than just a means to help improve our understandings and/or our (potentially) innate awareness of our ability to achieve absolutely anything: As it is a T.O.E. (theory of everything). A wise prophet once said that the truth shall set you free and in consideration of their telling—a full understanding of reality may be recognized as synonymous to the end of all suffering.

Often it is said, "You only miss things once they are gone," but it really does not take a great deal of imagination to get a sense of that potential future reality before actually experiencing it. This is one clear benefit of the modern mind—that of its ability to simulate potential future realities, albeit with some relative flaws as discussed throughout the book. However, with mood disorders I do not think this is the case, as only those who experience them can understand how profound their feelings really are. They impact their experience of reality in ways that are practically impossible to relate to unless you have also suffered such a condition.

It does not help that the term depression denotes sadness as well as the profound emotional state and disease. To say they differ in the way the common cold and influenza do is a gross understatement. This is a serious and growing epidemic and is now the number one cause of disability in the world. It deserves our full attention.

I will make an argument that, although there are certain distortions of perception caused by depression, it can actually also provide 20/20 vision, illuminate inconvenient truths, as well as reveal deeper perspectives of reality that ultimately point us towards answering the age-old questions about the meaning of life. I think the implications are even more far-reaching than the incomplete theory proposed by Charles Darwin that we are mere naked apes descended from basic creatures via the evolutionary process. The discussion is based on science and logic, so although a past or present experience of depression may be required in order for someone to "feel" that the content being presented in this book is true when it comes to mood disorders and what they tell us about meaning, an empathic non-sufferer could still nonetheless see and understand these perspectives of experience through personal reflection and/or by reflecting upon the information as it is presented.

Again, this is far more than a book on mood disorders. However, it is often disease and malfunction that leads us to greater understandings of anatomy and physiology; as mood disorders are a deviation from the norm, they should encourage us to peer deeper into the sense of meaning that most take for granted. As mood is inextricably linked with a sense of meaning, a disorder presents to us the opportunity to explore what a state of meaninglessness can infer to us about the nature of meaning. An exploration of mood disorder is, therefore, critical but humans' sense of meaning is only a part of the overall meaning of life picture, while this book covers a multitude of other relevant subjects. When people ask, *"What is the meaning of life?"* there are at least three things they could be asking: "What is the purpose of life from a scientific perspective?" "What is this experience we label as meaning that is unique to humans and, perhaps, to a lesser extent, experienced by other higher life forms?" and "What is the ultimate cause for everything? Why is there something as opposed to nothing, as well as so much order?" The book addresses all of these questions.

The "Black Dog" refers to depression and is the term one of its "bite victims," Sir Winston Churchill, used to describe it. The phrase, "When the Black Dog Is Barking Up the Right Tree," is a deliberate twist on the common phrase *"a dog barking up the wrong tree"* (i.e. wasting time pursuing a wrong assumption; the cat ran up a different tree). The tree, in this instance, refers to the "tree of life," although it is purposefully illustrated sprouting from mind/consciousness rather than soil. The Black Dog is deemed to be barking up the right rather than the wrong tree because depression can lead to insights that tend to cruise under the radar of most people who are fully focused on the process of living. On the one hand, the condition removes the rose-coloured spectacles worn by those totally engrossed in the minutiae of what goes on in "the bubble" and thus can provide a clearer picture by providing a detached perspective. On the other hand, an encounter with meaninglessness, that often accompanies the condition of depression, can grant experiential evidence that may reveal to us—by contrasting evidence and lessons learned through experience, what meaning actually is, how it arises, and from where it originates.

Some of the contents of this book are highly emotive and will likely clash with your belief system. As parts of it are a journey into existential angst, it is not entirely recommended for those who are faint of heart. Ignorance can be bliss, and maybe those who are pretty fulfilled most of the time should steer clear of the rabbit hole. Conversely, Socrates expressed his view that: *"The unexamined life is not worth living."* And besides, although there will be darker aspects of reality that you almost certainly will not have considered until you have read the book, there are revelations concerning scientifically proven "magic," which I believe are also key in understanding the meaning of life in its broader sense. Furthermore, this journey will present to you the information necessary—to realise that the true nature of reality differs from our instinctive perception of it by an unimaginable degree and shall provide insight(s) into the ultimate cause(s) that mainstream science currently regard as either speculation, or delusion.

Parts of my worldview may differ from yours, but the possibility of slight deviations from the truth would not alter the overall paradigm shift that is being presented. It should be noted that there are many highly qualified academics, who have dedicated much of their lives to the matters discussed in this book, that have rigorously defined certain conclusions that concur with my own ponderings, and that, accordingly, serve as a reality check. Although countless hours of deep thought were needed to assemble the jigsaw puzzle of what I have evidenced as being the meaning of life, I am not claiming to have special knowledge or skills—but to have merely collated the thoughts of many past and present giants in science and philosophy in order to decode base reality.

Hopefully, sound logic and strong empirical evidence (i.e., Buddha's: *"...But after observation and analysis, when you find that anything agrees with reason..."*) can counter the human predisposition towards confirmation bias (filtering evidence so that only information which fits one's worldview is permitted a place in the mind). I think that even the most reputed scientists are often guilty of this.

For example, Professor Richard Dawkins mistakenly believes that all roads lead to Darwin. There is no doubt that Darwin had identified a pattern that only a small percentage of people would have noticed through the evidence he had collected, including the fact that selective breeding, at the time, was demonstrating the genetic plasticity of living entities. However, for Dawkins to assert that the potentiality for reality, space-time, life, and the total driving forces yielding the process(es) of evolution itself, etc. can all be explained by reductionism, is nothing more than a belief. There is no credible scientific explanation for the emergence of these arbitrary phenomena. In fact, there is evidence to suggest that Dawkins' atheistic worldview is incorrect, and that a belief in methodological naturalism as a fundamental truth has prevented him and any other atheist scientist or philosopher to understand ultimate cause.

In other words, despite this non-exhaustive list of potentialities being the miracle of all possible miracles, they are simply accepted as axiomatic. The existence of such potentialities encoded into the "laws" of nature do not reveal anything about their ultimate cause and neither do the manifestations of such potentialities. Atheists' worldview is that nature/reality exists because *"it just does"* (along with all potentialities which are now manifest) and refer to any objections to this absurd position as, *"Looking for God in the gaps."*

However, whether the anthropic principle(s) discussed later in the book are applied or not, there exists still a miracle at the root of our reality. Even if you assume that it has all come about without Divine Intervention or Universal Consciousness, the ultimate cause of reality and all its inherent potentialities being chance or an inevitability would effectively be a miracle. After all, this fits the definition of miracles: Things that do not conform to our perceived cause-and-effect reality. Also, if it was inevitable, rather than chance, this would mean the apparent randomness observed is actually pseudo-randomness because inevitability by chance is an oxymoron unless every possibility can be played out in alternate universes. And even this infinite physical universes explanation would still leave unanswered questions about the origin of the arbitrary laws of nature, energy and matter, etc. as well as the origin of the multiverse. Contrary to the assertions of mainstream scientists, the "infinite universes" world-view also fails to properly address the issue(s) concerning apparent randomness appearing as pseudo-randomness, as there would have to be a mechanism that directs the allocation of the infinite possibilities into each and every universe. This allocation may be seen as random from an observer's perspective, but what determines which of each universe gets its version of the infinite possibilities? And what mechanism is there to assure the "rule" is never broken? It is always assumed that true randomness just exists and that there is no need for an explanation regarding its ultimate cause and, yet, there is, paradoxically, high order in terms of how it works. There is a distinction between apparent randomness in events within space-time, such as tossing coins and the seemingly true randomness witnessed in quantum mechanics, and it is the latter form that I am referring to here. A more detailed explanation of the difference appears later in the book because it is highly relevant to how our universe has evolved as it has. For now, I will say that the word intent is more than a clue.

The reason that all phenomena have been depicted and categorized as seen through the looking glass by most scientists and non-scientists alike is because of how pattern recognition has been mistaken for true understanding. There is significant difference in observing a process unfold and/or of identifying its patterns/order and of knowing why that system and order should even arise in reality in the first place (and/or of why the theatre that is reality should exist, let alone play out its inherent potentialities). The process of evolution itself, for example, is not so difficult to follow. The miracle lies in the potentiality for such a process. Einstein said, *"The most incomprehensible thing about the universe is that it is comprehensible,"* but I think that from a scientific viewpoint, the whole of existence is incomprehensible also, as are the potentialities that manifest as comprehensible phenomena. Reductionism has served science well and is, no doubt, a useful method. However, it is nothing short of a display of hubris to believe that the gaping holes will all be filled via the same method. This belief is known as scientism and, like all fundamentalism, it treats partial truths as though they were the total truth.

Despite the shortcomings of science, the book is not about religion, although religion and spirituality are relevant and receive more than a passing mention. Much of the meaning of life can be discussed without reference to a potential spiritual element or the mysteries surrounding the origin of reality and life. However, whether atheist scientists like it or not, this "rabbit out of the hat" reality from nowhere and the origins of the arbitrary, comprehensible, laws of nature are currently and will always be beyond materialist-based science. As scientism faces an attack from which it shall never recover, there is mounting evidence to suggest that everything is ultimately consciousness emerging from a timeless and spaceless realm.

A spiritual dimension is not easily provable, although there are many reasons to believe that it does exist, that do not require a blind leap of faith of the kind Buddha cautioned against. Spirituality is discussed near the end of the book, for the benefit of those with an open mind. For the most part, this book is intended for believers and atheists alike, because it focuses primarily (although not exclusively) on the processes that are consequences of the potentialities inherent to nature itself, rather than of how these potentialities came into being.

Of course, there is a possibility we are living in a simulated universe and that all is contrived—but the exploration of the true base reality, whatever that is, would lead to a similar discussion on spirituality anyway. Who or what created the base reality and the simulation programmers? Given that we experience certain things as profound as pleasure and pain, and do so as actual sensations rather than as mere measurements taken from some kind of instrument, it would not matter so much even if this were a simulation. The difference between us being authentic entities or simulated ones are indistinguishable from our perspective. In other words, we are real in some sense, even if our reality is a constructed simulation.

I believe people are hyper-normalized, taking all commonly experienced phenomena for granted. The term hyper-normalized is based on the BBC documentary title, *HyperNormalisation*, made by British filmmaker, Adam Curtis. The documentary argues that governments, financiers, and technological utopians have, since the 1970s, given up on the complex *"real world"* and built a simpler *"fake world"* run by corporations and kept stable by politicians. My use of the word hyper-normalization is much broader and refers to the fact that everyone is born into a world with arbitrary phenomena that quickly become all too familiar because, due to the preexistence of these phenomena, how to engage with them is all that matters. How things came to be as they are is rarely questioned by most people. Einstein said, *"There are only two ways to live your life: as though nothing is a miracle, or as though everything is a miracle."* Due to the impact of hyper-normalization and the human ability to recognize patterns and adapt to our environments, many people think that what they encounter in their daily lives is nothing extraordinary. A belief held by most scientists, that all the order we witness in reality comes about through self-creation, as does the universe itself and everything therein, strengthens this common worldview.

Hyper-normalization is as prevalent within the scientific community as it is within the population as a whole. Scientists are generally all too willing to accept countless axioms as non-metaphysical and this is closely related to the belief that reductionism will, ultimately, reveal all of nature's secrets, which was mentioned earlier. When we look to science to explain ultimate causes, it becomes clear that science has no answers. Is science merely observing and attempting to explain that which is an illusion operating by certain principles in this reality?

A simple example of hyper-normalization is to consider how a child learns about the effects of gravity. The child can see a kind of pulling force in action but, of course, the way in which gravity actually works is far more profound. Newton "created" a mathematical frame-work that allowed for a good approximation, then Einstein viewed it as the bending of space-time and brought us a more accurate, and in depth, account of gravity. But how it actually works and came to be is still not understood by practitioners in mainstream science, though it is explained in my theory of everything (T.O.E). Most simply accept all that is and busy themselves within the constructed "bubble"—little different from animals that simply act in accordance with the way evolution programmed them. Understanding reality at its deepest level does not significantly affect mortality, happiness, or genetic fitness, which is discussed later in this book. Accordingly, the main incentive to philosophise lies within our capacity to do so—thanks to our evolved intelligence and creative thinking combined with a sense of curiosity that we all have, and express, to varying degrees.

Hyper-normalization, however, is not limited to an incomplete understanding and, often, unquestioned acceptance of external phenomena. But also includes how our own thoughts and behaviours work, as well. Even our senses do not work in the way that our experience of them would have us believe, in the absence of some deep thinking and experimentation. For example, when you look at a red rose—you are actually seeing the map and not the territory. Although the eyes (sensory organs) can distinguish the relevant wavelengths of light coming into them, the brain is closed off in the dark. It is the electrochemical impulses received in the brain that, in turn, provoke specific regions of the brain to "manufacture" the red you "see" through your mind's eye.

In other words, the perception/experience of colour is formed by consciousness and is effectively a form of imagination (although different wavelengths form different mind-created colours because the resulting electrical impulses vary depending on the wavelengths, and this informs the mind what colours to add into the picture/mind projection). This is doubtlessly quite a profound realisation for the majority of people. Most see a red rose and wrongly assume that red is a characteristic of the petals, as well as a phenomenon that exists "out there" in our so-called physical reality. In other words, they naively believe they "see" a kind of photographic facsimile that is indistinguishable from the true "out there" phenomena. The illusion is so strong that some doubtlessly believe that eyes simply receive direct/unpolluted information, which would mean no further phenomena play any role in relation to the activity including the brain or, ultimately, the mind.

The colours are—"paradoxically"—made real because our mind and consciousness create that reality through the processing of "simulated" waveforms, yet the colours themselves are rather illusory by phenomenological definition. In other words, without a conscious observer there to convert wavelengths into the waveforms that we experience as colour, there would be no such phenomenon—at least not in the apparent physical material realm. The whole of what you see is, in fact, a virtualized reality, simultaneously reflecting and maintaining the accuracy of each of its locally distinct features in total unison. The fact you can see distant skies and stars (a huge depth of field that is projected by consciousness in such a way it is perceived way in front of the skull) has led some to postulate that it is not simply a recreation in the mind but that the mind projects out to what is seen. In short, there exists a two-way interaction between observer and the observed, whether it is animate or inanimate.

It is theorized that our consciousness weakly interacts with matter, while simultaneously feeding information back to us that is processed from within our respective conscious domain(s). Even if this relatively controversial hypothesis turns out to be wrong and the process is strictly one-way (the mind creates our virtual reality in such a way that it just appears to be re-projecting beyond our skulls onto corresponding "objects" within reality itself), reality itself is likely still a *"virtualized"* reality. At the very least because, as mentioned earlier, no photons/light get into the brain from the external environment, as it is an "individualized" and closed-circuit unit. It will be shown throughout the book that this hypothesis is not really controversial after all. And, in fact, does not go far enough. Because the perception of separation is illusory itself, as the observer resides in a singularity with everyTHING else, they are not only interconnected but ultimately One.

This is correspondingly true of all senses even. The smell of bananas, for example, is derived from the molecules of the banana itself, yet, the final scent creation that is recognized as "a banana" may also be recognized as a naturally "simulative" construct of the mind and consciousness based from upon and throughout the stimulation of certain areas of the brain that, in turn, creates the sensation/experience we label as smell. The molecules themselves do not enter the brain but a process almost certainly involving quantum mechanics, as well as a molecular lock and key type mechanism that translates that chemical/molecular information into a sensation within the conscious experience, is adopted. All smells are "invented" and kind of arbitrary although, as with all sensory experiences, I believe they are fundamental given their specific nature and overarching ubiquity.

Your blue may differ from my blue to some degree because of slight variations in the anatomy and physiology of the eyes and brain, and even things that affect perception such as mood or limitations created by language (some languages offer a broader set of colour descriptions and this can mean more shades are experienced). But we certainly still share a genuine visual experience of colour that is formed by colourless light waves of certain wavelengths—a creation that, for all intents and purposes, cannot be considered an ordinary phenomenon of our material realm. Unsurprisingly, evolution has led to some smells being accompanied by emotional reactions (to assure attraction or repulsion), e.g., rotting food is automatically experienced as a "*bad*" smell.

This kind of revelation is consistent throughout the book and is why I believe it is a novel take on the meaning of life. The conclusions are a mixture of good and bad news. On one hand, life is finite and meaning appears to be a human construct made real by consciousness. On the other hand, knowing what we really are and what the big picture looks like does greatly enhance our potential and motivation to take meaningful action that can enhance our experience(s) of life while we still exist within this hard to decode reality. For example, knowing about landmines, such as *"impact bias,"* *"focus illusion,"* *"freedom to choose"* (that are also discussed in this book) can help to enhance happiness and fulfilment similarly to how knowing ways to alleviate mood disorders, until future cures arise, can help mitigate suffering. The power of intent and subsequent action has been wholly underestimated by mankind and a deep understanding of how this works is not only life changing it is paradigm shifting.

Although depression is a disease, unlike anorexia, the sufferer is not always fully captivated. With anorexia, there is a huge amount of evidence demonstrating one's underlying psychological delusion: Belt size has shrunk, the mirror shows unhealthy thinness, friends and medical experts assure the anorexic that there is a problem, the weighing scales provide information which shows that (for their height) the sufferer is medically underweight. Yet, all of this evidence does not always halt the delusion or awaken an understanding of the facts.

A person experiencing depression tends to minimize positive experiences and outcomes, while conversely maximising negative ones. This may reinforce bundles of pessimistic thinking habits (including an eager jumping to false [negative] conclusions) that had already begun to arise as a result of one's own underlying emotional turmoil. However, it is noteworthy that depressives also happen to have a more realistic take on chance and self-assessment in terms of their perception of performance. This is known as depressive realism. Furthermore, when nihilism strikes and they feel or recognize no pleasure or meaning due to their condition: This demonstrates, inversely, that it is the anatomy and physiology of the brain supported by consciousness that "create"/provide access to the positive feelings that they no longer enjoy. Like colour and smell, these feelings are (in a sense) illusory and, yet, made real by the mind itself.

Like all diseases, the logical aim is to provide a cure for the underlying physical condition that will in turn alleviate any or all symptoms. Unlike any other disease, the condition of depression shows us that a "normal" state of consciousness may be normal from an evolutionary perspective but that it is also actually a naturally enhanced state: That assures motivation, meaning, and a sense of well-being. Given that this enhanced state is a potential—actualized and enjoyed most of the time by most people—this illustrates that human beings have the literal capacity to experience these natural benefits. And so, there should be a remedy for all sufferers even if the know-how and technology are currently too primitive to fully assist those in need.

The truth, in part, is that there is a lot perceived by the mind as being terrible about life. And I think most people have a guard up against this. The terror management theory suggests that people will sometimes suppress these inconvenient truths. It is my belief that people who suffer from depression are more finely attuned to this reality and, in short, that the condition itself results through the disintegrating of necessary illusions. Clearly, humans need a certain amount of illusion to live. If there is a positive side to depression, I would say that it can be very humanizing and can serve to enhance our empathy, although it is a very significant price to pay. Hopefully, soon, the disease will be banished and this singular positive can be retained.

The question of the meaning of life does not even occur to some people because they are so engaged within the "bubble" that they have very little space, time, or mental energy left over to ponder on all that they, others, and also nature are. This lack of curiosity applies to all human endeavours and experiences from work and luck to reproduction and child-rearing. However, experiencing life with no feeling of meaning can understandably lead some to question what meaning itself really is. Losing the sense of meaning does not guarantee such a quest but would surely make it more likely.

While a depressive is in remission, they will probably forget just how profound and real the feeling of no meaning is. It becomes to them as though it was the meaninglessness itself that was the illusion. Conversely, when everything seems permeated with meaninglessness, it is hard to imagine how "normal" people cannot see that there is no intrinsic meaning and that life is absurd. The so-called "normal" go about their routine, human-centric behaviours as though it all makes sense. Who is right? I would argue that both are, but even when there is apparent meaning, it is a kind of human construct nonetheless. From a big-picture perspective, there is an ultimate meaning that we will explore in detail, but the predisposition for humans to experience a sense of meaning has clearly led to a multitude of unrelated and arbitrary ways to enjoy it.

At its worst, depression results in a sense that life is pointless. This perpetual pain arises from a nagging feeling that the world is somehow not right—and although sufferers may know the "rules" and can maybe even appear to fit in, the nagging feeling remains. I believe that this can also be a symptom of a lack of spiritual awakening. Any and all animalistic behaviours can no longer fully pacify an evolved being that can see the futility of polishing the brass on the Titanic as its fate manifests. I think the fine-tuning that many depressives experience similarly to the spiritually open-minded extends to a recognition that society as a whole is off-kilter. Perhaps, this is not surprising given the unquestioned rituals and traditions, hyper-materialism, and vast deviations from evolved ancestral behaviour. It is not so difficult to detect the immoral and selfish drive that is almost ubiquitously casted over much of the world.

With politics as a catalyst, we have also seen the demise of community spirit and a rise in social isolation, along with the unashamed encouragement of selfishness. Where kites were once held, we see selfie-sticks; where children playing outside together used to be the norm, we now see mobile phones and gaming addictions. Jiddu Krishnamurti expressed this well in a quotation saying, "It is no measure of health to be well adjusted to a profoundly sick society."

Even though many people may live their lives believing there is nothing wrong, they have to accept that global warming, deforestation, plastic infested seas and wildlife, wars, rape, violence, genocide, homelessness, drug addiction, and a thousand other indicators of a descent into hell on earth are ever present. This part of the nagging feeling that the world is not right is far from illusory. Yet, does focusing energy on what appears real create more of this physical reality?

This nihilistic thinking is dangerous territory and as the possibility to sense meaning is real, this is clearly where the key focus should be. Whether a spiritual awakening is part of the remedy is less important than a return to the sense of meaning, at least to a sufficient enough degree that a full awakening could potentially occur. Indefinite meaninglessness is the ultimate thief when it comes to quality of life and so various potential remedies for mood disorders are discussed near the end of the book. As mentioned earlier, although this is not a book about mood disorders, they are highly relevant because they not only help us to understand what constitutes human meaning but they can also encourage deep thinking about the big picture.

Meaning requires both consciousness and the brain to function in such a way that meaning is felt. However, in the absence of some kind of spiritual dimension, there can be no ultimate meaning. The fact that meaning is contrived by the human mind does not mean that the meaning is not real though. In the same way that pain is merely represented by brain activity, the existence of consciousness makes it very real. A robot could mimic the response to pain and be made to respond to different pressure levels indicating the damage being sustained, but it would never actually *feel* pain in the absence of consciousness.

Just because emotions such as distress, love, and a sense of meaning appear to have evolved in a similar way to physical traits (evolved and harnessed for biological reasons), does not mean that they were not experiences of a predetermined nature and that the evolution of the brain and mind are merely providing greater "access" as they develop. In the same way that altruism may have developed from symbiotic/selfish behaviour—it is still real in its final form. The advent of consciousness and rational thought means that altruism can be viewed as an independent state and real in its own right. In other words, true empathy has emerged in most humans. And as the human mind and consciousness has developed so, too, have our range of emotions and desired personal experiences—so that there are essentially countless things that can provide us with meaning. This includes a sense of meaning that is associated with our animalistic behaviours as well as the nearly infinite number of contrived human activities—provided, of course, that the ability to feel meaning is present.

I believe, too, that a sense of meaning arose as an evolutionary necessity and that it has continued to be harnessed for various reasons. One probably being a spandrel (a consequence of the evolution of our consciousness), but a key reason is that extreme nihilism would be selected against by evolution because suicidal behaviour does not perpetuate gene transfer. To counter the emergence of self-awareness and, in particular, a sense of our own mortality, the coevolution of a sense of meaning and possibly religiosity may have been a necessity to avoid extinction. For similar reasons, most agricultural ancestors probably didn't ponder the probability of crop failure. There is clearly an evolutionary advantage to being optimistic and motivated and so it is universally innate to varying degrees.

A game of pool to a depressive is an observation in physics. The winning or losing and the concept of competition are understood but it seems a futile pastime—after all, the outcomes are soon forgotten and it is only the hardwired instinct for competition that makes a win more pleasurable than a loss for someone who can experience meaning. The problem, of course, is that the feeling does not stop at games like pool—but can extend to all activities undertaken by humankind.

Being aware of our own mortality adds weight to the nihilistic feeling for most depressives because it is clear that whatever one does in life it will be extinguished, from the achiever's viewpoint, when life is over. From the perspective of DNA, this is all irrelevant, as long as the drive for survival and reproduction is maintained. But for many egocentric beings that are seemingly just mortal gene transfer mechanisms, it is a hard pill to swallow.

A fear of harmless spiders is somewhat irrational, albeit the response is explainable from an evolutionary perspective. Existential angst is more rational, despite it being equally pointless (the cause of fear, in this latter instance, has the direst of consequences but cannot be changed). As Andrew Solomon pointed out in his TED talk, sufferers of depression and existential angst often say things like, *"No matter what we do we're all going to die in the end"* or *"There can be no true communion between two human beings when each of us is trapped in our own body."* He suggests that all we can really say to this is, *"That is true.... But I think we should focus right now on what to have for breakfast."* This is humorous and tragic in equal measures because the swift changing of subjects to the most trivial of matters is not just a distraction to lighten a heavy conversation, it is also a kind of admission that the morbid insights cannot be disputed.

For those who have experienced existential angst, the almost ubiquitous ability for people to block out these deep and disturbing truths is quite surprising. After all, many trivial events cause huge upset for many people and, yet, the actual consequences of these events are generally miniscule by comparison to permanent de-animation. It seems that some have an acceptance of this inevitability and compartmentalize it, keeping emotionally arousing thoughts on any issue(s) at bay, often subconsciously. This is part of the terror management theory referred to earlier. Others are pacified by their beliefs in religion or spirituality.

Of course, most people do not enter Disneyland lamenting over the fact that the day's experiences will soon be over. And so, for the majority, the journey of life provides enough fulfilment to justify living despite knowing it is finite. This is why the need for a sense of meaning is necessary – and, yet, it is conspicuous in its absence in Abraham Maslow's theory of sequential development (i.e., human needs). I would suggest that it is as vital as all the basic needs he identified. With no meaning, many people would no longer care about all of those other identified, needs—they would rather not "play" at being human at all.

Meaning was added into Maslow's theory as revisions were made, but it refers to a need to seek and achieve meaning, whereas I am referring to a fundamental need to have a sense (strong feeling) that life is other than pointless. People generally have a sense of connectedness within reality even if they are bored or sad. If this capacity is lost and nothing provides pleasure or meaning, the world is not only mechanistic, it is sadistic. Or in the words of Shakespeare's character, Macbeth, "It is a tale told by an idiot, full of sound and fury signifying nothing." Why existentialism can lead to meaninglessness or vice versa is discussed in more detail in the chapter on Leo Tolstoy's life and his desperate search for meaning.

Although the book contains well-considered and reasoned arguments throughout, I anticipate diametrically opposing views from much of the scientific community on some aspects. Science is a wonderful institution with the best available means of accruing reliable knowledge about the physical world. However, scientists tend to grow attached to their theories and hypotheses. Not only considering which explanations truly reflect the nature of reality but also their careers and intellectual legacy.

This means, in consequence, that sometimes new ways of thinking are treated with suspicion and often hostility. It is important not to let these emotions cloud the scientific debates, and also just as important to try to let the scientific ideas be evaluated on their explanatory merits and experimental evidence. Of course, conflicts arising due to differences in beliefs is not unique to science. All animals experience conflict over scarcity, territory, and are subject to the fight and flight response. This involves the oldest part of the brain called the limbic system (the *"lizard brain"*) and in particular the amygdala. As we have evolved many languages and with this, the ability to communicate ideas that will primarily have centred around natural and sexual selection, ideas can also become just as potent as physical interaction at triggering these primitive emotional centres.

Specific neurons and neurotransmitters, such as norepinephrine, trigger a defensive state when we feel that our thoughts have to be protected from the influence of others. If we are then confronted with differences in opinion, the chemicals that are released in the brain are the same ones that try to ensure our survival in dangerous situations. In this defensive state, the more primitive part of the brain interferes with rational thinking and the limbic system can knock out most of our working memory, physically causing *"narrow-mindedness."*

We see this in the politics of fear, in the strategy of poker players, or simply **when someone is stubborn in a discussion. No matter how valuable an idea is, the brain has trouble processing it** when it is in such a state. On a neural level, it **acts as if we are being threatened, even if this threat comes from harmless opinions or facts that we may otherwise find helpful and could rationally agree with.** But when we express ourselves and our views are appreciated, these defence chemicals decrease in the brain and dopamine transmission activates the reward neurons. Self-esteem and self-belief are closely linked to the neurotransmitter serotonin. When the lack of it takes on severe proportions, it often leads to depression, self-destructive behaviour, or even suicide. Social validation increases the level of dopamine and serotonin in the brain and allows us to let go of emotional fixations and to become self-aware more easily—making us feel empowered and increasing our self-esteem. Our beliefs have a profound impact on our body chemistry and perceptions. This is why placebos, which are discussed in great detail later in the book, can be so effective.

Science is about pattern recognition and truth seeking and so it would be ideal if everybody involved was objective and rational. However, scientists are people and so certain biases are unavoidable and many new ideas are threatening, causing the problems of the kind I have outlined. I am less optimistic than one of science's greats, namely Carl Sagan. He said,

> "*In science it often happens that scientists say, 'You know that's a really good argument; my position is mistaken,' and then they would actually change their minds and you never hear that old view from them again. They really do it. It doesn't happen as often as it should, because scientists are human and change is sometimes painful. But it happens every day. I cannot recall the last time something like that happened in politics or religion.*"

I am more than happy to hear opposing views on anything that is presented in the book, as I have no vested interest in what turns out to be the true account of the meaning of life and our reality. At the very least, I think all readers of this book will see the world in a very different light by the end of it and realise that things are far from what they seem. Before we begin our journey into what has to be the most complex "Who done it?" mysteries of all time, it should be noted that the answer to the book title is not revealed in any individual chapter but comes into focus by piecing all of the chapters together. Reading the conclusion alone will certainly not provide complete answers to the meaning of life, as there are too many interrelated subject matters involved—each of which contribute significant amounts of evidence that quickly become overwhelming when aggregated, to be able to answer the question summarily.

In one key chapter: The highly complex argument involving the fact that natural selection cannot be the sole mechanism and driving force of biological evolution leaves a potential vacuum. That of which, a later chapter on the primacy of mathematics and intelligence helps to fill. Decoding the meaning of life, especially in its broadest sense, was bound to unveil a blueprint that is somewhat difficult to comprehend. Some chapters may even require multiple reads, especially if you are not familiar with the processes of evolution, or if lateral thinking is not one of your main strengths. However, I hope that you persevere because some of the key truths are revealed in the latter half of the book and I am sure that you will feel a sense of satisfaction by rising to the challenge. It is surely worth it to get to see reality at a much deeper and richer level than you ever thought possible and to explore the deepest question of mankind: One that has stubbornly remained unanswered since time began. In answering the question, "What is the meaning of life?" in its broader sense, the book essentially presents *a theory of everything*. It also discusses the more metaphysical side of life and details how the interaction of intents impacts your world and how your individual intent can change it for the better.

2

THE MEANING OF LIFE —
THE SHORTER ANSWER

*"There is a superior Mind that reveals itself in
the world of experience."*

Albert Einstein

O ne writer had concluded that the meaning of life is to leave the world in a better state than it was found and to contribute to society, even if that means sacrificing individual happiness. I would suggest that this is generally mistaken on two counts. Firstly, when people want to know the meaning of life, they want to know if there is something more than birth, sickness, ageing, and death. They want to know if there is something beyond our biological and societal functions. In other words, this explanation does not go deep enough in exploring what meaning itself actually is. Secondly, the conclusion is clearly subjective and a prescription for how the writer believes all humans should act in accordance with his own evolved moral compass. It is more of a generic political manifesto than an exploration of the meaning of life.

From the DNA's perspective, everything is about survival and reproduction. As mentioned earlier, all animals including us are essentially DNA baton passers. There are hardwired drivers to assist and assure this; although, people can still choose to refrain from the reproductive function and/or the act that was "designed" to facilitate reproduction.

Evolutionary psychology proposes that it is not only our physical traits that have evolved but our cognitive and behavioural traits as well. This may seem to make us mere puppets and to remove most, if not all, the possibility of free will. Being conscious of this perhaps offers a sliver of free will. But most people are seemingly not "*awake*" and are unaware of the fact that pretty much all our physical endeavours are governed by the process(es) of evolution.

For a more basic animal, such as the peacock, in addition to its survival behaviour, it displays rudimental mating behaviours. Its beauty and, to some extent, gene quality (fitness) are displayed via energetic movement, bird noises (including ones outside the range of human hearing), and quality of tail. The peahen is discerning/choosy but not via human-like rational thinking. This demonstrates a process, known in the field of evolutionary biology as sexual selection, although many evolutionary biologists and evolutionary psychologists believe it is merely another form of natural selection. In other words, they see these traits arising as adaptations which assure the fittest survive (by creating a kind of test that those lacking in fitness will fail because of the inability to produce immaculate displays, thus providing visual and auditory cues used by peahens known as fitness indicators). In the same way that adaptations have arisen out of environmental challenges, it is theorized that the capacity for mate choice/sexual selection has resulted in further adaptations that work in the same way and is, therefore, natural selection at work via an indirect process (i.e. weeding out the weakest).

Together, natural and sexual selection form Darwin's theory of evolution. Many biologists see his work as infallible, yet, there are questionable aspects that will be discussed throughout the book. Ironically, Darwin did not see sexual selection as a part of natural selection, as nearly all biologists presently do. He made his view absolutely clear, that sexual selection is all about the creation and advancement of beauty, for beauty's sake (resulting in traits and behaviours that usually affect survival chances in a detrimental way). The chapter entitled "Beauty" concurs with Darwin but also explores what beauty is, why it exists, and what really drives it. Here is just one of Darwin's quotations about sexual selection and its role in the creation of beauty:

> "A great number of male animals, as [is the case for] all our most gorgeous birds, some fishes, reptiles and mammals, and a host of magnificently coloured butterflies have been rendered beautiful for beauty's sake."

When Charles Darwin considered the characteristics of the peacock's tail, he said, "The sight of a feather in a peacock's tail, whenever I gaze at it, makes me sick!" Those were his exact words which he wrote in 1860, the year after he published his Origin of Species (words that inspired my peacock cartoon illustration earlier in the chapter). It wasn't until 1871, 11 years later, that Darwin provided a detailed and comprehensive account of his theory of sexual selection in The Descent of Man in an effort to provide a naturalistic (evolutionary) explanation for peacock feathers and other "seemingly useless" male ornaments.

He'd thought that he could explain two of the animal kingdom's most conspicuous and puzzling features—of weaponry and adornment. Sometimes males who compete fiercely for females would enter a sort of evolutionary arms race, developing ever greater weapons—tusks, horns, antlers—as the best-endowed males of each successive generation reproduced at the expense of their weaker peers. In parallel, among species whose females choose the most attractive males based on their subjective tastes, males would evolve outlandish sexual ornaments. It is now well known that all sexes exert many different evolutionary pressures on one another and, that in some species, males choose ornamented females. But to this day, many of the best studied examples are of female preference and male display.

Darwin seemed happy to accept that beauty simply happens, thanks to some kind of innate aesthetic appreciation belonging to females assuring that beauty is constructed from millions of random mutations (effectively assembling a microscopic jigsaw puzzle over countless generations). This might account for some of the cruder expressions of beauty but cannot explain the mathematically complex, ornamental pattern we see in the male great argus pheasant, for example.

In sexual selection, the choosiness trait is heritable meaning females will seek the beauty and quality of genes that are often indicated in males by the optimum displays of beauty within their respective species. Furthermore, the choosing of greater beauty and potentially better genes will result in more attractive and sought-after males. Both male and female offspring will also benefit from having a father with good genes in terms of improved survival rates. Thus, mate choice assures that choosiness ongoingly perpetuates the same way that the beautiful traits of males also do.

The aesthetic nature of the whole pattern of the tail and/or other showy traits appear to be the result of hardwired unconscious *"goals"* that assure beauty over time (from a starting point of drab). In other words, beauty does not arise through blind chance. And given that beauty is ubiquitous amongst thousands of species of birds, to say nothing of countless other animals, there is clearly something more than chance at work.

Gene fitness could feasibly be displayed as the masterpieces are fully constructed (or well underway). However, the idea of gene fitness being the cause of beauty whereby random mutations simultaneously (and/or purportedly) "construct" such beauty, blindly, and afford some apparent improved fitness with each microscopic step from proto-ornament to complex ornament (with no functional reason that the new abstract partial marking could signal/provide any greater fitness than a specimen without such mutation(s) or a specimen sporting any other random alternative marking) is seriously flawed.

The "handicap theory," while associated with gene fitness indicators, also presents serious flaws. These flaws, detailed in the chapter on beauty, also infer profound implications about the ultimate cause of beauty. This current chapter, however, is introducing natural selection and sexual selection to contextualize the meaning of life in terms of their ability to shape traits without the need for free will.

In bowerbirds, beauty and (possibly) gene fitness is displayed mainly by behavioural above physical traits, although, indeed, they are physically beautiful and also display energetic mating rituals. Each male builds an elaborate and colourful garden, including a collection and arrangement of strategically placed flowers and berries. The predisposed choosiness of the female steps in to assess the male bowerbird's garden (and the inverted nest-type construction known as the bower). This construct offers a quick and easy to exit viewing spot for the potential mate to see the bird's handiwork, as well as a mating area should she signal her consent. The prize awarded to the "*winner*" is sex. It is quite astonishing to see how evolution can shape not only the physical traits of an animal but also its mating rituals and general behaviours, growing ever more elaborately in accordance with the female's preference and/or to keep fitness indicators consistently evolving, as the theory goes.

The bowerbirds' gardens look both attractive and man-made, demonstrating how their beauty can be appealing to the human sense of beauty as well as that of the female bowerbirds. It is more than a coincidence though as what manifests as beauty and/or gene fitness is provably mathematical by nature and observably a presentation of order and often striking colour arrangements. These are the deeper reasons their "appeal" presents itself and why two very distinct species get to agree upon what could easily be thought of as a subjective experience.

We favour facets like symmetry, for example, in human faces, art, and archaeological structures—a throwback from sexual selection in other species that ultimately manifested in us. Beauty also associates with order (the antipathy of randomness) and consciousness appears to appreciate this state—as though Mind (unmanifest consciousness) enjoys conspicuous displays of mathematical forms and order (manifest consciousness). In other words, consciousness attracting consciousness creates masterpieces that are, themselves, manifest consciousness happening throughout the world of experience. Before the materialist scientists amongst you are too quick to judge this additional definition of beauty, I refer you back to the quotation by Einstein at the beginning of the chapter: "*There is a superior Mind that reveals itself in the world of experience.*"

Gene fitness indicators and sexual selection, like natural selection, have always felt like incomplete theories to me. This will be more than obvious by the time you have read this book in its entirety as there are countless pieces of evidence showing the difficulties that arise once you resist hyper-normalization. What actually appears to be going on becomes quite obvious, as it is not the processes that are blind as many scientists believe but seemingly the scientists themselves.

The fact that mate choice seems to correlate with the selection of mates sporting the *"best"* traits, deemed as gene fitness indicators, makes the theory of gene fitness indicators as a cause of beauty appear credible. But this assumption is merely based upon what has been observed and, as ever, ignores ultimate causes. It is worth noting that a 2012 meta-analysis of 90 studies on 55 species found only *"equivocal"* support for the good-genes hypothesis, and so it appears that many of the so-called gene fitness indicators are not so reliable advertisements of fitness after all. This, of course, casts further doubt upon the idea that all animal beauty/mathematical order/patterns and ornaments have arisen as a result of random mutations leading to greater and greater indicators of gene fitness due to natural selection in the form of sexual selection.

With zero free will, these animals are merely a part of nature, morphing over generations due to external forces in a highly ordered fashion—en route to striking beauty. It is difficult to see how anyone can believe that this process is completely unguided, as micro "improvements" leading to such mathematical beauty and wonder cannot happen by chance alone. Similarly, animalistic preference alone cannot explain the drive toward the nearly incomprehensible order apparent in much of the pattern and ornament we witness.

The best display of mating behaviour and possibly gene fitness has to be that of the sand-based artwork of the pufferfish (see the link below). There is no doubt that we are witnessing an expression of intelligence and yet the intelligence is expressed through the organism rather than being something the organism is consciously manifesting. The chapter dedicated to the primacy of mathematics and intelligence explores the ultimate cause(s) in greater detail.

🔗 **https://youtu.be/B91tozyQs9M**

The same principle that applies to peacocks and bowerbirds applies to humans but the number of aesthetic developments through sexual selection and possibly "gene fitness indicator" evolution is far greater. There are still physical considerations such as build, breast size/symmetry, facial symmetry, etc., but behavioural traits have become a huge consideration and now dominate the process. The gene mutation load (potential for faulty genes) in the brain/mind will be significant due to its complexity and so is the best place for gene fitness/sexually selected traits to be revealed. As such, wealth, intelligence, generosity, power, wit, sense of humour, story-telling skills, and creativity are the main currencies in human sexual selection.

When referring to gene fitness here, I use this term to include the intent/choice of a mate for worldly benefits rather than just the overall gene quality in light of the fact that selected for attributes of certain members of a species are not necessarily reliable indicators of genetic superiority, as we have discussed at length. Although a good-looking male may have above-average gene quality (i.e. lower quality genes may have diminished the beauty potential), I suspect that looks will not prove to be a great indicator of long-term immune system prowess or mortality. Accordingly, what is often attributed to gene fitness really includes the choosers' innate taste for beauty, as well as conscious and subconscious assessments of attributes that are beneficial to the chooser and/or their potential offspring.

What complicates the assessment of causes of traits and behaviours in humans is that our access to higher consciousness means that there are so many interacting forces in play that it becomes very difficult to pinpoint specific causes. And often, as with genetics in general, there are multifactorial considerations and so the algorithms are too complex to allow for precise cause-and-effect revelations. Likewise, issues such as love are difficult for biology to quantify because they involve immaterial consciousness and so they came to be through a form of emergence. In other words, the experiences only became possible as the brain has evolved (or preexisted, with the evolved brain gaining the necessary structure to facilitate access to certain fundamental unmanifest experiences, which this book shows to be the more accurate account).

This makes the area of human sexual traits and behaviours (and traits and behaviours in general) a minefield where some of the potential causes put forward are highly speculative, with the work and conclusions of some scientists being dismissed as false by others. As such, the actual causes of some traits and behaviours outlined may differ from the scientific theories presented. What is certain is that sexual selection and natural selection (and the existence of fitness indicators, to some degree) are real phenomena—albeit, as I will show, incomplete causes of all that is manifest in life.

A lot of the display behaviour (and sexual selection behaviour) happens at a subconscious level and so it is not so obvious that everyone is an algorithm assessment machine (as well as a gene fitness/aesthetic display machine) when it comes to human sexual selection. Most people know that certain individuals are good looking and others less so and do not look deeper into what makes the difference.

Of course, some that crudely show off their gene fitness/"aesthetic" in order to be "selected" often experience the opposite of their intended results (flaunting wealth and success and boasting often devalues the facets possibly, in part, because it shows the potential for greater self-interest as well as a diminished ability to care for a mate and potential offspring). Besides, higher consciousness and advanced theory of mind mean there is an ability to sense too much showing off and interpret what it says about overall personality. Having said that, most people are also aware that wealth and power can attract higher quality mates (in terms of arbitrary beauty).

Evolutionary psychology is not politically correct—it suggests that penis size and breast size do matter according to taste. As humans became upright, it is a small wonder that these physical attributes became a focus and thus the peacock's tail equivalent. Through sexual selection, these selectable attributes changed shape and size over time although there is a great variation across different races and even within races illustrating that taste is a dominant influence (strengthening the argument against them being fitness indicators because natural selection tends to result in uniformity).

In recognition of what is deemed beautiful and/or sexually attractive, it is no wonder that in the modern world cosmetic surgery is frequently used to enhance what nature provided. The problem is that this often results in over-exaggerated versions that are considered attractive only by the minority (e.g. massively oversized breasts, super thick and highly false-looking eyebrows, bizarre over-inflated lips etc.). When a woman believes cosmetic surgery is purely used to increase confidence and nothing to do with sexuality, the choice of body parts they enhance suggests otherwise. It is unlikely plastic surgery will be used to enlarge kneecaps or some other obscure body part. It is quite clear, however, that the enhancements are made to body parts typically associated with sex and/or feminine beauty.

The obsession many women have with shoes is related to all of this too. With high heels, legs can appear longer and so this is why they are frequently worn despite often being uncomfortable and difficult to walk in. Shoes are also an accessory that can enhance beauty similarly to nail polish, lipstick, eyeliner, etc.

There is little correlation between breast size and milk yield and so the idea that larger breasts indicate a greater food source for offspring has little credence. However, large breasts highlight symmetrical differences and symmetry in nature is often associated with beauty (despite the fact that the idea of symmetry being a reliable fitness indicator has been severely discredited). They are, of course, used in sexual activity, too, affording pleasure to both parties and so this provides a motive for gradual enlargement over time through the process of sexual selection. Again, male taste varies and so size preferences vary significantly, which impacts the size variability amongst women. The male penis is proportionally much bigger (including width) than other primates, as well as having an evolved shape variation—all thought to have arisen through female sexual selection to enhance her pleasure in the experience of sex.

Of course, there are so many "fitness indicators" in humans, it is a marketing mix, and varying tastes have created many complex relationship patterns. People possessing fewer positive attributes are more likely to end up with mates that have less positive attributes rather than go without and so there are often many compromises that take place in the process of sexual selection.

With some species, such as the peacock, the sexual selection process occurs in groups known as leks. The so-called fittest male specimen(s) gets to mate with many of the females while the other, less aesthetic males go unmated. It has led to what is known as the "lek paradox" because it is surprising to many biologists that the mating does not result in indistinguishably fit/aesthetic male offspring arising from all the fit "chosen" fathers. In other words, they believe that all the next generation males should gain fairly equal attention when their time to attend a lek group arises based on the fact they all had "winning" fathers. However, only a small percentage

33

of peacocks get to mate in each new generation and so there is clearly a genetic (or fundamental beauty) variation within each successive group of males. There are various theories proposing why a select few peacocks acquire better genes/beauty in this *"winner takes all"* process, but regardless of the reasons, the peahens continue to be choosy and to favour more beautiful males.

Gene fitness can often be revealed through the quality of an inherited preexisting pattern and ornament/complex mathematical manifestation. However, there are examples demonstrating that mate choice must sometimes be based upon illusory gene fitness indicators. This is because mate choice behaviour indicates there must generally be some value in what is being selected for and, yet, we know for sure what is selected for has no fitness information whatsoever in certain circumstances. These examples manifest as irresistible *"pseudo fitness indicators"* that are, in fact, man-made and are acted upon as though ultimate fitness is being displayed. They just happen to be visually or socially appealing to some capacity, triggering the parts of the brain/mind participating in the choosiness process.

Biologist Nancy Burley had found that female zebra finches are attracted to males that have tall white plumes glued on top of their heads. In other words, it caused the females of that species to act as though the *"costumed"* males were the Casanova of zebra finches. Of course, we know because the white plumes are fake in that it shows no real additional gene fitness that the behaviour can only be based on aesthetics and taste.

Research into another example gained The Biology Prize at the 2011 Ig Nobel Prize Ceremony for discovering that: *"A certain kind of beetle mates with a certain kind of Australian beer bottle,"* as their award stated. It seems it was the colour of the bottles (brown) that was attracting these male Western Australian beetles, which coincided with the colour of the female of the species. The tiny tubercles at the base of the bottle seemed to emulate the wing covers of the female which have similar dimples and reflect light in a similar manner.

Bigger females mean bigger eggs and so sexual selection assures that the males seek larger females (it is possible the bigger eggs are a genuine indicator of fitness). This *"evolutionary trap"* is something that was never *"intended"* to be in nature and so, understandably, the hyper-exaggerated dummy female has proven irresistible.

This was such a widespread issue that it was severely disrupting the reproduction of the beetles. Since the publishing of the research, the manufacturers no longer include dimples on the bottles.

There is also some inherent (random?) animal taste, which led to the acceptance/choice of some colours that form the pattern and ornament via mutations while rejecting others. In some cases, cues from the environment can affect mate choice, e.g., an orange fruit in an animal's environment may make that colour sought after and so it becomes adopted when it arises via mutations in a mate and enhanced via sexual selection thereafter. Likewise, conditions in an environment can affect mate choice, too, e.g., shiny fish versus super colour-saturated fish arise due to differing water conditions. However, on the whole, it seems pattern and ornament and colouration arise purely based on beauty as a fundamental truth—part random, fully mathematical, and highly ordered.

Some animals live in harem groups where the dominant alpha male has access to all the females in the group and gene fitness/dominance is expressed by the male via their ability to beat out the competition. This form of sexual selection is relevant to human sexual behaviour as well as other animals. Natural and sexual selection have led to huge variations in the mating game, making it extremely complicated to identify some of the evolutionary *"force(s)"* that lie behind all its manifestations.

However, once you see that survival and reproduction appear to be DNA's only functions, there is nothing in animal behaviour that is particularly surprising. Some things may appear counterintuitive at first but if you observe the basic drivers and the consequences of these (read *"selfish gene"*), there is always a rational explanation. For example, a male redback spider putting itself at risk of being eaten by the female after reproduction would seem contrary to the survival instinct. However, when it becomes apparent that the spider's risk also assures more efficient reproduction and more offspring (each carrying 50 percent of the genes of the male), it is no longer a puzzling move. Nature is merciless.

When it comes to human gene fitness indicators, there is a theory that the female orgasm, which is far from assured, is a subconscious response to gene fitness. The theory posits that the orgasm corresponds to male fitness and the process enhances the likelihood of reproductive success (by the movement of the egg into a more receptive position and/or an up-sucking effect that brings the sperm into a more favourable position). In other words, it is a sensation which happens to be pleasurable (a motivational factor) that arises in accordance with the gene fitness of the person in the sexual encounter. This theory has been discredited by various people, but if gene fitness indicators prove to be a real phenomenon in some cases, this would provide a plausible reason for mechanisms such as these to arise through evolution, whereby the gene fitness *information* is acted upon.

A more plausible explanation for the female orgasm is that the sex of a fetus is only determined at month two of the embryonic process and so there are huge commonalities between the sexes. This means that the male organism could, through heritability, lead to a similar experience amongst women. This happens in other traits, e.g., bird pattern and ornament, and in the case of humans the functionless male nipples and the dilution effect seen in the opposite sex would perhaps explain why there is variability in the capacity to experience the orgasm in women.

What is known is that the predisposition for females to experience orgasms is heritable and that there seems to be a correlation between the closeness of the clitoris to the vaginal opening and the capacity to experience the orgasm.

As mentioned earlier, there is so much debate over fitness indicators, it makes sense to explore what is believed by both sides before looking at the various flaws in logic (especially the flaws relating to the questionable capacity for fitness indicators to create and develop beauty).

The human female menstrual cycle has become almost undetectable unlike in, say, dogs. This *"clever"* evolved tact has the consequence of a long-term mate more than likely ending up being the father of her child (and long-term mates are statistically reasonably likely to hang around for the long-haul co-rearing of children). Evolutionary psychologist Geoffrey Miller did an infamous experiment that revealed strippers earned double the number of tips at their most fertile in the cycle, which indicates that there are cues picked up by males favouring them at this period and so peak fertility is clearly not as well concealed as first meets the eye. Furthermore, at their most fertile, women have been reported to prefer more manly faces (and odours) and when they are less fertile more feminine faces which would indicate a preference for more feminine and nurturing types.

According to one scientist, even human sperm displays behaviour that has evolved to enhance reproductive success on the basis that our species is not wholly monogamous. There are suggested to be three types of sperm—fighters, blockers, and egg getters. According to observations made by the person who put the theory forward, the third represents only a very small percent. The function of the other two is to block or attack imposter sperm in a bid to protect against fertilization by another male. In other words, there are lesser-known systems *"designed"* by nature/evolution that assure the efficiency and effectiveness of DNA in its bid for survival and reproduction. This is apparently another discredited theory that requires further evidence to be taken as scientific fact.

Likewise, the shape of the glans of the human penis is said to have evolved like the end of a mushroom because it sucks and draws back preexisting sperm in a woman (another form of sperm wars). There are mixed reviews on this theory and it could ultimately prove to be that sexual selection by female mate choice determined the shape merely as a means to gain enhanced pleasure. It is quite apparent that many scientists have put forward their hypotheses before they are fully tested and before results have been replicated to such an extent, they prove their worth—an issue which has been particularly problematic in the adaptationist program, discussed later.

There are different strategies adopted by males of differing gene fitness/aesthetics. For example, a lower fitness male is more likely to seek a long-term mate and invest energy in protecting that relationship. A fitter/more attractive male is more likely to spread his genes via multiple mates. It is no surprise that women are often considered the choosier of the sexes as they have limited eggs, a long gestation period, and children that take many years to become independent (and so having two parents to raise the children is valuable). Choosiness by the female(s) of many species, in addition to the human species, is also likely to have evolved for the same reasons—namely, the limited number of eggs available and the fact that further reproduction is impossible during the pregnancy period. Both of these are clearly nonissues for males who can reproduce with multiple partners.

In most species, the gene fitness/aesthetic displays, therefore, develop in the males in accordance with choosy female taste. This is why it is normally the male that sports striking beauty and mating displays. Male humans cooperate in the long haul raising of children and so this is thought to be a key reason why choosiness applies to both sexes. Of course, the capacity that men and women have to identify and seek pleasure and beauty in accordance with taste will also influence mate choice. It is worth noting that some non-DNA based "material" (epigenetics) is purportedly left behind in sexual encounters amongst flies meaning when offspring arise some of the traits can come from previous "lovers" and not exclusively from biological fathers. This phenomenon is called telegony and was proposed long ago by scholars such as Aristotle. Advances in the understanding of epigenetics are bringing some lesser-known mechanisms to the fore.

The loss of the male penis in most bird species is considered to be one of the main reasons female choosiness in birds became so prolific and caused the evolution of beauty in the males. Forced copulation became rare, meaning that enhanced traits and behaviour(s) arose through increased male competition and the heightened freedom that the females gained to create and/or select changes in accordance with taste (as well as the theorized "*guiding*" forces that appear to assure the order of complexity). This likely resulted in more pair bonding as well as male investment in parenting.

The display and choosiness behaviours relating to gene fitness indicators and aesthetics amongst humans are, of course, varied—as human reproduction and sexual selection is considerably more complex than it is for, say, peacocks. Taste factors, such as girls sometimes liking boys with their father's eye colour, are one of many such examples of how complex the selection process is.

From one perspective, survival and reproduction constitute the meaning of life in its simplest form. The individual functions performed by us all are directly and/or indirectly a result of the survival and reproduction process, at least in accordance with how the physical material realm appears to the vast majority of people. The fact that the human brain has developed many ways of experiencing pain and pleasure means that there are thousands of ways to invest time in seeking fulfilment. Many work activities and pastimes are indirectly linked to survival or reproduction (even soccer is a gene fitness display platform as well as a throwback to tribal competition and a display of mastery and live art). If you consider any sport, you will see that, although there are underlying laws of physics governing the processes, the difference between a novice and a professional is the difference in the levels of mastery. There is always a level of randomness in all sports whether it be snooker, golf, tennis, etc. But consistent practice (often referred to as the "10,000-hour rule") assures that mastery is delegated more and more to the subconscious which, as we will see, is in a different league when it comes to the capacity for intelligence. This mastery and the mathematical order that are present in sport, music, etc. seems to be the key ingredients in their aesthetic appeal.

Art and poetry are forms of gene fitness/aesthetic displays, too, whereby the wasteful and yet skillful work variably demonstrates the gene fitness of the creative. They are also a display of order that follows mathematical rules and this translates to beauty at a fundamental level.

Poetry, as with all gene fitness indicators/aesthetic expression, is considerably both wasteful and inefficient from a survival-only perspective because, while the use of language aids survival, poetry is arguably an unnecessary extravagance. It seems counterintuitive until the concept of showing off that romantic behaviour and aesthetics is brought into play. It is no coincidence that the subject matter of a lot of poetry and art is of a romantic or sexual in nature, but even when it is not, their origins are rooted in the concept of sexual selection fitness indicators and beauty.

Even activities that do not seem to relate to survival and repro-duction are pursued due to a mind that has developed the capacity to experience pleasure and meaning, which in turn had arisen due to survival and reproduction progenerating such a capacity. Or, more aptly, it had arisen through our evolving anatomy and physiological complexity thus granting access to these novel emotional states.

As mentioned earlier, many narrow-minded people perceive that we are mere puppets within this evolutionary system and have a very nihilistic outlook. The good news is that the development of external pleasure perception and a sense of meaning shows us that there are many more ways to enjoy the journey of life when compared to lesser animals that appear to have limited behavioural maneuver-ability. However, it does not address the question of if there is intrin-sic meaning to life. There is good news here as well but this becomes apparent as the truth unfolds.

The story so far suggests that, from the universe's perspective, there doesn't appear to be an intrinsic meaning of life. It could not care less whether life on earth became extinct or not. It cares no more for humans than it did for the dinosaurs. Even if life on earth survives extinction from numerous potential global disasters, it cannot survive the future expansion of the sun and so in the long term, it will be extinguished. Colonizing around other stars is merely delaying the inevitable—entropy and the accelerating expansion of the universe suggests that, eventually, the universe itself will become starless and uninhabitable. But this is billions upon billions of years away and so does not say much about the meaning of life that each of us inhabit in the meantime.

Freud suggested that the meaning of life is to work and to love. I would contend that these are human endeavours that may provide a feeling of meaning for many but that the brain has to be functioning in such a way to facilitate that feeling in the first place. In other words, the evolved capacity to perceive meaning has to first exist as this is what permits the experience of it. This capacity correlates with the evolutionary advancement of the biological brain and so meaning exists in a lesser form amongst lower animals and not exclusively amongst humans.

But when the conditions are right: Meaning is just as real as it is personal. It may be that the meaning gained through a certain activity is seen as absurd by an observer, for example, the Jewish tradition of kissing the Western Wall. Its meaning is gained through tradition and belief and so it really does not matter if the basis of the belief is true or false for it to be meaningful. The problem is that it is all too easy for humans to ascribe meaning to things/rituals—although, if it is not harmful to others, then the object of meaning is perhaps not so important. This does, however, show how we are *"programmed"* to see patterns and assign meaning to almost anything. When you closely analyse what brings pleasure to a gold medalist sprinter, for example, it is clear that it is only our human-centric nature that provides a sense of meaning to this absurd activity (read sport). In reality, what does it matter if one human ran 1/100th of a second faster than another? Likewise, what does it matter if one team scores more goals than another? Competition is pleasurable for biological and aesthetic reasons and, accordingly, participation and spectating make for entertainment, including a form of gene fitness indication/display of aesthetics.

Some find meaning in video and mobile device games as they harness the predisposition to enjoy problem-solving, skill mastery, mock conflict, and competition. Ask a successful entrepreneur what gives him or her meaning and it may be the trappings of success such as a big house, car, and holiday home (as well as the mastery element). He/she will think a monk's view of meaning is odd because they have abandoned what is deemed pleasurable by most in the material world. A Christian will think that the entrepreneur and monk are both misguided when it comes to meaning—as this person believes that the answer is Jesus.

Of course, they are all experiencing real meaning even if the subject of the meaning itself is only meaningful to a specific person. Logically, the ones that have a happy and fulfilled life are surely the real winners. If the entrepreneur has outward success but is unfulfilled then this, to me, is a failure to gain meaning in life. The trade-off of hundreds of hours of unfulfilling activity for short bursts of pleasure in the form of successes is also questionable. If all the hours are fulfilling overall, providing a sense of mastery and control and there is a positive flow of experience(s) where the ends justify the means, in terms of overall life fulfilment, then this is clearly a win.

I think that those who do not believe meaning exists from a human perspective confuse the fact that our ability to explain the evolutionary origins of the feeling (an explanation I will question later) does not mean that the emergent feeling is not a real experience. The formation of clouds is explainable and yet it doesn't make the existence of clouds questionable. It is possible that no meaning has "any" intrinsic meaning as the universe is an objective stage where phenomena occurs in accordance with laws of nature but meaning is more than a belief. It is as real as any physical phenomena (more so, in actual fact) and arises in the same way that colours do: mind-made but a very real experience all the same.

Emergent consciousness and evolved higher intelligence may be necessary for the feeling of meaning but the feeling is not illusory. It is the same with pain. The universe does not experience pain itself and nor does anything within it except for living forms with a certain level of consciousness, but pain is both real and at the same time an illusion. It is more than just brain activity too—for it is a real experience within consciousness. A very real and describable sensation and not, as mentioned previously, simply some instrument of measurement where the brain provides information about the damage being sustained. Brain activity indicates that a sensation is being detected but who/what is genuinely experiencing the distinct *"creation"* (in this case, pain) that could never have existed without consciousness? In other words, the brain activity correlates with conscious experience and the conscious experience depends on the brain. But they are a separate and radically distinct phenomena.

By asking these kinds of questions, it becomes apparent that the brain activity informs consciousness of an experience so that it, in turn, allows a person to experience this novel, highly unpleasant sensation within their very being, in the case of pain. And because of hyper-normalization, this all seems kind of ordinary.

So, the bad news for many is that meaning appears to be dependent on the human mind and is only made real by the combination of consciousness and evolved brain anatomy and physiology, including brain chemistry. The good news is that it is still very real, albeit somewhat taken away from us all due to our finite nature. Our mortality is the ultimate tease and illusion—born into a form with the ability to sense meaning (possibly the only source of meaning in the universe) and yet this form is exterminated all too soon, regardless. Who wants to live forever anyway? How long would living with the human condition, with certain limitations defining how long meaningful behaviours and states can remain meaningful, be satisfying?

I think what is quite obvious is that human evolution doesn't favour happiness and fulfilment particularly and that the human mind is not quite so adept at predicting what will result in happiness. Having said that, happiness is more about pleasure and I would suggest that meaning is more about fulfilment and vitality, although both states require the absence of depression. Meaning is defined in more detail in the following chapter.

Impact bias—the tendency for people to overestimate the length or intensity of future emotional states lead us to think that winning the lottery will mean long-term happiness or that becoming paraplegic will mean long-term misery (hypothetically speaking). The evidence shows that, after an adjustment period, people generally return to their prior *"happiness set point"* irrespective of which of these two extreme experiences they have potentially had. Likewise, focus illusion—the cognitive bias that occurs when people place too much importance on one aspect of an event, causing an error in accurately predicting the utility of a future outcome—shows that people who single out a key goal in the pursuit of happiness generally find disappointment. Thinking that the material experience of money or love alone will provide happiness is shown to be flawed. The formula is far more complex—and likely to vary according to beliefs, values, tastes, and personality type. Jim Carrey said, *"I think everybody should get rich and famous and do everything they ever dreamed of so they can see that it's not the answer."*

Of course, this does not account for the fact that meaning differs vastly for us all, and that there will be some who will have achieved "success" and enjoyed the journey as well as the trappings. Jim Carrey has sensed the shallowness of conspicuous consumption and that our behaviours and emotions are hardwired as a result of evolution and so he likely feels that a spiritual path is the way to assure satisfaction and meaning. Due to impact bias, a huge proportion of people think of success and the accumulation of wealth as the Holy Grail and wind up dedicating huge amounts of resources and time to this in the pursuit of happiness. And even when faced with evidence, they will feel that they are an exception to the rule—such is the power of impact bias and the focus illusion.

It is rather apparent that, for most people, the ego does tend to lead them along the donkey and the carrot trap. Happiness is usually deferred and always fleeting—such that even the successes do not provide long-term meaning. But some may also genuinely find meaning in what Carrey claims is not the answer. As a past depression sufferer, he will almost certainly have felt meaninglessness and, therefore, will have questioned what is meaningful to him and people in general. However, even if his statement is true for the vast majority of people, including many who do not believe him (thanks to impact bias), I am not sure people like Donald Trump would agree with him.

There is another, more synthetic form of happiness worth a mention, despite already highlighting that happiness and meaning are quite different. Along with impact bias and focus illusion is the freedom to choose, which also affects happiness to a lesser extent. In one experiment, people were asked to put six paintings in order of preference. They were told that one of the paintings either number three or four, were available for them to keep and when asked which one they would like, not surprisingly, the third is selected in most cases. Several weeks later, the same individuals were asked to rank the same six pictures. On average, the one that was originally in third place moved to position two and the rejected choice moved from fourth to fifth. It is as though the subconscious endorses the choice by enhancing its ranking and lowering the ranking of the rejected painting (somewhat artificially inflating the satisfaction levels by effectively endorsing a previous decision). This even happens with amnesiacs who cannot recall the choice of painting they originally selected—which seems to add weight to the thinking that the subconscious mind is what synthesises the "satisfaction," doing so because it is a more logically favourable experience from an egoic mind perspective.

In a different experiment, two groups of photography students were provided with two distinct opportunities. One group was told that they would have a choice to keep one of their two favourite pictures with a chance to change their mind within a few days, while the other was told that they would get to choose one of their two favourite pictures with no option to change. The ones that had the option to change generally regretted which photograph they had chosen (both during the change permitted period and after) and the ones that had no option to change remained happy with their choice. This demonstrates that more freedom to choose and switch and change, counterintuitively, can be less satisfying than having to stick by a choice.

If people mean there is no purpose to life when they say there is no meaning of life, then I think they are wrong as the purpose is survival and reproduction. If they mean that there is no such thing as meaning from a human perspective, again, I think they are wrong, for the reasons discussed earlier. If they mean there is no ultimate meaning besides meaning contrived by the animal mind, then they are possibly right, although significant evidence to the contrary is presented later in the book.

Without some kind of spiritual dimension, it all appears to be a blind and uncaring process. But the fact that meaning has emerged as a human experience means that it is "real," just as the capacity for pain is real. However, unlike pain, what creates meaning for each person differs significantly and also requires the brain chemistry/anatomy and physiology to be optimized so that meaning can be perceived. It is beyond disorienting to feel no meaning in a depressive state, though, as not only does it result in perceiving and experiencing only meaninglessness in the many pursuits of the masses, it even means those activities that are normally endowed with meaning at a personal level are "*shown*" and/or felt to be ultimately meaningless. It reportedly feels like an absolute truth, too, as both emotions and logic interdependently *"show"* that there really is no meaning without the mind having evolved as it has—to function optimally.

As mentioned at the beginning of the book, depressives find it hard to articulate how that undisputable truth feels as even verbal and/or written communication fails to capture its essence. The revelation of such a *"truth"* (absolute meaninglessness) could be described as being like a child finding out that there is no Santa, although significantly more profound. Knowing that the inevitable death of each individual will level achievements and nonachievements alike, is only a small part of it because it is also about the apparent fact that all activities in life only appear meaningful as meaning ultimately helps assure survival and reproduction (or more accurately, it is just a product of the evolutionary process). It is a real paradox that meaning is a mind-made illusion on the one hand and, yet, because of nonmaterial consciousness that has emerged, is also as real as anything physical on the other hand (which, of course, is also illusory when you enter the quantum world). This is one of many apparent paradoxes that the book gradually solves.

Perhaps most do not question the meaning of life unless there is something lacking. It's like the fox in Aesop's fable that declared the grapes were sour because they were out of reach (i.e., meaning is generally questioned only by those who do not have it in their grasp). But meaning is either contrived, or not, and whether the journey is enjoyable and endowed with potentially illusory meaning, or not, is irrelevant in terms of the truth. In other words, being contented within *"the bubble"* does not mean that there isn't potentially some deeper, disconcerting, truth—but because behaving in accordance with how our societal conditions have evolved does not require introspection about the meaning of life, there is less incentive to do so than for someone who is contented to spend much time philosophising.

How many people analyse the origins of the pleasure of sex for example? Most just accept the status quo and act accordingly.

Having said that, our power of rationality coupled with conscious-ness has led most to, at least occasionally, ponder on the meaning of life but perhaps just not with the same frequency and intensity as the discontented, highly curious or depressed.

Although I have covered the broader aspects of the meaning of life in this chapter (both biologically and from a human experience perspective), there are many related subjects which add far more detail and depth. Many of the secrets of how the mind works which, after all, is what makes individual meaning possible are revealed by assessing the damage to different regions of the brain rather than the assessment of a normally functioning one. Accordingly, many examples of this will be explored along with how the minds of autistic savants differ from the norm and of what this indicates about the untapped potential of consciousness and intelligence.

Likewise, seeing how visual illusions work, including the result-ing brain activity revealed in fMRI brain scans, are also very informa-tive as they help to show how the brain and mind help to create our reality. Some great examples are included in this book. The remain-der of the book aims to build on what has been discussed so far, as well as to explore the potential meaning of reality that underpins "the *meaning of life*" (perhaps what many people mean by this term).

3

TOLSTOY AND EINSTEIN'S TAKE ON THE MEANING OF LIFE

"What is the meaning of human life, or, for that matter, of the life of any creature? To know an answer to this question means to be religious. You ask: Does it make any sense, then, to pose this question? I answer: The man who regards his own life and that of his fellow creatures as meaningless is not merely unhappy but hardly fit for life."

Albert Einstein

Before looking into Tolstoy and Einstein's valuable insights, it is worth looking at what is meant by meaning. In particular: What is meant by meaning from a human perspective? In its basic form, the notion of "meaningful," is captured by the expression *"something worth doing."* In other words, the behaviour should not be seen as pointless and so needs to serve a purpose and remark value. Extrapolating from actions to whole lives, this history of actions results in a meaningful life (a life worth living) when, on balance, these actions are perceived as meaningful.

If there is a sense that a person's life is meaningless, it would suggest that they see life as pointless, without purpose, empty, etc. Instead of perceiving life as meaningful, they see it as flat, stale, and

unprofitable and more than likely weary—*"a tale told by an idiot…
signifying nothing."*

Clearly, there is a potential for a meaningful life because many people experience this state. They are able to gain instrumental, intrinsic, and spiritual value in what they do. Instrumental value is where a person does X to achieve Y (where X is undertaken not for its own sake but because it is seen as instrumental in getting to what actually provides value). A reporter may go to work to feed his family and to inform the public of current affairs relevant to their lives. These reasons to engage in work are what constitute the instrumental values also known as drivers. The reasons can be so highly valued that their whole life is organized around them, e.g., to venture into space, to show religious followers the apparent error in their ways, to become a gold medalist, etc.

Intrinsic value is where a person does X for its own sake (where value is derived from X itself). The list is endless: Watch a movie, listen to music, play games, chat with friends, etc. A person who enjoys certain behaviours that are really just a means to an end, as well as the fruits of their behaviour, is lucky and when this fulfilling instrumental behaviour is what they do for a living then they would not consider what they do as "work." As Robin William's character, Mork, once said, *"There are things you are good at and things you enjoy—if God is looking down on you, and you are blessed, they are both one and the same thing."* In other words, whatever constitutes instrumental values can be intrinsic in their own right. And so, most people who build a business, create art, care for others, etc. do so because the process itself is predominantly satisfying and challenging to them.

Spiritual value is more about life purpose and so goes deeper than instrumental and intrinsic values that do not fully explain the cause(s). Spiritual value is, psychologically, much deeper as it is not so much about the purpose of daily actions but more about a person's life and/or the universe as a whole. What is the meaning of life? What is the meaning of reality? To date, spiritual value has not been a primary focus in psychology.

Leo Tolstoy, best known for his classic novel, *War and Peace*, spent much of his life in a pit of meaninglessness, lacking spiritual value. Persistent suicide ideation meant he had to steer clear of his shotgun and ropes in order to avoid the overwhelming temptation to leave this reality.

He wrote about his experience and thoughts on the meaning of life (or lack thereof) in his book, *A Confession*. His plummet into existential depression began some 10 years after the writing of *War and Peace*, although the issues had been brewing since childhood. He was a wealthy landowner, well known, had written literary master-pieces and, yet, had a sudden realisation that the whole *"game"* was absurd. If someone with so much of what so many people aspire to have (and be) questions the meaning of life, then what hope do those who are less successful have? He makes a strong case for a lack of true meaning and, given that writing was his profession, presents it in such a way that is literally, arguably, difficult to dispute.

His book does overlook a key issue though, so his logic may not be as airtight as he'd believed. He had discovered something later in life that pacified his mind and this, in my view, adds weight to what seems to have been his oversight. He was still searching for the meaning of life—looking for truths within religion—up until his death in 1910, and so he was plagued with a sense of meaning-lessness for most of his later life. His full account is very dark and he harbours on the seemingly inescapable truths that kept him from meaning. This comes across even in my brief overview of his account but, hopefully, detailing what I believe was the oversight that will steer it away from being an exclusively morbid account.

From an early age, he began to see flaws in the religion he was brought up within and in particular felt that most people in his social class realised that the teachings were not aligned with real-life behaviour. There was no way of distinguishing between the behaviour of those of the Orthodox faith and of nonbelievers and so there seemed little value dedicating time and effort to something that did not confer any benefit. In fact, he felt the believers were more selfish, immoral, cruel, and of lower intellect than the nonbelievers.

His faith was not only lost in religion but also in his fellow artists and writers. There was no agreement in whose works were right and so there could be no teaching of the truth. They all felt their work was right and everyone else's was wrong. He started to see these people he was amongst as a horror and that he was no different. He also realised the drive in all his fellow writers came from a love of money and notoriety and that the fruits of their labour were actually pretty worthless. But it was rationalized as worthwhile because the thought of it being meaningless was too painful to consider. Tolstoy felt that had there been agreement in their teachings, the false belief in it all having value may have perpetuated, but there were always diametrically opposing views and so it was clear to him that they were all deluding themselves.

This madness, as he called it, went on for six years. And when he visited Europe, he saw the same belief driving people there too. He saw that people believed in a concept we know as "progress." But really it is a rudderless boat that carries us to places we have no real say in. The sight of an execution in Paris made it clear to him that so-called "progress" was flawed and that there was no justification for such brutal actions—and he vowed his morality must come from within and not in accordance with societal norms. The slow and painful death of his young brother made a mockery of the so-called "progress" too. His brother neither knew why he had lived nor why he was dying at a young age. Extremely negative experiences like this understandably led to him questioning progress, and even life itself.

Despite these seeds of doubt, he carried on with a sense that the development of everything, including himself, would become clear at a later date. It was only engagement in family life that deferred his descent into despair. Fifteen years passed and his life had become about improvements in his material situation. Whilst he wrote during this period, he considered it a trivial endeavour (this was the time when he wrote *War and Peace*). He admits that he stifled any inner yearning concerning the meaning of life during this period.

He then began to experience periods of depression. These became more frequent and left him wondering: Why? And what next? They seemed trivial and something easily solvable if he were to ever get the urge to apply his mind to them. But then he realised: The questions may be trivial but the answers are not. And they became urgent to him—he wanted to know why he did anything that he did. He wanted reasons for doing all that he did, from educating his son to writing and tending to an estate.

All sense of satisfaction had vanished. His fame meant nothing. He said that if a fairy arose and could give him anything, he would not know what to have wished for. He had reached the conclusion that life was meaningless and that it was all a delusion. During the times meaning seemed to return, he saw these as habits of old desires and not as true desires. And in times that he proclaimed full clarity, he'd thought that all desires were a delusion. This was accompanied by thoughts of suicide as strong as his prior ones for improving life.

Life was nothing but a joke. He'd fantasized about some being outside of life, amused at the realisation that he had spent some 30 to 40 years evolving and progressing only to find there is actually nothing in life and never will be. He was astonished that he had not seen this much earlier. How could he not realise that any achievements will one day be forgotten and that he will be dead regardless? He was also amazed that all people are aware of it and yet live.

The idea of accepting that there could be no answer to the meaning of life, and carrying on regardless, was unpalatable as he had already endured too many years living like that. The one truth to Tolstoy was the inevitability of death. He saw life as per an Eastern myth where a traveller is chased by a beast into a well – with a dragon at its bottom. The traveller clings to a branch between these two points of certain death as black and white mice appear and gnaw at the branch. However, there was honey on the leaves of the branch and the traveller reached out and licked the honey. For Tolstoy, the honey had no appeal anymore because his fate, and the processes leading to his fate, were his primary focuses.

Tolstoy knew that some horror awaited (death), and even though he knew that it was not relevant to him immediately, it was an inevitability all the same. He could not stand the tension of this knowing. His search for an answer to the meaning of life was far from trivial. He spent day and night on his quest. He had many connections—access to some of the best sources of knowledge available and was still unable to find any useful answers.

He found that science could not provide the answers he sought and neither could the more speculative *"science"* subjects (which made unsatisfactory guesses). He said,

> *"Should experimental science run into a question concerning ultimate cause, it stumbles over nonsense."*

Great minds of the past such as Aristotle, Socrates, Schopenhauer, Solomon, and the Buddha were of no help either, as they came to much the same conclusions as he. As such, he turned to life for answers instead of knowledge. However, he found no solace here either.

He talked of four means of escape from the terrible situation he and those of similar education and way of life endure:

1. **Ignorance:** Failing to see meaninglessness. Failing to see the problem of life identified by Socrates, Schopenhauer, Solomon, and the Buddha. He felt this group consisted mainly of women, the very young or very stupid men. They see neither the dragon nor the mice gnawing away at the branch and simply lap up the honey. But he felt sure something would eventually turn their attention to the dragon and mice.

He had nothing to learn from these people as you cannot un-know what you already know.

2. **Epicureanism:** Enjoying blessings while ignoring the dragon and mice. This was what Solomon's advice was despite knowing the absurdity of life. This, according to Tolstoy, was the most popular means of escape. But this is only really possible while the balance beam of good and bad favours the good, and he reminds us that, for every palace like Solomon's, there are thousands who built it by the sweat of their brow. Also, even the privileged can experience negative changes in circumstance(s).

   He felt these people lacked imagination and that they somehow forgot the gravity of what kept the pre-enlightened Buddha from peace—sickness, ageing, and death. The positive psychology instinctively adopted by these people made them no different from the ignorant. Tolstoy could not imitate these people because he did not lack imagination and so the mice and the dragon could not simply be forgotten.

3. **Suicide:** In his view, the strong way out. Knowing life is pointless and a *"joke,"* this was the most logical way. And he stated that more and more in his class were choosing this route. He also suggested this was mainly done by those in the peak of life when they had strength of soul and fewer habits that undermine reason. He wanted this route for himself.

4. **Weakness:** Despite knowing life is meaningless (and nothing will come of it), carrying on regardless. Sometimes there is a delusional hope, and these people wait as though something will happen but really the true motive for avoiding the means of escape number 3 is weakness.

He chose means number 4 and hated himself for this, resulting in attempts to rationalize his behaviour. He knew that it was reason that led him to declare that life was irrational, and there appeared to be nothing higher than reason, meaning it is what makes life itself real.

Yet, there was a paradox because it makes life real and yet allows for the realisation that life is irrational. Likewise, no life would mean no potentiality for reason—so life was real, for sure. Until you get to see the solution, the paradox is real. The solution arises from knowing that our life essences are real but all life circumstances are not. Obviously, if you are unfamiliar with this truth you will need huge amounts of evidence which we will get to later.

He pondered on the fact that humans had been around for millennia and found meaning in life even though he had concluded it was meaningless. It felt to him like he was missing something and, yet, he could not see any solution. Some people may not understand Tolstoy's predicament, and a modern philosopher once wrote that feelings similar to those expressed by Tolstoy were existential snobbery and that the romantics were to blame for this. However, what bothered Tolstoy was not illusory unlike, say, an irrational fear of a small harmless insect and so the fact that some people can consciously and subconsciously inhibit emotional reactions to an issue of such a magnitude does not mean the thoughts and emotional reactions of those affected are in any way irrational.

For those who cannot see the gravity of Tolstoy's predicament, maybe a few thought experiments may help illustrate his worldview. Imagine you have not been given long to live and knew that if you embarked on a degree course, you would die 2/3 of the way through the course. Would you still enroll? I think this would depend on whether the attending of lessons and learning is meaningful in its own right rather than just a means to an end. For those who want the knowledge and qualification solely for a brighter future, they would probably change their priorities and perhaps use their remaining time on *"bucket list"* items and with friends and family.

Or imagine you were tasked with building an architectural masterpiece that takes years, knowing in advance it would be destroyed shortly thereafter—most would think that this prior knowledge of the building's fate makes the work pointless. This is how those who see life as pointless feel about life itself. In other words, it is a destruction of the self, not the fruits of one's labour, and unlike a destroyed building that can be rebuilt, this destruction cannot be rectified and marks the end of the potential for pleasure, love, and meaning for infinity. Or so it seems.

Tolstoy felt that consciousness of life, over reason, was what kept him from means number 3. This metaphysical force is what took him from despair, into a direction that was away from reason. It had also occurred to him that his social class did not represent all of humanity and that the answers he sought may lie in the life of humanity as a whole. Up until this point, he considered all the lower classes as animals.

Before going into more detail about what he felt was the solution, I think he missed another means of accessing feelings of meaningfulness, possibly two. Whilst he clearly acknowledges having suicidal depression, it does not seem to have occurred to him that the capacity to experience meaning comes with the prerequisite for a person to be free of the symptoms of depression. Although there is nothing wrong with his reasoning, he somehow fails to see that, with no symptoms of depression, there is a capacity to feel meaning as well as a sense of interconnectedness; although meaning is in some sense subjective, it is also objectively real because the mind and consciousness make it so.

Evidence of this is that many people are equally aware of what he waxes lyrically about and yet are unaffected. Not because they lack imagination and are living a purely hedonistic life to avoid thinking about the reality of the situation—but because they do have a strong sense of meaning. Some people have speculated that meaning is merely a phantom arising via the evolutionary processes and probably unique to the human mind, evidenced by the diversity of what is meaningful to any individual(s), but as mentioned previously, this unique and distinct experience is as real as pain. This trend of erroneous thinking does not account for the fact that true meaning is deeper than the counterfeit meaning experienced via the engagement within the apparent "out there" reality, which grabs at most people's attention every waking hour.

Another means could also be via enlightenment, which can potentially arise through certain practices, intuition, or possibly even from a mental breakdown that somehow resets the mind so that it becomes free from torment, leaving it to experience the extraordinary power of presence (an awareness of being aware). In other words, the kind of state that spiritual teacher and writer Eckhart Tolle enjoys. His enlightenment came via the latter route, although he is an advocate of meditating on the present moment as a means to experience the "Power of Now." Given that this state is effectively a form of mindfulness meditation which is proven to alter the brain anatomy and physiology and, in turn, immunize or help cure people of depression—some of the people Tolstoy would have placed in categories 1, 2, and 4 may have actually had a deep sense of meaning due to being *"present"* most of the time.

If my understanding about this is correct, then whatever later pacified him (his solution) will have simultaneously lifted his depression and/or coincided with the lifting of it and so the sense of meaning could be attributed to this, even though it would be seen as a direct consequence of what it is that he had felt pacified him. There are millions of atheists who are fully aware of what Tolstoy became obsessed with, and yet most have a sense of meaning despite it, and despite *"knowing"* that they will ultimately face the fate that obsessed him—therefore I would suggest that the mood disorder is the most relevant factor and not whether you are a believer or nonbeliever.

Having said that, many of those who ruminate on existential nihilism may find it results in existential depression and so what they conclude (ultimate meaningless) will be felt as well as known intellectually. This will then lock them in a vicious cycle because the lowered mood will likely lead to further meaninglessness as a key symptom. It would make sense that nonbelievers should be more susceptible to this because they do not have faith that there is a bigger purpose. However, the mood disorder hits believers and nonbelievers alike and so believers can also fall into a pit of meaninglessness.

His personal solution arose out of exploring the lives of the lower classes. He realised they were not as stupid as he had assumed— that they were aware of the question of the meaning of life and could answer it. They were not Epicureans as most of their lives were marked with deprivation and suffering more than pleasure. These people also saw suicide as a great sin.

The solution lay in the irrational (God) because knowledge seemed to exclude rather than add meaning from his perspective. But he struggled with an acceptance of this because it meant to have blind faith. It seemed you had to have reason in order to have meaning and so to turn away from reason and act according to faith was practically unthinkable.

He saw faith as a genuine and real force of life though and he realised that everyone must have faith in something or they would not live. So, he studied various religions, especially the one he was already familiar with, i.e., Orthodox Christianity that existed in his class of people. But he saw an error in all their teachings and that they did not live as they professed and so fell back into despair. He looked again at the lives of the poor and adopted their faith. He spotted superstitions within the Christian teachings but noticed that this class of people embraced them and made it all a part of their daily life.

He observed that his class of people, who had spent their lives in idleness, hedonism, and discontent, was contrary to the poor who, despite all their hard labour, were generally much less dissatisfied. He, ironically, came to similar conclusions as Jim Carrey and realised that the Epicurean life sought by so many was the opposite route to the one leading to happiness or meaning. He had seen life as evil because of his life situation, rather than because of his thinking.

It became clear to him that animals appear contented and humans are the ones who, often, are not. And so, he felt we should be more like the animals but with the key difference that we should live life for all and not just the self. It seems he was able to rationalize about meaning in some sense after all.

Months of a *"believing in God and then not"* cycle followed and he describes a long period of corresponding elation and depression. And it became obvious that he only enjoyed a sense of meaning during his periods of belief. When settling on the Orthodox Church, he had issues with the claim of past miracles, inconsistencies in teachings, and each sector of the church claiming any other was *"the enemy."* The Church even condoned killings and prayed for weapons. The final move by Tolstoy was to spend vast amounts of time trying to establish the difference between the truth and the lies.

In short, a return to a faith in God restored a will to continue living along with a recognition that his life had lacked meaning because of the behaviours he had engaged in, rather than any faulty logic. Either way, I think the pacification of the mind and the thoughts it created for him would have impacted his mood disorder and that this would have been a key contributor to the restoration of a sense of meaning within him. This is not reported on and so seems to have been overlooked as a key potential contributor to the restoration of meaning. A quiet mind finds meaning in existence itself.

It is interesting to hear the thoughts of such a knowledgeable and well-educated man of such reputation. I think the main *"take home"* message is that human meaning is personal and that despite his belief that religion is the only salvation, atheists are clearly just as able to gain a sense of meaning. Tolstoy seemed to overlook depression (anatomy and physiology/chemical issues in the brain) as a key contributor to his meaninglessness—perhaps not fully appreciating that meaning is a state which is severely inhibited by mood disorder in the same way happiness is.

To highlight how important mood is, a bipolar sufferer will freely admit that life circumstances need not change for their whole sense of meaning to change—it can be completely dependent on their mood. A rapid-cycling bipolar sufferer can literally go from a feeling of meaning and connectedness with a drive to clean, create, engage in rapid pattern recognition, multitask, etc. to feeling suicidal within minutes—stripped of any meaning with a sense that the whole process of life is mundane and, in fact, absurd. Consciousness is clearly a prerequisite for the capacity to enter a state of meaningfulness and, yet, it also requires that the brain is operating within the capacity it has evolved to, i.e., to sense meaning. This is how critical mood is to the meaning of life.

Of course, there are a huge number of actions that can be taken to enhance or alter mood. But genetics is known to play one of the biggest roles, because with two long alleles in certain genes, a person is three times less likely to become depressed when faced with two or more significant, negative, life events.

Despite the critical omission in Tolstoy's account, his insight into the meaning of life does, in fact, reaffirm that without some spiritual dimension, the capacity to feel meaning does not guarantee that there is any intrinsic meaning, even though the potential for a sense and experience of meaning cannot be disputed.

How the potential for there to be no intrinsic meaning in the universe impacts a person is very much likely to depend upon their individual nature. A pessimist would more than likely feel that no intrinsic meaning makes human meaning somehow counterfeit and certainly will be right in knowing all pleasures of the flesh must end as life ends. An optimist will realise how short life is and that the capacity to have a sense of meaning as well as pleasure and happiness is a gift—that every moment should be cherished.

Einstein's view on the meaning of life is much more upbeat. Whilst he suffered later in life with depression himself as did Newton and Darwin, he is responsible for the quotation at the start of the chapter, namely;

> *"What is the meaning of human life, or, for that matter, of the life of any creature?*
>
> *To know an answer to this question means to be religious.*
>
> *You ask: Does it make any sense, then, to pose this question?*
>
> *I answer: The man who regards his own life and that of his fellow creatures as meaningless is not merely unhappy but hardly fit for life."*

Despite what Professor Richard Dawkins seems to believe, Einstein made several references to his view that science and religion were not mutually exclusive. For example: *"Science without religion is lame, religion without science is blind,"* said Einstein in his 1954 essay on science and religion.

Einstein was a pantheist and was an advocate of Spinoza's philosophy. He rejected a personal God with human attributes and equated all of reality with Divinity. Dawkins refers to Einstein, in light of his beliefs, as a *"sexed up atheist."* However, Einstein also referred in his writings to a superior spirit/mind vastly superior to the mind of man. In an earlier quotation, he expressed Buddhist-like beliefs too: *"The true value of a human being is determined primarily by the measure and the sense in which he has attained liberation from the self."* I believe what Einstein meant by the self was the same egoic mind that Buddha recognized was responsible for the illusion of self (and physical reality).

This theme of liberation from the self to glimpse life's true meaning is also echoed by Einstein in a 1950 letter to console a grieving father, Robert S. Marcus:

"A human being is a part of the whole, called by us "Universe,' a part limited in time and space. He experiences himself, his thoughts and feelings as something separate from the rest—a kind of optical delusion of his consciousness. The striving to free oneself from this delusion is the one issue of true religion. Not to nourish it but to try to overcome it is the way to reach the attainable measure of peace of mind."

Einstein also gives his views on money and wealth:

"I am absolutely convinced that no wealth in the world can help humanity forward, even in the hands of the most devoted worker in this cause. The example of great and pure characters is the only thing that can lead us to noble thoughts and deeds. Money only appeals to selfishness and irresistibly invites abuse. Can anyone imagine Moses, Jesus or Gandhi armed with the money-bags of Carnegie?"

To summarise the chapter, it seems to me that the rational mind is both the making of mankind and its number one enemy. Whilst theory of mind and rational thinking are the jewels in the crown of evolution, it is also the reason we can ruminate and ponder our own mortality. Emotionally charged rumination can cause and perpetuate depression, as can habitually thinking of the past and future instead of the now. Similarly, the logic underlying the conclusion that life ultimately lacks intrinsic meaning can remove the sense of it.

The evolutionary advantages of rational thinking are clearly huge and so it is a small wonder that the evolutionary process has *"harnessed"* it, as it has incrementally come to be. However, this has also led to incessant thinking known as the *"thought stream."* An automatic and largely negative subconscious habit that can be observed during mindfulness meditation—a practice that has scientifically been proven to help people experience more peace of mind by altering the brain anatomy and physiology as mentioned earlier.

It is worth mentioning here that 5000 years of Asian knowledge does not enter mainstream science and neither does the know-how of the indigenous people of America, South America, Australasia, etc. It is truly arrogant to believe that the modern Western scientific method is the only source of knowledge on the workings of reality. Alan Wallace jokes about the question of whether there is any other intelligent life in the universe, and he answers, "Yeh…Asia!"

Western science studies what is related to the mind but no branches of science study it in a direct way. Asia has done so for 5000 years and the Buddhist tradition for 2500 years. Western science is great at what it does but it has so many blind spots that it is unwilling to recognize and rectify. Methods exist to analyse thoughts and layers of consciousness but, in the meantime, the skills/capacity of Westerners' focus, in general, have fallen into an ADHD-like state and so the chances of getting deep within the self are next to impossible. This is a state that is worsening and may very well be irreversible now that mobile phones are ubiquitously perpetuating a constant flow of trivial information.

The mind-body connection and the measurement problem in quantum mechanics remain unresolved and the reason seems quite obvious. There is no scientific approach to the nature of the observer and it is the biggest shortcoming of modern science. The West is great at objective science but is ignorant of rigorous and refined first-person enquiry into the nature of the Mind. Fortunately, for those who care to follow all the evidence that science already provides, there is good news: as the true nature of reality can be understood via science itself.

4

WHAT DARWIN, DAWKINS ET AL APPEARED TO MISS

"There is no matter as such. All matter originates and exists only by virtue of a force which brings the particle of an atom to vibration and holds this most minute solar system together. We must assume behind this force the existence of a conscious and intelligent mind. This mind is the matrix of all matter."

Max Planck, Quantum Theorist

The fundamental *"laws of nature"* used to bewilder me until a candidate for how reality actually works, rather than how mainstream science *"believes"* it does, came into focus as part of my experience of self-realisation (and more importantly an ability to access pure logic; more powerful than the language of mathematics). Take a magnet and observe how iron filings react to it; how seemingly arbitrary does it appear that this force of magnetism exists? I have to accept that the probability of what happens is one (i.e., certain) because it is indisputably a part of perceived reality. But only hyper-normalization makes it seem anything less than extraordinary.

In accordance with Darwin's theory, evolution is generally accepted to be a blind bottom-up system that leads to vast manifestations/biodiversity. What is not mentioned is that all the manifestations *"created"* via evolution already had to be potentialities. They were/are all, without exception, not only feasible potentialities but ones that always conform to the *"laws of nature"* as they arise through the evolutionary process which is ultimately a non physical (mind) phenomenon. They could not have been impossible potentialities because, like magnetism, they are actual manifestations within reality and so their probability of existence within reality is one.

Impossible, by definition, means something that can never manifest. Not improbable beyond comprehension where near-infinite time can still manifest what seemed to be near impossible but nothing short of an absolute miracle. Due to the laws of nature, a human will never be able to jump from the base to the top of the Eiffel Tower without changes to the laws of physics or the assistance of an artificial aid—it does not matter if you allow a million years, a billion years, or an eternity.

So, the potentialities underlying phenomena such as the mind perceiving the colour blue, meaning, nonrandom movement, the development of the various senses, etc. all had to be possible and not impossible as did the manifestations that arose from these potentialities. All of them being potentialities during the infinite time, or no time, leading to the Big Bang(s), despite them all being a long way off being manifest at the infancy of our universe (multiverses). As mentioned, evolution has to abide by the laws of nature and so both the process itself and emerging manifest *"creations"* must abide by constitutive, yet dynamic parameters inherent within physics, chemistry, etc.

It is akin to a voyage of discovery, uncovering many unimaginable manifestations whose potentialities already preexisted, but would have remained unmanifest without the process blindly, or seemingly blindly, leading to their manifestation through mutation made *"feelers."*

The paradox is that many of the "paranormal" manifestations that arise appear to infringe upon the laws of physics, e.g., the existence of nonrandom willed movement. Many also defy the laws of probability, e.g., all the distinct senses in the animal world supposedly have arisen as a result of the notion that the properties of life are so accommodating, that in cahoots with an inherent but super-rare predisposition for beneficial mutations which exists in replication, biologically unwitnessed phenomena such as photons and olfactible molecules transform from unidentified data in flux to being information transmitted and received, encoded, and decoded by biological formations. One remarkable example of this is the European Robin's ability to sense quantum entanglement to aid navigation via the earth's magnetic field. Another being the retired Scottish nurse who can "*smell*" serious diseases, along with certain dogs who have been documented (having been trained) to be able to smell cancers. These are both discussed in detail later in the book.

Some manifestations also operate apparently beyond cause and effect, e.g., smells, colours, and other qualities are mind-made but somehow fundamental because they are independently real and rooted in physical phenomena. They are as distinct as the phenomena that trigger them but ultimately not "caused" by the phenomena—consciousness is required for their existence and, in fact, for the apparent cause (trigger) as well as the respective experiences.

In other words, many phenomena appear impossible yet their possibility is proven by their very manifestation. Once the straight jacket thinking of automatically assuming that methodological naturalism (a belief that phenomena are always free of any kind of directing influence) underpins our reality, is cut away, these apparent impossibilities disappear, and a much clearer picture of what is happening comes into focus.

In biological evolution, not only is it an extraordinary fact that mutations have incubated the alteration of an organism's form to allow it to experientially "capture" and make sense of independent phenomena (e.g. photons), it is extraordinary that, additionally, certain inventions/creations have manifested through such evolutionary processes. I am talking about phenomena such as colour that did not preexist in nature for use in this novel and *"comprehensible"* way until such creation/arbitrary interpretation (experience) occurred. In other words, the creation of certain arbitrary phenomena seemingly arises due to a combination of evolution and consciousness, resulting in real magic (conveniently arming organisms with more and more complex abilities and senses).

Although the magic perhaps seems less obvious when we observe the process itself (the algorithms and creations of evolution coming into being), we should still be mindful of our conditioned hyper-normalization. This is a deep cognitive bias, a veil raised by our ability to describe theory with simplicity and logic. But in truth, the whole manifestation of animated complex clusters of energy is quite bizarre, as are the existence of all complex structures in the universe, especially ribonucleic acids, proteins, and the genetic input-output, self-modifying system. However impossible, it must be possible, for it undeniably exists. We should be able to accept that. As we, our very understanding and ability to accept that, are manifestations of the system itself. Its potentiality was and is encoded into our reality alongside the potentialities of the many manifestations emerging as the process carries on, seemingly blindly.

I cannot stress enough—this does not mean that the whole process of evolution itself is not a manifestation of a potentiality, heretofore unexplained in terms of an ultimate cause. It is typically hyper-normalization that makes everyone feel as though our experiences of reality are meant to be as they are. As if they are inevitable results of stochastic permutations declaring matter-of-factly "nothing to see here, folks, keep moving along."

Another aspect of evolution which, when scrutinized is profound and extremely improbable, is the selectivity of female reproduction in many species (seeking and shaping better gene fitness indicators/ beauty). Given that animals already have the capacity for mobility and/or a conscious/subconscious adaptability to sensory information, allowing discernability among mate choice, in addition to predator, prey, and gender identifiability—it is not so surprising that mutations arise to effectually cause heritable choosiness. This is assuming you accept that will/goal-orientation is inherent in choosiness and any other nonrandom action and is axiomatic and possible without some hidden external intelligent force/agency. By assuming this, there is an automatic challenge to methodological naturalism because the assumption automatically means there has to be a primacy of consciousness and intelligence.

It then only takes a binding of sexual choosiness to coincide with a selection for improved environmental fitness and/or social beauty for the perpetuation of the trait or behaviour, passing from generation to generation (including the resulting exaggeration of the relevant fitness indicator/aesthetic traits on the basis that each level of exaggeration provides more accurate information about fitness and/or beauty).

If we look at a few of these seemingly impossible manifestations separately, the oversight to which I refer in the chapter title should become more apparent. As mentioned earlier in the book, colours are a mind-made illusion as well as real and distinct once manifest. Red and blue objects do not have an inherent red or blue nature— the experience differences arise due to the varying wavelengths that are perceived as red and blue in the mind. Consciousness is required to bring these colours into reality, but nobody could dispute that— just because they are mind-made, this does not mean they are not also real. All colours appear in our reality as distinct and, although they exist in the mind alone, are still somehow real. Just as real, in fact, as phenomena outside of the mind which, as we will discuss, are not as real as they seem anyway.

It is as though the causation of this type of manifestation (experiences) is not limited to the building block method of evolution, which may surely be the case for physical manifestations at the very least, because when certain conditions are met, seemingly impossible and novel manifestations emerge like colour perception, smell perception etc. (genuine creations).

This gives the illusion that evolution is the cause of all manifestations when "correlation" is a more accurate description. Many manifestations are novel, metaphysical states that are quite independent of the evolutionary process; that is necessary only insofar that it facilitates the apparent creation of the sensory organs that are required in order to experience, via augmentation, qualia in our physical realm.

Because perception-based pattern recognition, as in observing what appears to be spontaneous fortuitous causes underpinning the whole evolutionary process, is hyper-normalized, the more trivial fruits of this phenomenon are assumed by most to be non-metaphysical. For example, the morphing of wolves into countless species of dog is seen as non-miraculous because the process can be observed and described in terms that even a child could understand.

It seems that not all miracles were born equal because the origins of the anatomy and physiology of sensory organs appears more miraculous than the diverging shapes and sizes of dogs through selective breeding. But in the final analysis, all of evolution is miraculous and it is hyper-normalization and an unwillingness to investigate ultimate cause(s) that makes it seem otherwise.

How we experience the differentiation between colours is arbitrary, in similarity to smells, and these differences are something the mind creates based upon sensing wavelength or chemical/molecular information respectively. Maybe evolution could have led to alternative, equally informative ways of us to experience these. Arbitrary or not, these experiences came about from a potentiality, and what we experience happens to be the manifestation that has conveniently arisen. As such, red and blue (as we perceive them) were always a possibility because their existence proves they were not impossible outcomes. However, the manifestations themselves cannot be explained by mutations because it would imply that the mutations were involved in creating and bringing red and blue, as an experience, completely into being and it is consciousness that plays this key role. This applies to all of our senses.

Evolution as we currently perceive it is the business of blindly altering traits due to mutations. This also constructs the illusion that it is a machine for creating new phenomena. What really happens is that the Mind creates a template for that which ultimately manifests into physical reality as an experience and object. Hyper-normalization makes us think that red and blue are in nature whether conscious observers exist or not. This is false. What you experience and see is an undisputed form of creation and its existence, even within the mind's eye alone, means that something that was not a part of the material world now exists from *"no-thing."* Furthermore, it has become as *"real"* as the invisible wavelengths that give rise to the mind-made experience. They are not merely the subjective results of the imagination but are the results of *"external world wave"* to an *"internal world experience"* transformations: Conversions and correspondences that can only occur thanks to an, as yet, unexplained phenomenon we call consciousness. If you still believe that red and blue just exist *"out there"* and always have, then you have failed to appreciate that they are not phenomena in physical nature at all. The fact you can experience them means creation was not entropically reserved solely for the time when the universe came into being, as in the so-called Big Bang. There is significant evidence later in this book that colour is a mind-made phenomenon and not something that exists as part of any object independent of minds.

Physicalism is the thesis that everything is physical, with consciousness being a kind of emergent illusory state. This means, according to this false belief, that all qualia such as pain, love, colour experience, etc. are deemed part of that illusion. The argument is that, because the physical brain is involved in the modeling of the world, it would be nothing short of a miracle for this model to exactly match the unprovable nonphysical phenomena (deemed to be a hallucination by physicalism advocates) that appear in the model. In other words, because the brain is producing a useful model based on algorithms, it could not as the argument goes, by chance at least, produce a model that coincidentally represents reality as it truly is. This means the colour blue, according to this thinking, neither exists in physical reality nor in a nonphysical reality but is allegedly conjured up by a brain-created model. Of course, it has nothing to say about who or what is experiencing the colour—it is just assumed that the experience is a phantom one. It is quite insulting because it is one thing to be experiencing an agreed upon hallucination which, for many, may devalue the experience—but to say it is just some phantom experience arising due to firings within the brain is another level altogether. Perhaps, those who share this worldview would reconsider their position if they faced a spell at Guantanamo Bay Detention Camp.

In truth, many of the Mind duality-based qualia illusions are created by Universal Consciousness, a manifestation of who or what we all are in physical form. The alternative possibility that a brain-made model uses some kind of extrasensory perception enabling the model to include experiences/phenomena that closely emulate true reality or even include actual phenomena from a nonphysical reality seems even less plausible, though, until considered more deeply. But even this is only a step closer to truth. It is somewhat like Newtonian gravity which, thanks to Einstein, shifted towards a more accurate model that describes how it is more of a bending of space-time. This is how it works in terms of the prescribed mathematics within the physical material realm we perceive but once we go deeper into the fallibility of our senses it shows us that even Einstein's model doesn't reflect the fundamental truth. I believe true love, for example, is fundamental in this sense and transcends the Mind-created duality.

However, the physicalism position overlooks a critical issue. If the brain is creating phenomena that arise via algorithms alone, then what is the reference used to model the illusory phenomena on? The first-person experiences are nothing like the causes that give rise to the experiences. Accordingly, this would imply that the models can spontaneously create illusions that are as real, if not more real, than anything physical and yet because proponents of physicalism are *"certain"* about their worldview whereby qualia, according to its advocates, do not have an independent existence in a nonphysical realm, they lack an explanation of ultimate cause. Not only that, they also lack an explanation for what first-person experience is and how it came about.

The algorithms that they believe are all that is needed for the magic to happen, apparently lack a reference/benchmark on which to base these vivid and distinct phenomena. Of course, the brain (mind) is capable of seeing colours that are not actually there, i.e. their invisible waveform equivalent can be absent in certain circumstances but the colour appears, nonetheless, and so optical (and auditory) illusions are common, as we will explore later in the book. However, the fact that the brain can be stimulated to produce the experience through *"false"* inputs does not explain how such distinct phenomena came into being, whether falsely triggered or correctly triggered, via some purportedly blind modeling system.

Because the brain itself is not passive in the perception process, it is a small wonder that areas giving rise to certain perceptions can be stimulated in "error." In other words, visual and auditory illusions show that the *"system"* (brain/mind calculations) is far from 100 percent reliable, but this does not mean that the distinct and universally experienced qualia are complete illusions. Likewise, as we will see later in the book, a key part of the visual information we access does not actually form part of our mind's eye image but is used for motor function. This system requires more detailed and accurate information than our virtual reality mind's eye imagery can provide and so it operates independently from it—albeit subconsciously. However, consciousness does not disappear from the equation simply because our motor functions are, generally, subconsciously controlled. Consciousness (awareness) is also a prerequisite to experiencing the world as any such motor function occurs.

If it transpires that the physical brain is a manifestation of localized consciousness, which is the localized mind, and the localized mind is a form of receiver that is capable of *"access"* to nonphysical phenomena, this will overcome the physicalists' argument that modeling cannot match reality by chance. This is because, as mentioned, the model would be using real phenomena and so could either match it precisely or would at least create a simulation that is a close approximation. In other words, if the mind uses real nonphysical phenomena, it could simply integrate them with the brain/mind-made model, i.e. the mind as a receiver—hypothesis would show that qualia are as real as what we perceive as material despite them being something that exists outside the physical world. This correlates with what Nicola Tesla observed in respect to Universal Consciousness. It should be clarified each step of the way that the distinction between "out there" phenomena and augmented experiential phenomena is ultimately illusory because even the former occurs in a singularity (Mind) and so it is only the perception process (illusion) experienced by life entities that creates the apparent distinction.

I do not believe that even the most complex AI robots will ever experience qualia because algorithms can only ever enhance functions and capabilities that are mathematical and/or based upon pure logic, while the subjective first-person experience(s) require consciousness. For this reason, I think it is also highly unlikely that brains create qualia through complex algorithms, as physicalists believe, and that it is only nonmaterial minds that are capable of experiencing phenomena from a nonmaterial realm via the primacy of consciousness. Even if it turns out that most qualia are mind-made and, as per physicalism, have no independent reality, unless someone has the capacity to transcend localized mind perceptions (e.g. expert meditators who can reduce or eliminate pain or make themselves immune to the startle response), they will always be subjectively real. Even though expert meditators may be able to mitigate or possibly even eliminate the experience of pain, they are unlikely to be able to override more fundamental qualia such as colour experiences or love. This is because certain qualia are absolute truths and are not localized mind-made. These are simply augmented into perceived reality within the mind's eye model.

Photons preceded photo receptivity by billions of years but clearly the potentiality for the ultimate "*sensing*" of them was there, otherwise something impossible has occurred, i.e. a miracle. As mentioned earlier, the paradox is that the potentiality and final manifestation(s) cannot be impossible because they exist and, yet, the potentiality itself appears impossible. Imagine a time that is in the pre-Big Bang illusion of duality and the idea that the arbitrary phenomenon, to be referred to as the photon, would "*one day*" be a manifestation— it is easy in hindsight to observe its presence and behaviour(s) but reality has basically brought this into being as though it were a non-conjuring version of the "*rabbit from the hat*" trick. It is often conveniently overlooked that the Big Bang and all fundamental phenomena were potentialities "*waiting*" to emerge, having all derived from nothing. Or if they were just preexisting states that arose from a permanently cycling system where quantum phenomena pop in and out of reality, then it is the same miracle coming in through the back door.

Now, picture a time where you had become hyper-normalized by (or to) the photon phenomena, i.e. you have got used to the phenomenon but don't really understand its ultimate cause, from the formless state of existence, despite being able to deduce it has somehow arisen and exists in our perceived reality. We are investigating a time that is still way before life on earth in our thought experiment. And now imagine the possibility that something would arise that could react to the existence of this fundamental particle— something that would, in fact, make sense of it and "*treat*" it as a form of energy and information. You may, because you already know something can come from noTHING in our reality, sense that there is more to come of the so-called "*laws of nature.*" In other words, more than photons colliding with inorganic objects and being affected by large sources of gravity but otherwise moving in straight lines emanating from their source. However, the idea of something so complex emerging that it would mean billions of years into the future, the phenomenon could become *"visible"* and be sensed in its capacity as an information carrier would surely be inconceivable. It would be highly serendipitous for compounds that *"react"* to the photon to emerge in an apparent evolving universe, but the idea of the concept/experience of vision being *"created"* to *"make sense"* of a prior phenomenon (the photon) would be nothing short of a miraculous coincidence. Not surprisingly, this simplistic and yet miraculous account of the sensing of a prior existing phenomenon is highly inaccurate. Not only this, linear time is also an illusion, since many great minds already acknowledged this factual reality. All events and experiences, as well as perceptions relating to them, only occur in the present moment. This means that the fairly complex evolutionary process just described is really just a hallucination because all evolution depends on linear time being other than illusory. It should be becoming apparent at this stage in the book that reality is a far cry from what our fallible senses and mainstream science would have us believe.

The illusion of time is illustrated in a beautiful poem by one of my talented friends, Marcus Thor Soderlund.

'Time is an Illusion'

Ebb and Flow of Energy and Mass
Is What Makes Seem Like Time Does Pass.

And at the Root of All Confusion:
Is Time,
A Grand and Old Illusion.

Without an End.
With No Beginning.

Circle of Time Keeps Ever Spinning.
Back to the End,
To a New Beginning.

The Endless Circle,
Keeps on Winding.
In Energy Endless
New Mass Is Bearing
A Birth
To a New and Fleeting Being:
Time
The Illusion All-Deceiving.

Order from Chaos
For Ever Seeking
For Time to Do
Its Own Undoing.

When Search of Order
Comes to a Finish,
The Time Will Come
For Time Will Perish.

The Order Balanced,
In End Will Attest:
That Time
Shall Have Its Final Rest.

In Infinity Endlessness
Time Shall Slumber.

...Never More Arise,
Tear Energy Asunder.

Universe in Time,
In a Time Long Passing;
Finality Finds,
With End of Time:
Its Final Fated Form.
Status Quo Sublime.
All Encompassing.
To Timelessness,
Will Then Time Conform.

The emerging complexity of inorganic and then organic matter meant photo receptivity was both a potentiality and, in time, something to be manifest. It is as though once the baseball was thrown (photon), evolution was *"installed"* to facilitate the manufacture of the perfect baseball glove (photo receptivity). You did not, therefore, factor in another potential creation event—this time life! Along with its inherent evolutionary process that can, apparently, blindly *"feel"* its way to hidden phenomena. It is able to create, despite statistical impossibility, the morphing *"keys"* (receptivity in various forms) to fit prior manifest *"locks"* (that which can potentially be *"sensed,"* e.g. photons, sound waves, olfactible molecules, etc.) to use, yet, another analogy. The sensing ability and resulting actions of basic creatures are truly profound; to say nothing of the 3D model of the world they are gifted that is consciously experienced due to such sensing by animals at the higher levels of the perceived evolutionary food chain.

In short, unveiling the patterns that exist within the process of perceived evolution, and unveiling some of the products of this fairly simplistic process, are a far cry from unveiling the ultimate cause(s), in which the unmanifest becomes manifest in physical form—all a part of the illusion of being duality.

Another seemingly impossible and, yet, perceived evolutionary manifestation is nonrandom movement. A leaf falls from a tree and has no influence on where it will land, or so it seems. The shape of the leaf and wind conditions are relevant but nothing *"within"* the leaf itself appears to have any bearing. Compare this with an ant or a bee. This is not suggesting that their apparently nonrandom movements are anything other than unconscious but the manifestation of this form of will is still extraordinary all the same. To move from point A to point B in a nonrandom fashion means that random became nonrandom through a basic common ancestor (or had arisen inter-dependently along a current beholder's ancestry). Observe bees moving in a swarm. Observe ants working together to bring food to an ant hill. All is ultimately working in synchronicity. What creates this synchronized movement? Is it a Universal Consciousness, something greater than and, yet, the same as a localized consciousness known as the mind of man or animal?

It would be no surprise that mutations which lead to nonrandom movement would be harnessed by the process of infinite intelligence—the survival and reproduction advantages for conscious agents engaged in this perceived reality are huge. But the fact it would be harnessed does not explain how such a potentiality could arise. It is the same paradox again: Mobile creatures (of which we are one) cannot be an impossibility because we witness them, and, yet, the existence of such potentiality is unexplained. The existence of anyTHING rather than noTHING is unexplained, let alone arbitrary potentialities (despite highly speculative theories about how reality could spontaneously occur, along with matter and energy, the laws of nature and the essential precise constants in the illusion of duality). In other words, the same *"impossible to possible"* paradox applies all the way down—in the final case, it is that reality exists and, therefore, cannot have been impossible and, yet, the cause has to be contrary to what is normally deemed possible in accordance with the rules of the physical world.

I would say the ultimate cause(s) and perceived arbitrary laws of nature are miracles—the unmanifest appearing in the manifest illusion of duality—pending some scientific proof that they are not. An atheist would say these all have scientific explanations and we just have not understood them. If an ultimate cause exists that itself has no cause, it is hard to see how this could be anything other than a miracle, even if it is science that unveils it through the observation of duality. I maintain that all that is manifest is miraculous, including the process of evolution itself. It is hyper-normalization that blinds those who believe that seeing patterns equates to true comprehension. Scientism is merely a pseudo-religious kind of belief that differs from metaphysics in that robust patterns can be observed and often harnessed in science, which creates a huge assumption that the ultimate cause(s) will also reveal their secrets via the same scientific method.

The fact that science has tended to bring us closer to *"the truth"* as time has progressed does not mean that it is any closer to decoding base reality/unearthing ultimate cause(s). Any scientist who believes that science is a done deal the moment they leave their institutions—grasping a part sexual, and a greater part social proof of intelligence, and knowledge fitness indicator piece of paper (read degree, BA, BS, MA, MS, or PhD, etc.)—is guilty of what Professor Dawkins accuses religious people of—Laziness! They have closed their minds to Eastern "know-how," which predates modern science by millennia and will have seen a multitude of past geniuses who knew things that are all too easily dismissed despite the fact that the methods these Eastern geniuses adopted were basically the same as Einstein's key method. Namely, connecting to an inner world and learning via the power of the mind and Soul rather than the teachings of third parties.

Ironically, the strength of science is also its weakness as it is founded on the concept of methodological naturalism. This means that nearly all scientists assume that all processes are material and always undirected. However, this arbitrary *"rule"* is nothing other than a belief and one which is proving to be a barrier preventing the revelation of TRUTH. The reason for this is that science is not permitted to follow the evidence due to its own fundamental mind-contrived *"rule."* The paradox is that the same scientists all use the mind in their assessments of phenomena and this calls objective truth into question. As we will see, the mind provides what appears to be a true representation of objective reality when it is merely an illusion. In fact, everything is a hallucination because of how minds work, and it is the consensus of agreement on certain experiences that allow us to deduce what we think is *"out there."* This consensus is what many deem as reality, when in essence it is an illusion constructed of the illusion of duality.

As the book consistently demonstrates: Evolution appears to inevitably lead to selective sensing and perception which is helpful for organisms, including us, but offers no assurance of truth. Accordingly, scientists have to admit that getting to objective truth is difficult, if not impossible. Therefore, their whole methodology is far from infallible. Their mistaken belief is no different than the controversial belief held by Catholics that the Pope is infallible. In other words, it may provide a useful and reliable approximation of reality, but even if we ignore the fact that methodological naturalism and fake Christianity arrogantly precludes the following of evidence (i.e. evidence that indicates the existence of a superior Mind), the necessary inclusion of minds in the scientific process prevents science, as well as egoic mind-polluted organized religions, from getting to TRUTH. This applies when it comes to the phenomena that are deemed fully explained and understood, let alone the ultimate causes relating to phenomena that scientists or these organized religious leaders admit are unexplained.

Regarding this very issue in the context of science, Charles Darwin himself wrote: *"With me, the horrid doubt always arises whether the convictions of man's mind, which has been developed from the mind of the lower animals, are of any value or at all trustworthy. Would anyone trust in the convictions of a monkey's mind…?"* (Charles Darwin, Letter to William Graham, Down, Kent, July 3rd, 1881.) Of course, the same argument can be used to question the validity of all the evidence for some kind of intelligent design. However, the unavoidable involvement of the mind is much more likely to produce a distortion of general reality and, therefore, a distortion of truth in many scientific conclusions than it is to bring about the undisputed mathematical order observed in the male great argus pheasant pattern and ornament, for example. The transition via evolution of crude beauty to striking beauty in the form of incomprehensible order needs to be explained, even if it is a product of consciousness and not something that is a true reflection of reality. In other words, mathematical order and signatures of intelligence and design exist even if the great argus pheasants prove to be radically different from our mind-made representations.

I do not think anyone could seriously deny that the process of evolution is real. But I also do not think the fact that the process unveils many hidden potentialities, as opposed to being the cause of them, has been fully considered. According to mainstream science, every novel feature, be it physical, behavioural, or mind-made in tandem with evolving consciousness, had to have been a non-metaphysical potentiality because the alternative is impossible.

Mutations alone cannot create new phenomena. We need to explore TRUE causation and what lies WITHIN the genetic mechanism, the spirit in the machine. A statistical analysis of complex biological forms such as "feelers" requires a frame of reference, a "simulation" spanning the entire history of the universe in infinite detail, or else we are just constructing an environment of assumptions and calling it "science." We assume there is a "hierarchy of fundamentality" to reality and we worship the atom and gravity as the fundamental beings. I think, like gravity, the seemingly impossible (created) manifestations that emerge via evolution ARE fundamental.

Consciousness itself is fundamental and perceived evolution is a delivery process that follows its arbitrary and logical rules. We live in a conscious universe arising from an infinite nonphysical realm flowering in a manner that sculpts apparent or perceived randomness with order. I am not alone in thinking that the primacy of consciousness explains how our reality is the way it is. We will dive into the details of this and you'll be presented with more supporting evidence than you can ever find in legal cases with smoking guns, bloody gloves, and the very judge as a witness. The verdict will be deemed *"beyond reasonable doubt."* This book you are reading is book 1 of 2. Sufficient evidence is contained in both books to prove the primacy of consciousness/intelligence to our shared reality. Of course, ultimate truth is immune to opinions and beliefs and, given that apparent truths can vary between observers within the material realm in which we presently reside, it is even more difficult to get at TRUTH. Examples of these diametrically opposing perspectives being *"correct"* due to perception are discussed in detail later and include examples taken from the deferred-choice double slit experiment in quantum mechanics as well as observations in special relativity.

Later in the book, I also discuss how the human mind has been proven to affect Random Number Generators (randomness based on nature and not computer algorithms) such that intended outcomes emerge that infringe the laws of probability. Why is this so? Even in laboratory conditions, 56% of desired outcomes were gained on average, when chance (without human intent) would result in 50%. This shows that randomness can be affected by mind/consciousness/intent. If the primacy of consciousness hypothesis proves to be correct, then the statistical impossibilities referred to in this chapter would no longer be impossible because there is, by implication, an intent/intelligence that can perform the *"magic"* required to impact perceived randomness (a more global and intelligent mind than that of an individual human—what Einstein referred to when he said, *"There is a superior Mind that reveals itself in the world of experience"*).

Although the idea of a superior Mind may be seen as highly speculative by those in the scientific community, it explains how natural selection often appears to create results that a Mind would also seek to engineer through supreme intelligence but does so via an allegedly blind process. On many occasions, it would seem to take more than blind luck to achieve quantum leaps in the necessary direction that the system needs to move in, to provide the end-fitting results we witness and experience. Furthermore, the idea of a superior Mind does not appear to be speculative at all when it comes to the sexual selection process. The chapter on beauty demonstrates that there really has to be a high degree of intelligent design that lies beyond the capability of the apparent agent (e.g. the female birds) and so the quotation at the beginning of the chapter by Max Planck takes an important step from philosophy to science, as does Einstein's assertion that there is a *superior Mind.*" Darwin's observation of beauty arising for beauty's sake was another important step of the same ilk, but every effort has been made since to try and fit what he said into a framework that conforms to methodological naturalism.

The subject of human intent impacting Random Number Generators and the like is discussed in the chapter on metaphysics, but strictly speaking, it does not belong in that chapter. Regardless of the views of sceptical scientists, this anomaly has been experimentally proven to exist time and again, yet the prejudice within mainstream science, sadly, has slowed progress down dramatically. The good news, however, is that experiments can be run infinitely more times and so the phenomena can be proven to be real even if sceptics dismiss the validity of the observations of others. This is not an "anything goes" perceived physical material realm and so it is understandable that evidence is sought. Both books only touch on the subject you will think of as metaphysics, although the irony is that the mere turning of a book page is metaphysics and it is cradle to grave mind model perceptions that make you take a very extraordinary phenomenon for granted.

The unexplained nature of many phenomena in our perceived reality begs the question of whether both the potentialities that come to manifest and the manifestations themselves have all arisen by chance alone. Indeed, the evidence indicates that consciousness creates the manifestation of physical experiences through a combination of localized, collective, and Universal Consciousness.

Although there are undoubtedly many potentialities that have not become manifest, have yet to do so, or have already done so but are beyond our detection—what about the ones that have? Are we the field of all that is possible in manifest human form? The weak anthropic principle suggests that conditions that are observed in the universe must, at least, "*allow*" an observer to exist. Are we the observers in our human form—just one of infinite life forms that collectively make up the sum of all observers (all part of the ONE observer)? The anthropic principle, for those unfamiliar, operates on the basis that it is an undeniable fact that we are able to observe all the potentialities that have manifest because everything is aligned perfectly for observers to arise (or else it would be impossible for there to be any observers). But this is the same paradox rearing its head again: It cannot be an impossibility or it would not be so, and yet it checks and stamps all the hallmarks of an impossibility despite becoming manifest in tandem with an arbitrary process called evolution which, itself, is accepted without knowing its ultimate cause due to hyper-normalization.

The strong anthropic principle goes a step further and suggests that the universe was in a way "built" for intelligent life. This inevitability is unlikely, by chance, given all the conditions that must align (immeasurable "fine tuning") to assure it, even in a universe with a couple of trillion galaxies or more, all consisting of over a hundred billion suns. How do all the trillions of molecules in your body know what to do so that you as a human being even function? There are several constants in nature that, even if varied by a fraction, would have completely prevented the possibility of life. This is to say nothing of the fact that the emergence of the arbitrary phenomena we call energy and matter, from nothing, is absurd until it becomes hyper-normalized by its observers.

As is such, some invoke the idea of the multiverse, which attempts to overcome the impossibility dilemma. The idea is that our universe is one of an infinite number and the conditions were perfect in ours (hence why it was inevitable). To me, this is fudging the maths. It is a supposition that, on the surface, appears to make our reality feasible. But as mentioned before, impossible is impossible—and infinite universes would not mean the impossible could become possible: Which is what appears to have happened according to the mainstream science narrative. It is the same as suggesting that what would be deemed as real magic by scientists can become possible in some universes, provided that there are infinite universes—yet, I suspect most scientists would also be the first to say that infinite universes would not alter the status (or considered potentiality) of real magic from that of impossible. There are actually multiple universes and how this works and how it impacts the agreed upon hallucination we call reality is discussed in detail in book 2 but this does not speak to the ultimate cause of such universes. The books are about ultimate cause and compelling evidence about what it is and how it works.

Both anthropic principles are simply stating the obvious: That things have to be as they are, as we could not be here to ponder them if they were not so. This pseudoscientific concept says nothing about ultimate causes and is like saying we can experience what we call blue because (despite it being a creation of minds) it must by witnessing its existence be a possibility within the real and/or arbitrary form(s) of experience. In other words, they acknowledge the phenomena but say nothing about its ultimate cause. Fortunately, this book does.

It is the origin of all the potentialities and manifest potentialities that remain unexplained by the anthropic principle, the origin of any of the universes in the multiverse and even the concept of infinity—

all that is—itself nothing short of miraculous when the term is truly comprehended, rather than hyper-normalized. Scientists should admit that the idea of self-created universes with self-created laws of nature is even more bizarre than the most extreme examples of so-called paranormal occurrences (that many people claim to have witnessed) most scientists are also quick to dismiss as impossible.

I do not think incomprehensible order can be ignored in attempting to understand the reality that we all inhabit and experience. There have to be patterns and order for the universe to have manifested as it has—this applies to all the laws of nature and not just the process of evolution, of course. But the logical state, if we blindly accept the existence of the universe itself as non-miraculous, would seem to be entropy (any random order, quickly falling into a state of disorder in what is observed as an ordered universe—one where the earth, sun, and moon appearing and operating in completely ordered, mathematically precise revolutions around each other). Yet, the creation of complex and ordered systems, including those that ultimately sense prior phenomena (e.g. photo-receptivity), stamps all the hallmarks of will, design, and Universal Intelligence. If the laws of nature happen to favour "emerging order" in certain circumstances, this still leaves us with a mystery…because the existence of order becoming more and more ordered defies probability once a certain level of persistence leads this *"running spree"* of order speedily towards *"statistical impossibility."*

Professor Stephen Hawking pointed out in several of his books that order is permitted within a closed system as long as the result was greater entropy resulting from such order. This is apparently why the ordered nature of life is, to him, *"permitted"* because it takes energy and converts it into a more disordered form (i.e. into heat). This is yet another example of describing what happens, as verified by our observations, yet says nothing of the ultimate cause of such *"rule."* It passes the *"pattern recognition"* off as true comprehension. Life may conform to the second law of thermodynamics (entropy)

THE MEANING OF LIFE

in the bigger picture, yet it appears to break the law in the most extreme way possible in the process.

One idea, that there exists at least one possible universe designed with the goal of generating and sustaining observers is still feasible, though, and it is a more plausible answer that negates the need to conquer a multitude of Mounts Impossible. However, most materialist scientists will not like this other possibility as there would still be a singular Mount Impossible in the way, in the form of a *"life force"* (consciousness) that created what is manifest by design with, as they think, randomness as a part of the fundamental reality, as opposed to a cosmic, *self-created*, progenitor known as the universe or multiverse. But for those who believe consciousness itself is up to this task, there is no Mount Impossible. This is very different from the atheist scientists' viewpoint where they believe reality must first self-create with all its *"set"* arbitrary constants in place, followed by the emergence of nonrandom acting clusters of energy manifest as life forms—but all without, of course, meeting the definition of *"miracles."*

In his quirky book, *The God Delusion*, Richard Dawkins seems bewildered that people should see the super improbable as a possible sign of something beyond coincidence—a potential sign of intelligent intent. Richard Feynman had a similar view and expressed it as follows:

> *"You know, the most amazing thing happened to me tonight...I saw a car with the license plate ARW 357. Can you imagine? Of all the millions of license plates in the state, what was the chance that I would see that particular one tonight? Amazing!"*

A bizarre and facetious comment from such a genius. He is saying that the chances of seeing any particular license plate are one in several million, but the chances of seeing any nonspecific license plate(s), since he was in an environment where seeing some was inevitable, were 100 percent. The one(s) he does see are just there by chance and so the license plate ARW 357 has no significance, and if it had been any of the other millions as he refers to, it would still have been of no greater significance either. Have both Professor Dawkins and Mr. Feynman forgotten about the Natural Law of Synchronicity as written about by Dr. Carl Gustav Jung, Chris Mackey (my good friend the Australian leading psychologist), as well as well as Dr. Deepak Chopra and many others?

However, an alternative version of Feynman's story will help explain why some people think that extraordinary coincidences (events with meaning as opposed to random events) could be a sign of something that is beyond mere chance:

> *"You know, the most amazing thing happened to me tonight...when I came to park my car in the car park, all the parked cars were grouped according to colour."*

Occam's Razor (a scientific precept which suggests that when presented with competing potential answers to a problem, one should select the answer that makes the fewest assumptions) would suggest human/intelligent intervention was behind the order observed in this hypothetical car park phenomenon. But if this was ruled out, we would have to accept that, although what presented itself is beyond the statistical probability of happening by chance (importantly), it is not physically impossible. We would be forgiven for thinking that humans were behind the ridiculous level of order observed in this story and would likely consider the notion of it happening by chance next to impossible. And yet, the pattern and ornament that exists in the male great argus pheasant plumage make the car park demonstration of order seem like child's play. Even some unexplained fundamental desire for beauty for beauty's sake within the females' psyche, which is what Darwin believed, could not begin to explain the precise mathematical order. Neither sexual selection nor natural selection can explain this; however, the reasons why are detailed in the chapter on *"beauty."*

When does order become ordered enough to be a reason to consider the possibility of conscious intelligent will?

Photograph by Off Grid Entrepreneur (Barcelona) ©2019 Matthew H. Forrest

In the summer of 2019, whilst working in a 5-star hotel in Barcelona, I noticed some odd smudges on my business partner's laptop screen. Upon closer inspection, it was amazing to see that some of the smudges bore a striking resemblance to an angel or Christ representation—manifest in artwork form. If you look at the photograph close up, which is completely untouched—from a Photoshop perspective—you will see something akin to human-created art. Art that appears to have been created by the hand of a skilled artist. Of course, I am not suggesting that this is anything other than a coincidence, but the level of similarity between the apparent random smudges and the type of artwork, which would be produced if an artist were given a specification to paint an angel/Christ, is quite remarkable.

Although it is improbable for random patterns to create such beauty (an illusion of ultimate order despite no apparent intelligent intervention), it is not definite proof of willful manifestation based on an external, intelligent driver. Randomness, in theory, can occasionally stumble upon states that appear as though they were anything but random. However, it is when statistically impossible manifestations come about that we need to look deeply into ultimate causes, especially when statistical impossibility followed by statistical impossibility occurs. It becomes obvious then that nature operates beyond statistical impossibilities and at the deepest level, everything is ordered.

Most people are aware that humans see recognizable images or patterns in otherwise random or unrelated objects, and this is called pareidolia. It is a form of apophenia, which is a more general term for the human tendency to seek patterns in random information. There are evolutionary reasons for our biological forms to pattern recognize in this way. However, some people may believe that the angel/Christ imagery presented is too similar to the human made art form to be an example of this condition. Either way, it is quite a trivial example of statistical improbability when compared to some examples of the statistical impossibilities that present themselves in our universe.

As already discussed, the photon has clearly preexisted in life for billions of years (or so our perceptions would have us believe—perceptions that are later shown to be highly unreliable) until, conveniently, evolution brought into play something that not only transformed the inorganic into the organic but also morphed the organic, by "*chance*" mutations, to be able to "*sense*" and identify this prior phenomenon we call the photon. A superior Universal Mind would surely "will" an identical outcome given the opportunity—and yet blind luck is supposed to have construed an outcome that coincidentally mirrors the will of such a hypothetical Mind. Of course, with no photons, there could be no receptivity of photons arising. But the fact that photons preexisting did not make the sensing of these inevitable at some future time. Or if it was inevitable, as proposed by the strong anthropic principle, this would imply that each step along the way has been too.

The laws of nature must have embedded that potentiality inherently within them, as numerous Mounts Improbable had to be climbed to achieve what the Mind wished for upon the outset. Accordingly, it is incomprehensible chance that purportedly and ultimately granted such a hypothetical wish. Why is there such a stance against entropy that conveniently leads to literally making sense of the photon phenomenon and the facilitation of all other senses such as smell?

How convenient! This property of the unexplained state called life, that it can, via mutations, sense photons and molecules and physical properties. All impossible without the "*onset*" of life, and yet life itself seems impossible considering its predetermined/inherent(ly) perfect plasticity, actualizing the potentiality to "*make sense*" of these phenomena. While in the meantime, this is all generally swept under the carpet due to science's belief that ultimate causes must exist AND be non-metaphysical, which will somehow ultimately explain all the discernible patterns and manifestations that exist.

What underpins reality and evolution does not necessarily affect the meaning of life in terms of the sense of meaning that humans have the potential to experience. As already concluded, this meaning is like pain and/or colour—and appears to exist only because of the potentiality for it to do so within consciousness, all of which are reliant upon the underlying process of evolution. Yet, what underpins evolution and the fundamentality of reality provide(s) answers to the meaning of why anything exists and/or what the meaning of life is in its broader sense. As it stands, the ultimate cause of the clustering and animation of biological forms, that are evolution's manifestations, still appears to be unknown to the naked mind, let alone the ultimate cause of everything. Yet, this book changes all of that.

Are you and all that you see a manifestation of the unmanifest expressing and interacting with ItSelf through the illusion of form? Explanations for the potentialities discussed in this chapter, including the potentiality that has clearly existed for the evolutionary process itself, are all left wanting for the naked mind. And although scientists may be happy with their *"billiard ball science,"* they have no idea whatsoever about the origins of all such potentialities; except the dubious idea some materialist scientists assert that a quantum vacuum, void of time, suddenly caused a chain of events via virtual particles leading to over two trillion galaxies. An idea that even a five-year-old child would see as preposterous, including the notion that it fails to explain the origin of these magic beans known as virtual particles.

I do not consider myself an advocate of intelligent design in the form of an Old Testament type *"God"* even though it is clear from what I have written that I feel there are many curious manifestations that have arisen as though evolution is the cause—when they are creations that, I believe, random mutations alone cannot facilitate. However, I am presenting abundant evidence of intelligent design by some form and that many of the manifestations of life appear too "beyond chance" to have formed by countless blind mutations. Many traits brought about by sexual selection, in particular, support this view, proving beyond any reasonable doubt that there is some kind of superior Universal Mind behind their construction. Are we a manifestation of the Universal Mind? Are we the Universal Mind in localized form?

The *"Panglossian Paradigm"* was coined in 1979 by Stephen Jay Gould and Richard Lewontin in what has become an extremely well-known paper amongst biologists, entitled: "The Spandrels of San Marco and the Panglossian Paradigm: A Critique of the Adaptationist Programme." The term is a deliberate abuse of biology's adaptationism. Adaptationism posits that all parts of an organism are useful unless shown otherwise. Some lose the usefulness and remain in place as the cost on the host is negligible, like the human appendix. There are even features that had emerged with no initial function or a function that had changed over time to allegedly drift into fixation by chance. An example of a changed function is the use of feathers, initially appearing on dinosaurs, probably for warmth and water resistance, potentially becoming larger and more ornate via sexual selection. They ultimately afforded another key function as they became an essential part of avian flight.

The reasons they were so critical of adaptationism was stated in their paper:

> *"We fault the adaptationist programme for its failure to distinguish current utility from reasons for origin (male tyrannosaurs may have used their diminutive front legs to titillate female partners, but this will not explain why they got so small); for its unwillingness to consider alternatives to adaptive stories; for its reliance upon plausibility alone as a criterion for accepting speculative tales; and for its failure to consider adequately such competing themes as random fixation of alleles, production of nonadaptive structures by developmental correlation with selected features (allometry, pleiotropy, material compensation, mechanically*

forced correlation), the separability of adaptation and selection, multiple adaptive peaks, and current utility as an epiphenomenon of nonadaptive structures. We support Darwin's own pluralistic approach to identifying the agents of evolutionary change."

They felt that many biologists were *"guessing"* at how presently useful traits came about. And when their seemingly plausible explanations proved to be flawed, they simply replaced one guess with another. In a sense, this is how science, in general, has progressed and so it is quite a harsh criticism. However, what they were alluding to is that organisms should be viewed as a whole and that by atomising them (breaking them down into all its separate traits and functions), their complex interdependence, that is a systemic interrelation and progression of their evolution over time, is often lost. In this sense, their paper was probably a success and forced deeper thinking and better experiments rather than continuing the habit of describing all manifestations through the adaptationist programme. However, the fact remains that mechanisms themselves (even if some aspect(s) appear [due to fallible perceptions] to arise by chance alone) are always worthy of explanation as some can seemingly be shown to arise from prior goals and blueprints. And the idea of manifestations from prior blueprints goes well beyond any and all of modernized evolution's *"capabilities."*

In their use of the term *"Panglossian Paradigm,"* Gould and Lewontin call upon Voltaire's character, Dr. Pangloss, and his comically deliberate over-the-top explanation of why Columbus suffered from a venereal disease. Dr. Pangloss reasons, *"It is indispensable in the best of worlds. For if Columbus, when visiting the West Indies had not caught this disease, which poisons the source of generation, which frequently even hinders generation, and is clearly opposed to the great end of nature, we should have neither chocolate nor cochineal"* (Voltaire, 1759). In other words, anyone other than Dr. Pangloss would consider the notion of looking at the venereal disease as anything more than a bad, totally unrelated incident as ridiculous. Yet, Dr. Pangloss goes even further to suggest that it was not only correlated but essentially caused the availability of chocolate back home! Voltaire's *Candide* is a satire of Leibniz' philosophy that we live in the best of all possible worlds.

Another example they cited, also attributed to the character Dr. Pangloss was, *"Things cannot be other than they are... Everything is made for the best purpose. Our noses were made to carry spectacles, so we have spectacles. Legs were clearly intended for breeches, and we wear them."* Yet, evolutionary biologists, in their tendency to focus exclusively on immediate adaptation to local conditions, do tend to ignore architectural constraints and accordingly perform such an inversion (or reduction) of explanation. The need for rhyme and reason drives this, as it results in biologists citing causes of phenomena, which are actually correlations that are presumed to be causations. And sometimes even the correlation proves to be illusory as a result of trying to make a trait or behaviour fit the adaptationist programme by putting forward seemingly plausible reasons for their existence. Gould and Lewontin clearly used absurd and extreme analogies and hyperbole to illustrate what they felt was going on amongst fundamentalist adaptationists.

They used another analogy in their paper too. The Spandrels (arc-shaped architectural support features used in St Mark's Basilica in San Marco, Venice) are adorned with striking mosaic art. Gould and Lewontin argue that the mosaic design on the spandrels is *"so elaborate, harmonious, and purposeful that we are tempted to view it as the starting point of any analysis, as the cause in some sense of the surrounding architecture."* We know the true reason the spandrels exist, but they are suggesting that the mosaic design fits so well that it could cause some to think that this is the true origin of the spandrels when there is, in fact, a greater fundamental cause.

I believe their criticisms were not taken far enough, however, because the same criticisms can be applied to evolution as a whole. As we will see: What they insinuated was certainly well-founded when it comes to sexual selection, as well as some aspects of natural selection. Most biologists fail to acknowledge the possibility of Darwin's belief in beauty for beauty's sake and they have proposed various theories to try and bring natural selection into the equation. Richard O. Prum, who is "William Robertson Coe Professor of Ornithology" and Head Curator of Vertebrate Zoology at the Peabody Museum of Natural History at Yale University, believes this tendency may be attributed to a kind of fallout from monotheism that has existed throughout human history. He suggests this may explain the constant need for a singular idea, natural selection in this case, to explain all phenomena—a replacement for the ingrained monotheism in the form of monoideism.

I believe there is a simpler explanation for this. Natural selection, on the surface, seems to offer a plausible mechanism for the trans-positioning of randomness into order without the apparent need for a *"superior Mind."* Darwin felt that beauty arising via sexual selection worked independently from this mechanism but, unlike Darwin, contemporary scientists are perhaps uncomfortable with the notion of beauty for beauty's sake as they doubtlessly see that the unimaginable mathematical order often present is such a radical stance against randomness that there must be more to it than the actions (arbitrary tastes) of some dumb animal at play. This all points to intelligent design, which is the antipathy of methodological naturalism, and so it is a small wonder why various theories would emerge that attempt to explain how unguided mathematical complexity in beauty arises.

Another example which is open to the same type of criticisms that Gould and Lewontin made, which is not sexual selection-oriented, is the construction of the middle ear in humans. Having formally studied audiology myself (the anatomy and physiology of the ear) random drifting into fixation is how we were taught that two of the middle ear ossicles (bones) arose. It seems they migrated from reptilian jaw bones located well away from the ear and although conferring no obvious benefit, they drifted, moving progressively through thousands of generations into fixation where they began their new "*use*" in crude form, leading to the more "*perfected*" form of today. The probability of such a journey would seem statistically impossible in hindsight, even with a liberal pluralistic mindset, but without the benefit of witnesses, we are expected/have to accept that normal evolutionary processes somehow did give rise to the positioning and reshaping of the bones by random mutations alone.

There are many more examples of traits arising via evolution that seem way beyond chance. And in addition to this, it is also hard to see how micro improvements can consistently apply to crude versions of traits, where each such mutation(s) confers no significant survival benefit. Does a 0.000001 percent improvement to a crude and well underdeveloped trait via a mutation(s) make any statistical difference to an individual specimen's odds of survival when "*survival of the luckiest*" (a notion discussed in the chapter of the same name) is infinitely more relevant to its mortality? Mathematical models have also shown that beneficial mutations are so rare, compared to mutations that are harmful or benign, that there has not been enough time for the accumulation of useful mutations needed to manifest as they have without some guiding mechanism. This does not mean that it is physically impossible for unguided evolution to occur but that the chances are so remote it is deemed statistically impossible. The anthropic principle was already stretched to the limit with all the statistical impossibilities that were "*overcome*" leading up to the onset of life. You have to wonder how many independent statistical impossibilities in succession there needs to be before a will is considered rather than chance alone, as discussed in the car park illustration earlier.

In many instances, it is also hard to see how certain traits came into play when a partially developed version would be useless. We know that, sometimes, uses can change but there seem to be many traits that had no prior use and would only become useful when their development was fairly advanced. This, of course, is one of the main arguments put forward by the proponents of intelligent design. As no physical witnesses who could have chronicled these events were present to see the true unfolding of evolution in these cases, it is difficult to say whether or not unguided evolution filled the apparent gaps.

By way of example, see the striking camouflage of the Orange Oakleaf butterfly that is illustrated in the video clip below and imagine the pattern and ornament when it was nothing like the leaf that it mimics. The prevailing view of what evolution is would suggest that the current pattern and ornament was acquired by a blind (unguided) process. However, when it was nothing like the object it mimics, even a multi-mutational *"jump"* adorning the insect with a few vaguely similar characteristics would seem to offer no useful camouflage effect whatsoever. Accordingly, there doesn't seem to be any basis to allow the camouflage effect to progress via further evolution. The progression, from the point it becomes useful to the point it becomes a mimic—indistinguishable from the leaf— is also highly impressive when you consider how a natural process observably assures such lengths of detail. The eyes of the predator(s) must be hyper-discerning to occasionally pick up on a 99.9 percent evolved *"incomplete"* mimic such that pressure remained to *"adopt"* mutation(s) leading to a 99.99 percent or more mimic perfection. The mimic in the video example is so accurate that we would have to conclude this level of discernment is present because it is uncanny how alike a leaf it really is in every minute detail. The paradox is that I have witnessed a cat capture and eat a resting example of this species of butterfly because, despite the millions of years of evolution *"creating"* an immaculate mimic, it flaps its wings occasionally when resting—revealing the conspicuous colours and pattern that are displayed when open winged. This makes a bit of a mockery of mimicry.

🔗 **https://www.youtube.com/watch?v=LE_ktrn8970**

Even if all of these more questionable aspects of evolution are eventually shown to be feasible by the application of the blind process alone, there are still manifestations that are fundamental in their own right; although, they arise via evolution, as creations, e.g. the experiences that are seemingly provoked by certain phenomenon via what we perceive through our physical sensory apparatus. This book shows that the whole evolutionary process/mechanism is guided and that Darwin's theory of evolution is only part of the truth. We have become so familiar with the natural selection explanation for the development of all traits that it becomes difficult for most people to even consider alternative forces. In short, we have become hyper-normalized to such an extent, that the idea that evolution always conforms to some immutable "*rule*," whereby organisms must be constructed in micro stages via random mutations over a vast sea of time—honing in on a proto useful anatomy and physiology that can then be further shaped by survival and reproductive pressures towards more "*perfected*" traits—that it doesn't cross many minds that this is a belief and not truth.

There are also unanswered questions concerning the origin of life itself, of course, and the origin of the process of natural selection, i.e. how these hyper-normalized phenomena happen to be part of the emergent fundamentals of our reality.

As mentioned at the beginning of the book, atheists accuse those seeking an explanation for these, as yet unexplained matters as "*looking for God in the gaps*" but conveniently ignore the fact:

> "*Modern science is based on the principle: 'Give us one free miracle, and we'll explain the rest.' The one free miracle is the appearance of all the mass and energy in the universe and all the laws that govern it in a single instant from nothing.*"

> –*Terence McKenna.*

An equivalent version of Feynman's anecdote, taking McKenna's quotation into account, would be something like:

> "You know, the most amazing thing happened to me tonight...when I came to park my car in the car park, all the parked cars were grouped according to colour. And, as if that was not miraculous enough, when I arrived at the car park it was empty—and it was only when I stepped out of the car that they appeared. Amazing!"

The evolutionary process is not only a key part of that *"one free miracle"* but it also adds a few of its own. Something that experts in the field of evolution somehow fail to see is not that the process isn't both logical and magnificent on its own but how the manifestation of both the mathematics underpinning the process and the clustering of matter in arbitrary forms facilitates nonrandom animation, the form of replication, and a Goldilocks proportion of useful mutations inherent to the evolutionary process—is what is truly amazing. As already suggested, they appear guilty of hyper-normalization and somehow seem willing to suspend the use of their innate investigative predisposition by accepting these unexplainable properties as axioms that, irrespective of the fact that they are supposedly unexplainable, 100 percent cannot be metaphysical in nature, according to their belief.

It seems that consciousness, in mind form, is an emergent property (a phenomenon that is in the world, as an observer, but not of it) that grows as organisms become more complex. Likewise, the organisms themselves also grow in complexity over time but do so via Darwinian evolution, at least in part. This gives the illusion that the properties of consciousness are caused by evolution. However, in the case of consciousness, evolution is not just simply progressing by harnessing the tools that nature already presents. It is, instead, apparently inventing/accessing new phenomena, as already discussed. In actual fact, it is more an access to infinite possibilities within the quantum realm where experiences/qualia/intelligence are there for the taking.

The taste of coffee, the colour blue, love, fear, pain, and the voices or music heard via the ears are all somehow fundamental and are more than just increased blood flow to specific regions of the brain. This is certainly what brings the experiences into consciousness, but the experiences themselves are *"made"* of something that is completely novel and does not behave even in the same ballpark as all prior phenomena. A more basic creature has lower levels of consciousness and possesses more basic *"gifts,"* e.g. a *"will"* under-pinning needs, albeit, an unconscious will, nonrandom movement capabilities (inherited from ancestors that first acquired this capacity), etc. Maybe consciousness that is more developed than what we have as humans will bestow even greater, unimaginable *"gifts?"* Some scientific research suggests that humans and other animals already have some such *"gifts"* despite what mainstream science refuses to believe. This is discussed in the chapter on the primacy of mathematics and intelligence as well as the one on metaphysics.

There are also greater lengths of discussion and presentation concerning the causal factor(s) underpinning the evolutionary process(es) later in the book. However, the idea that consciousness, from within the human mind, can influence the illusion of random-ness and the fact that a congruently equivalent but infinitely more powerful force in the form of Universal Consciousness (collective minds) can, too, and would essentially explain how statistically impossible states continue to arise despite them seeming to defy the laws of probability. It would also fit with Einstein's intuitions/observations, *"There is a superior Mind that reveals itself in the world of experience."*

The conclusions of this chapter are relevant to the question of the meaning of life in a number of ways. On the one hand, many believe that we are the products of biological evolution and so gaining an understanding of how it works at its deepest level provides us with knowledge about what we really are. On the other hand, the idea of individual points of consciousness residing in temporary biological forms gives rise to the possibility of some level of will, which transcends nature and nurture as well as the illusion of linear time. Also, if there is an inherent intelligence within all that is manifest, it would seem to suggest that there is also an overall purpose/intent/order and that there may be clues indicated by and throughout our reality about what those really are.

5

SURVIVAL OF THE LUCKIEST

*"How unlucky I am that this should happen to me.
But not at all. Perhaps, say how lucky I am that I am not
broken by what has happened, and I am not afraid of what
is about to happen. For the same blow might have stricken
anyone, but not many would have absorbed it without
capitulation and complaint."*

Marcus Aurelius

We live in a cause-and-effect universe, while this property of physics also extends to willful cause and effect too. This means that a person can decide (or is compelled, if free will is an illusion) to pursue a profession of choice or to start a new business knowing that their efforts will directly influence their journey. In practical terms, this also means if you want to win the lottery, you must also meet God halfway…and buy a ticket!

However, notwithstanding willful effort, there is also a huge luck factor that impacts everyone's life to varying degrees every single day. I call it *"God's Dice,"* although it really just relates to the apparent randomness (luck) element inherent in the laws of nature. On the bright side, it can mean that *"trying"* (intent) to get pregnant works out as *"planned"* or that the love of your life can manifest at some unexpected time and place. However, it also means a huge array of undesirable outcomes are inevitable—unfairly distributed and often, seemingly, through no fault of the person enduring such bad luck.

Most people know of the phrase Herbert Spencer coined that relates to Darwin's natural selection, *"survival of the fittest,"* but it tends to draw attention away from a more powerful force of nature. Namely, *"survival of the luckiest."*

In the cartoon illustration, *"God's Dice,"* has bestowed greater gene fitness upon the largest of the three ants which, on balance, should aid survival and due to heritability would assure a similar position likely arises in its offspring. However, *"God's Dice"* has also placed the ant in the path of a predator and so this effectively nullifies the potential advantage and, assuming it is yet to reproduce, means its genes will not be passed on either. Such potential and yet a *"loser"* as far as the game of life is concerned, as it failed to survive and failed its function as a gene transfer mechanism.

Failure to survive and reproduce due to this "luck factor" means that many useful gene mutations never got (and will never get) to impact the species of which the specimens are a part of. Nature is such a hazardous playground that this will have likely occurred trillions of times to life on earth. Yet, the question arises, is a lucky experience a manifestation of an individual's consciousness when it comes to human beings?

On a more positive note, this "failure to reproduce" scenario has not affected your own bloodline—all the way back to the basic organisms that were your original ancestors. It is quite mind-blowing as well to think that you were "the one" of millions of sperm, each of which were potentially alternative children your parents could have had instead of you, that "won." And this is only part of the history because there is still a series of millions upon millions of ancestors that ALL had to survive up until sexual maturity to reproduce successfully in order to arrive at you. Any of the sperm of all these ancestors other than the one that "*won*" would have meant a different you. And, if you now imagine some fish that eventually led to you in the perceived physical material realm, it had to have survived many treacherous conditions and predators, at least until reproduction, or otherwise the bloodline that led to you would have been severed all those millions of years ago.

Without exception, some males in your bloodline will have died before the birth of his/its offspring leaving behind a widow, but none of these countless millions of males could have died before reaching sexual maturity nor before the process of reproduction occurred. Likewise, some female ancestors will have died at childbirth or during the child's infancy but will have had to have survived until after sex and gestation.

The probability of you being here right now is one (where one, in probability theory, is defined as a certainty). But if you were to look at the probability of you coming to fruition based on the odds of what needed to happen from an early basic organism to now, including the odds of each set of mates surviving long enough to pass on genes that led to you and the odds of the right sperm "*winning*" in each process of reproduction, it would be so incomprehensibly small that it would be deemed a statistical impossibility. This is *"God's Dice"* in action too. As we will later learn, the so-called God's Dice perception is ultimately an illusion—everyTHING is based on intent (of Universal Consciousness, collective conscious agents, and individual points of consciousness interactions).

This necessarily implies that there is an inevitability about all these events aligning to assure the existence of you. However, the description of perceived randomness highlights the immeasurable improbability of your existence when there were, seemingly, trillions of potentialities that would have resulted in there being "no you." This same stance against randomness is far easier to detect in the pattern and ornament of the male great argus pheasant, where there is also an inevitability in the form of order. But even in this instance, mainstream science is so preoccupied by observation and measurement that its practitioners pay little attention to ultimate cause. Even though the design aspects and colouration could easily have varied, the output has come about through a nonrandom process. It is obvious when scrutinized that the phenomenon of hyper contra-randomness had to be intended, thus being an indication of intelligent design.

In a documentary some time back, Professor Richard Dawkins disputed the fact that Darwinism was relevant to business in the same way it is *"standard"* in animal behaviour. For most, business is all about competition and is often a fight of tooth and nail—albeit with official and unofficial rules. Large businesses are really just complex organisms—often seeking mergers or takeovers to afford it greater strength. Even CVs and interviews are about selecting for fitness, less about sexual selection for gene fitness, and more about fitness in terms of best fit for added strength for the business/organism.

Dawkins talked with a senior city executive who concurred with his view that business is no more than a casino where luck is the key ingredient. I do not think that people like Sir Richard Branson or Simon Cowell would be in agreement. They would be the first to admit that luck certainly appears to be a factor but intelligence, resilience, persistence, and will are vital aspects too. Are these successful businessmen really consciously or unconsciously manifesting businesses and business results? Concerted intelligent effort in meeting the demands of human's pain avoidance and pleasure-seeking predisposition (human needs) has more to do with bringing about success than luck has. This is not to say that there are not many failures but very few business leaders will have reached their position without a prior goal and will to accomplish such, i.e. consciousness creating order against a background of chaos.

"God's Dice" affects the meaning of life in various ways. On the one hand, how it works and how it is inextricably linked with the process of living means that it affects everyone. I was fortunate enough to have attended a talk by spaceman Chris Hadfield in Budapest, the astronaut made famous by singing a David Bowie song that was transmitted from the Space Station. Most of his talk was about risk (negative *"God's Dice"*) mitigation. All the checks. And checks on top of the checks. Alas, *"God's Dice"* hit the Space Shuttle missions on a number of occasions, including two disasters that killed the occupants. Of course, it is logical to mitigate but there is no such thing as zero risk, regardless of the brilliance of the collec-

tive minds on the task in hand. By focusing attention on risk, are the "*risk-mitigators*" increasing the likelihood of manifesting the result they seek to eliminate? Not only is human error a factor in space flight missions but so is the potential for problems with any of the other thousands of parts. Luck can potentially conspire to have many rare events align, which collectively result in horrific outcomes, occasionally.

For some people, it is quite disturbing to realise that every minute of life comes with an inherent risk of something bad happening, including the potential of fatality. The high-frequency bad events are on average of low severity, whereas the high severity bad events such as plane crashes, fortunately, happen at a much lower frequency. And so, the risks of major drawbacks, or of a fatality, are much lower than the general slings and arrows of life. But they do eventually affect everyone without exception. This realisation, understandably, can cause existential angst in many people.

The other way "God's Dice" can affect the meaning of life is by a series of what appear to be bad events eventually leading to mood disorder. As pointed out earlier, a person with two short alleles of a certain gene, who also experiences two or more major negative life experiences, is three times more likely to suffer depression. And so, given that depression affects meaning on a personal level, "*God's Dice*" is a highly relevant factor. Of course, it is "*God's Dice*" that bestowed the two short allele(s) on some and not others, and so the phenomenon is not restricted to the bad events that ultimately trigger the mood disorder.

I doubt that anyone reading this has not considered the "*God's Dice*" element of reality. But I think a lot of people, understandably, do not ponder on it and have an "*it won't happen to me*": attitude— the kind of mentality that leads many to drive without a seat belt or to smoke whilst knowing full well about all the potential dangers.

The luck factor is not all negative, of course. To some extent, the risks for potentially bad outcomes can also be mitigated while effort can be applied to enhance the likelihood of good outcomes. However, the luck factor plays a significant role in all our lives and can result in the difference between a meaningful life or not (especially if multiple negative outcomes trigger mood disorder, which in turn may diminish one's capacity to experience meaning).

As with one's own mortality, people are aware of this potentially devastating *"luck"* (*"bad luck"*) factor, but most compartmentalize it and deal as best they can with whatever arises. In other words, the terror management theory referred to earlier applies to negative *"God's Dice"* events also. To ponder on all the negative events that *"fate"* may have in store cannot alter how reality works, and so there is solace to be found in focusing on the now and planning for the future: Hoping that not too many such events will manifest. Hope is a weak word though. Even intent is not necessarily set in stone and so setting inevitabilities is the most powerful route to manifestation. Of course, despite being cocreators, there are conflicts in intent and so absolute certainties are impossible in this physical material realm.

Believers in the Law of Attraction, discussed later in this book, claim that what the mind focuses on manifests in reality. As such, they would say a lot of bad luck is created by thought. The impact of human intent on Random Number Generators would seem to evidence that the mind alone can influence certain outcomes to some extent via intent, as already discussed. What is certain—is that thinking, attitude, and actions can affect certain outcomes, and that when negative outcomes are accepted as they arise, they much less severely affect the person's mood and, therefore, reality too. Does the Law of Attraction work because, ultimately, we are all manifestations of the unmanifest from which form manifests?

The only way to behave in light of this invisible *"force"* (*"God's Dice"*) is to follow the first part of the Serenity Prayer (for atheists, simply remove the word God):

God grant me the serenity

to accept the things I cannot change;

courage to change the things I can;

and wisdom to know the difference.

Living one day at a time;

enjoying one moment at a time;

accepting hardships as the pathway to peace;

taking, as He did, this sinful world

as it is, not as I would have it;

trusting that He will make all things right

if I surrender to His Will;

that I may be reasonably happy in this life

and supremely happy with Him

forever in the next.

Amen.

This prayer reminds me a little of Eckhart Tolle's teachings. His genius is not in question, but his teachings are over-passive. It is true that it is futile to try and reject the *"isness"* of all that arises, but given that we are in the world and not necessarily of it, every effort should be made to overcome negative manifestations. Acceptance is a last resort. Placebo(s) and other metaphysics should be used to assure more favourable futures.

Without a spiritual dimension, this present reality would be a temporary experience/illusion and would mean nature is, at best, amoral. Without a deeper knowledge, there appears no way to fully prevent negative oncoming events no matter what we do but we cannot accuse nature of being vexatious. Given the underlying truth concerning mind duality, manifestation is in the will of the beholder as well as Universal Consciousness as a whole.

Randomness, in general, is another hyper-normalized phenomenon that is more complex than first meets the eye. With modern technology, multiple images per second of a tossed coin can be captured, and so the outcome of the coin toss can be predicted (although once it hits a surface the predictions become considerably more difficult). This means that, although it appears random to an observer, it is merely acting as physics dictates and so the outcome is not actually random at all. Of course, thousands of throws where the conditions of the throw are not controlled/known to individual observers will result in approximately 50 percent heads and 50 percent tails. Algorithms from the quantum realm assure that, with large sample sizes, binary outcomes, such as a coin toss, are evenly spread in the absence of any impact from individual or collective points of consciousness.

When it comes to the double slit experiment in quantum mechanics, the randomness observed may seem like true/objective randomness from an observer's perspective but all the collapsed particle allocations are based on intent (Universal Consciousness intent influenced by observer intent). Only the probability of where a particle could appear is available to any individual observer in advance of the event because until it has manifested it cannot be known. Unlike the behaviour of physical matter, the probability based wavefunction determines that the outcome of any particle's path or "set" of characteristics appears through the "workings" of the invisible immaterial world, although human consciousness can still influence this "world." There is more about the origin of randomness later in the book.

In light of hyper-normalization being ever present: What I have termed "God's Dice" could potentially be radically different from some luck factor that most people perceive. Our true nature resides behind the scenes of space-time but also resides within the universe in human conscious agent form, meaning that our true essence here is real but, also, that the space, time, and our life circumstances are not as much. In other words, the "God's Dice" events are ultimately Mind-made along with everything else in this realm and are simply just a part of the immersive experience. It is maybe a little premature to be introducing such a radical idea at this stage in the book because, so far, there is insufficient evidence of this. For now, I ask that you suspend your disbelief until you are presented with all of the evidence.

6

FREE WILL

*"Man can do what he wills but he cannot will
what he wills."*

Arthur Schopenhauer

I think it is appropriate to discuss free will in a book that addresses the meaning of life. They are inextricably linked. Without free will, it may still be possible to experience a sense of meaning, but if everyone is acting in accordance with an accumulation of outside influences that results merely in an illusion of free will, can that sense of meaning really be authentic?

There are various definitions of free will, as there have also been many debates on whether or not free will exists. Many scientists, including many neuroscientists, believe free will is an illusion. The idea of being able to do otherwise than what one does is, to them, fanciful—and so their view is that we are all automatons that sense free will because our evolved ("emergent") consciousness gives the feeling of agency. A number of modern scientists were asked to mark the proportion of free will that they think exists on a large piece of blank paper. They unanimously drew a small dot.

There are a lot of potential barriers to free will, from "time-slicing" in a so-called block universe to nature and nurture. Chemicals, including drugs and alcohol, can influence free will, as can some diseases. If genetics over the eons of time have evolved to enslave us into this pseudo nature of freedom, governed by natural and sexual selection, then it would be "reasonably" fair to assume a step further: That all human moods, as a result of involuntary responses to stimuli causing brains to release neurotransmitters (governed by DNA programming), are really set in strict immovable patterns—that all further serves to riddle our control and ultimately any opportunity to direct our own lives. Take an extreme case such as bipolar disorder, a disease where the sufferer's behaviours are almost exclusively based upon the "puppet master" (i.e. the symptoms of the disorder with its extreme states).

Free will is emergent in the same way as meaning, in that the brain and mind have to be of the right size and type to allow "access" to these capacities. A combination of consciousness and our contemplative capabilities suggest that a degree of free will appears possible. Some believe that animals can only act in accordance with their "function" via genes and/or learned behaviour and that it would seem impossible for them to act otherwise when presented with any stimulus that provokes action. Even if some small element of randomness applies it means that, although they will act slightly differently in identical situations, this is not free will either. However, intelligence exists throughout the whole food chain of the animal kingdom (see the chapter on the primacy of mathematics and intelligence) and so this "force" (of free will) provides some genuine agency even for nonhuman animals. Do animals act in a nonconscious manner, thus being rendered seemingly unable to experience much, if any, free will?

Humans are able to turn their back on what nature "intended" and choose directions that seem to exhibit true free will. It could be argued that nature and nurture dictate all tastes and choices, and so each individual is acting in accordance with their will but as per Arthur Schopenhauer, there being no will to will (other than an inherent subconscious will that works to represent itself in the form of nonrandom, directed action). Whatever the true answer is, it is clear that we do not have anything like the level of free will that most people perceive we have. Simply wishing for a huge level of free will does not make it so. At least, not unless the egoic mind is transcended. Likewise, intuition would suggest that there is some level of agency and free will but intuition is neither wholly reliable nor heretofore scientifically defined.

The whole judicial system operates on the basis that we have free will. But even behaviour that is deemed immoral is vastly, if not completely, influenced by genes and environment. There is little doubt that violence begets violence or that experiencing sexual abuse as a child increases the likelihood of that child eventually becoming an abuser themselves. Is this a negative experiential example of the Law of Attraction? As we will see later in the chapter, there are even diseases that can cause immoral/illegal behaviour.

It is not out of the question, either, for nature, nurture, and uncontrolled circumstances to neutralize free will altogether. Of course, this would make praise and punishment meaningless because all behaviour would be mechanistic. However, this does not mean that systems should not be in place for prevention and rehabilitation but that administering punishment, itself, would be immoral.

A big challenge to free will comes from the implications of Einstein's theory of relativity. According to Professor Brian Greene: If an alien were to travel towards earth from millions of light years away, they would experience future time in relation to an inhabitant of earth's perspective and if it moved away, it would experience past time from the same relative perspective. Not in terms of what the alien would see but in terms of actual now time. The information carried by light would clearly need to travel many light years to reach the alien's senses, and so it makes essentially no difference whether the alien is in a past, present, or future spatiotemporal relationship to that of the earth dweller because that light information is millions, if not billions, of years away from reaching any said alien (and not only that but the expanding universe will cause additional delay(s) on top). And, of course, it is highly unlikely that the alien would have equipment capable of picking up such a small amount of information from millions of light years away—but even if it could, the alien will be a long time dead before the relevant information could reach the relevant destination.

This means objects/consciousness moving in space can "experience" past and future time depending on their speed, distance, and relative direction. This implies that one's future has already happened but has yet to be experienced through one's own timeline. It is like a movie on a DVD: It doesn't matter where you are up to, the past and future aspects of the movie exist simultaneously. Einstein was well aware of this implication of his findings and knew that this made our perceived reality an illusion, albeit a stubborn one.

If the future has happened already but has yet to be experienced in its perceived physical form by our waking consciousness, then a person cannot do anything other than what they already do. This is because every decision and event is already set, despite not becoming aware of them until they unfold in the perceived now time of the observer. Because of consciousness and brain chemistry and their facilitation of meaning, there does exist a capacity to experience meaning during the universal passage of time. However, the concept of free will is theoretically annihilated, as you will have already done all you are going to do until death and, accordingly, there is no opportunity to do otherwise (which is what true free will theorizes against).

This concept may seem bizarre, but then so is relativity, which we know to be true in our reality. Imagine a man standing equidistant from two women—one near the front and one near the back—on a fast-moving train. If he strikes a match, photons moving at the speed of light will hit both women at the same time from his perspective. An observer off the train, however, will see the woman at the back of the train moving towards the photons approaching her and the woman at the front moving away from the photons approaching her. This means that from the stationary observer's perspective, the event of these photons hitting the two women happens at slightly different times. As such, there are two coinciding and, yet, varying realities that depend on the status of the observers themselves (in this case one where photons hit the women simultaneously and one where the photons strike one before the other). This is highly counterintuitive but is the consequence of light speed being fixed and space-time being malleable.

This effect impacts satellite navigation and has to be accounted for, otherwise your positioning as indicated by the GPS display screen would not be in-keeping with your actual geographical position (there are actually two competing effects in the case of GPS satellites: One being Special Relativity, whereby the speed of the satellite causes on board clock-rate to run slower, with the other being General Relativity, whereby reduced gravity [in space] causes the clock to run faster—yielding a net result of the GPS clock-rate advancing faster, with the reduced gravity effect having the greatest impact of the two). As such, this phenomenon is adopted in everyday life and is not illusory.

When you take on the perspective of the photon in this thought experiment, things get even weirder. Time slows down as objects approach the speed of light in a process known as time dilation, whilst the distance they travel through space-time appears to minimalize. At the speed of light itself, the time experienced is "zero" with the appeared distance traveled also being "zero." This means the simultaneous creation and annihilation of the photon (from the observer's perspective) coinciding through an evolving space-time. Which, in turn, means that space-time exists as a construct only for slower than light speed phenomena/objects that weigh in below infinite mass; in other words, singularities and light-speed can be observed but these phenomena appear in the world but are not of it. It is, in fact, minds/consciousness that paint space and "linear time" into the augmented mind's eye model that we experience as reality.

Time dilation has to be one of the most counterintuitive aspects of our physical realm. It means that a spaceship traveling at a speed close to the speed of light will witness all human events here on earth in fast forward. The construction of the Himalayas occurring in minutes as well as the passing of thousands of generations of humans (with decades of life circumstances occurring in each heartbeat of the traveling observer). Viewed from a photon's perspective, the sequence of events is no longer in a hyper fast forward mode; sequences cease to be phenomenon as do space and linear time. Everything is all at once. What was seen as sequences from one perspective is infinite happenings in a singular moment from an equally valid alternative perspective. Because time dilation is not generally in our everyday experience, this profound phenomenon is only known by a very small percentage of people and yet the implications are huge in terms understanding reality.

There is no doubt that Einstein was correct when he realised that past, present, and future are all illusions. There is simply an infinite now. However, this does not mean that what we perceive as the future, in illusory linear time, has happened in the same way as the perceived past. The past can be influenced by individual observers under special conditions which are discussed later (including the which-way deferred choice double-split experiment in quantum mechanics). The future can be influenced to an even greater extent because it is probabilistic, and so even though the flowering of consciousness is always in the now, the becoming is in accord with the intent of infinite points of consciousness. In view of the fact individual points of consciousness possess separate wills, this makes for a very complex becoming in the agreed upon hallucination we call reality. However, not all wills are equal and they strengthen as the beholder moves towards enlightenment (or learns of the power of intent by chance). It is too early in the book to expect any reader who has focused all of their past attention on mainstream science to consider this metaphysical viewpoint as anything other than woo-woo. However, more and more evidence will be presented to assure no leap of faith is necessary in order to accept the upcoming, inevitable, paradigm shift. Time dilation alone is so at odds with our intuition and yet has been proven to be a valid phenomenon, that this should force us to be open to other radical revelations about our reality provided that they are well evidenced.

It could be argued that even if the future has already "happened," because it exists in the way already described, there must have still been agency to the "building" of it. In other words, there was a free will element that was involved in creating the journey: Even though the journey, in a sense, has already been completed and is simply yet to be experienced from the "now" of the experiencer's perspective. Given that we know that linear time is an illusion and so ALL events are concurrent in our physical material realm, it means that the apparent cocreation process of all points of consciousness assures a flowering of information that is fundamentally predetermined (infinite inter-actions causing information and perception to emerge simultane-ously that are governed by infinite intents). It is not the volition-sens-ing aspect of humans that leads to actions but inherent intent that drives neuronal encoding which, in turn, augments a predetermined observer reality into the agreed upon hallucination we see as reality.

Given that space-time appears to be an illusion (hypothesized as a construct of consciousness), an eternal "now" rather than clock time would be the only truth anyway. And so, the life forces (plural because we are individual points of consciousness separated by minds/egos) are real but everyone's life circumstances are not (they are akin to virtual realities appearing as real but are "designed" to engage the senses without realising that any virtualization is contrived). This does not mean that each point of consciousness is not real—but that the experience of time, and all that appears to happen in space-time, is experientially illusory—contrived differentiations of conscious-ness. That, when in human form or lower, are generally too immature (insufficiently evolved) to transcend the illusion(s) of perception. Only an enlightened minority get to transcend mind/ego. And because they are "mind" manifest in human form, I do not imagine that even they could completely escape the illusion, as they have to play a human "role" in this form to eat, sleep, defecate, and undertake most of the basic privileges of being human.

This is similar to the Matrix, where the illusion experienced is so compelling, it is almost impossible to prove that it is an illusion— except, in our "reality," space-time is equivalent to the "machine-made" virtual reality of the Matrix, while a superior Mind (pure consciousness originating outside of space-time) is the equivalent of what is portrayed as true reality in the movie. Even if the concept of free will in the flowering of consciousness within an eternal now is true, the impact of nature and nurture that are real forces in our universe, as are societal forces, certainly remove most of our free will anyway, regardless of whether our life circumstances and space-time are illusory or not.

Another scientific phenomenon that virtually destroys the concept of free will, if determinism proves to be a fundamental part of reality, is cause and effect. Ever since the Big Bang, every event has arisen due to a prior event. Despite the complex manifestations that make weather patterns quite simplistic, everything at the non-quantum level behaves in predictable ways (and even in quantum mechanics, the probability of events is measurable to an unimaginably accurate degree). Humans are made of matter, as are our neurons. As such, unless consciousness gives rise to an infringement of this fundamental "rule," then every birth, car crash, manufacturing of a birthday candle, etc. were all predetermined. There is no room for free will to manoeuvre in such circumstances.

Many scientists, who fail to see that randomness is always just a lack of observer information, believe that complex emerging phenomena are not just near-impossible to predict but are actually impossible. For example, neurons sitting on a knife edge could go either way, according to this viewpoint. Other scientists take the opposing view and believe all effects are wholly deterministic and all outcomes can be predicted by looking at all the prior causes. Neither position is correct because intent appears to be the true underlying driver. But as already mentioned, the infinite interactions between infinite points of consciousness make apparent randomness seem valid when there is no such as thing as random.

Even if human perceptions about randomness being a valid phenomenon, despite evidence to the contrary, were true: Evolutionary psychology can provide very accurate nonrandom predictions about human behaviour in light of the evolved biological drivers within us all. This is surely one of the biggest blows to the idea of us having a significant measure of free will.

There are behaviours that are adopted by all humans, in light of the fact that we are indeed animals, albeit highly evolved ones. For example, sexual arousal is just a motivational tool bestowed on humans as it is with all higher animals—an inherited and embedded system of sensual transaction that is nearly impossible to override. Squirrels mate with squirrels, owls with owls, and so on. Humans can be sexually aroused by many things (some rarely even by cars, although this is clearly a deviation from the norm) and so we, too, like animals engage in related activity and invest time in predictable ways accordingly. Many human activities are because of this type of "programming" and this is described in the science of evolutionary psychology, as discussed earlier. Most, if not all, of our behaviour is the result of subconscious drivers.

We may be quietly amused by the idea that nature has deceived some insects through the lure of sex, when it has other uses for the insect in *"mind"* (e.g. when it *"begets"* the insect by harnessing its inherent sex drive to facilitate pollination) but are we really so different? Evolution has created such an attraction between higher animals that assures certain behaviour also, but even when it is not for deception purposes, it is still, *"essentially,"* just a lure and evolution's assurance of the perpetuation of DNA via gene transfer mechanisms. Thus, humans are counted among the *"lured."*

I think many people are aware that they are puppets to such drivers. However, because these behaviours are associated with pleasure, not only the act of reproduction but also the evolved sense of meaning gained from parenting, their true cause is seldom a concern. Ask most parents why they chose to have children, assuming it was planned, and they would answer: That it is what we are here to do, to bring joy and guidance to life. From a scientific perspective the whole process is solely about the "selfish gene" and DNA is the true puppet master "using" life forms as relay race runners. In the end, is it just instinct or is there something more going on?

If anything, the display of free will is more likely to come from those who choose to abstain from this conditioned reproduction behaviour, or at least question it even if they do conform. If it is due to concerns about having resources, or due to the state of the world, e.g. terror, war, violence, greed, etc., then it is a free choice that could not be made by any other animal. If it is because the idea of bringing another entity into the world that must ultimately face birth, sickness, ageing, and death seems absurd and/or cruel, then this decision has arisen due to some deeper thinking based upon fact(s) and logic that is unique to humans. It is clearly our ability to see what nature and reality appear to be, via true rational thinking, that affords us a way to control our behaviours in ways not accessible to lower animals.

Some scientists invoke the results of the Libet experiment to show that free will is an illusion. When subjects were asked to spontaneously hit a button and note the time that they felt they were going to hit it, brain activity had actually begun up to two and a half seconds earlier, though usually around 500 milliseconds before. In other words, the subconscious mind instigates the choice and the conscious mind feels as though it made the choice after. Importantly, the feeling of volition does still precede motor action itself. They seem to overlook the fact that the individual is given instructions, rationally processes them, and engages in fulfilling the requirements of the experiment, albeit around 350 milliseconds before the subject consciously thinks they are acting. The commencement is not as a result of some third-party influence and truly is based on a nonrandom choice, so the idea of free will is not lost, in my view, just because the subconscious mind is harnessed as it is in many "*tasks.*" A more detailed analysis of the Libet experiment is explored in book 2, which shows how intent (operating outside linear time) leads to prescribed manifestations that are augmented into our mind's eye model of reality.

Rationalising about having children and "*deciding*" when to press a button are worlds apart but intent is the common thread. There is no doubt that the subconscious mind runs algorithms and that rationalising often follows: So, it would make sense that some of the more complex algorithms are done by running simulations within conscious awareness and that all of the outcomes are based upon rational and conscious decision-making. This does not necessarily mean that the decisions are founded upon platonic logic because the egoic mind is far from infallible. However, in all cases, it is ultimately intent that drives our perceived reality.

There are a few other potential blows to the concept of free will that should also be discussed. In one case, an American, Charles Whitman, committed one of the worst mass murders in US history. After stabbing his mother and wife to death, he traveled to the University of Texas, killed about a dozen people, and wounded more than double this number in a shooting spree. He left a suicide note saying he wanted to have a postmortem as he felt there was something wrong with his brain compelling him to act *"evil."* He was found to have a large tumour in the hypothalamus pressing on the amygdala. This should change our view of him and should also change how the law is designed to handle such cases. He is no longer evil but an unlucky victim of biology (read "God's Dice"). It is not beyond reason to think that the structure of different people's brains can differ in such a way that we are not all on a level playing field when it comes to morality and behaviour.

Although there indeed is a lot more access to free will than most scientist *"deniers"* will acknowledge, there are also a few important impacts of the kind discussed that undermine the general conception of free will and so it hangs by a thin thread. One is the influence of other points of consciousness (e.g. people) asserting their own free will measures and affecting that of others. This is rather like alpha male behaviour.

Another example where disease caused a form of mind control was when an egg-sized brain tumour in a 40-year-old man caused sudden uncontrollable paedophilia. When it was removed, the behaviour disappeared. The tumour was in the right lobe of the orbital frontal cortex, which is used in judgement, impulse control, and social behaviour. Neurologists Russell Swerdlow and Jeffrey Burns of the University of Virginia at Charlottesville believe it is the first reported case linking damage to the region with paedophilia. They confirmed that "We are dealing with the neurology of morality here," and because even severe damage to this area does not impact the ability to function, a doctor would not suspect something is wrong.

Correlation rather than causation was ruled out when the problem returned along with the tumour sometime after the original one had been removed. The behaviour subsided when the first was removed and then the return of the tumour was noted when the ill behaviour also returned. It was not that the man did not know his acts were immoral, it was merely that the "pleasure principle overrode restraint." The gravity of the desire was clearly far more compelling than the ability to terminate his wrongful actions. He was still aware of the moral position but had some force akin to mind control acquiescing him and rendering resistance futile. A person who is not suffering the condition will doubtlessly see this as an excuse and believe there is always the will available to overpower what is morally known to be incorrect. Probably the person suffering the tumour would have believed this, too, until he became under the control of the consequences of it.

Most Catholic priests will believe unquestionably in God. They know that paedophilia is morally and legally reprehensible and that it will be against the will of God with foreseeable dire consequences that they are sure are true within their own mind, if not true in reality, and again the pleasure principle clearly overrides constraint in those who offend.

When Parkinson's disease sufferers are given dopamine to reduce symptoms, they often begin new *"addictive"* habits that are alien to their normal nature. For example, habits of addiction such as gambling arise in their life, and when the dopamine administration stops, so do their new habits. So, it would seem that we are more easily controllable than we dare believe.

These cases do not mean that there can be no free will, but they do show how easily behaviour can be influenced. If physical problems can alter behaviour, then it is quite clear that nature and nurture can, too, as the brain anatomy and physiology are affected by these two forces.

Not only are we bound within our animal nature but we are also constrained by societal behaviours too. There are official and unofficial rules. You cannot choose to walk the high streets naked, for example. This being an example of society-imposed restriction upon free choice and not something naturally imposed upon us, since clothing is a human innovation.

One particularly evolved predisposition is of learning through others within a hierarchical social structure. This means that humans are capable of sharing and corresponding essentially anything; although, this has also led to immoral and amoral corruptions of truth and people's ability to discern it throughout history. The Milgram experiment, for example, had shown how the majority of people will blindly follow the instructions of those with authority or perceived authority. Subjects were asked to administer electric shocks to people answering questions incorrectly with the voltage increasing following each wrong answer. Even though the ones receiving the shocks were actors faking the shocks, most subjects carried on administering shocks despite evidence it was causing great pain that was seen to be worsening as the voltage was increased. This experiment was repeated recently: It was assumed that much of the public knew about this famous experiment and so would act accordingly. However, this was not the case as the results were even worse, with fewer people objecting to participate further as the voltage was raised more and more.

It is worth mentioning as well that most of the subjects who were following the instructions of the conductors of the experiment had shown signs of distress, and so it was not, necessarily, that they lacked a moral compass. Although, they had allowed the perception of higher authority to override their own feelings on the matter and generally proceeded despite these feelings.

Even exposure to the concept of "no free will" can affect behaviour. In a psychology experiment, two groups were given different essays to read. One took the position that free will is an illusion, and that nobody can act other than how they were going to, so are mere puppets in a mechanistic world. While the other essay took the opposing view. In tests undertaken immediately after the reading, the "free will is nonexistent" subjects had demonstrated higher degrees of selfishness. Having been primed with the idea of being puppets, they clearly adopted the idea that they were not really responsible for their own actions and thus concluded that they may as well just look after themselves. This has serious implications because it means that beliefs surrounding free will actually impact behaviour and choices.

Societal conditioning is one of the many factors that appear to diminish the possibility of free will. In Thailand, for example, the King's Anthem is played in all cinemas before the movies are screened. The majority of the audience stand immediately in a Pavlovian type manner. Some may do so out of respect, but for the majority, it is a reflex. Despite royalty being nonelected and the result of genetic chance, they are worshipped in Thailand in a kind of religious manner. Their belief system is "*programmed*" from an early age and is set in stone for the vast majority. Of course, this predisposition applies also to organized religion, and it happens to be geography that is most likely to determine a person's religious "*choice.*" There are hundreds of different religions. Which are right, if any? Do they contain some truths while distorting other truths? Regardless of the answer, billions of people are predisposed to being psychologically conditioned, and this illustrates yet another blow to the general consensus of free will.

In addition to the many factors already discussed that diminish perceived free will, temporary, or even permanent, changes to it can arise from the use of drugs or through alcohol consumption too. Again, it shows how fragile our behaviours are and if alcohol can do it, nature and nurture certainly can as well.

I think some of the philosophies I have read on addiction are off the mark. Many experiments have shown that mice, for example, can be addicted to the pleasure in *"wire-heading"* (where the pleasure centres of the brain can be stimulated at will, due to being wired a specific way that facilitates this effect) to such an extent that they neither look after themselves nor feed offspring. This compulsion overrides the very strong maternal instinct. Consequently, the addiction is very real and causes compulsive, destructive behaviour. Does the cause of addiction in the mind always have some physical aspects as well? Alternatively, when rats are given sociable and abundant space with varied activities, they are shown to avoid certain addictive behaviours. Of course, with humans, intervention and support can help treat an addict. However, the potentiality to become addicted is real, and genetics clearly plays a large role toward who is more likely to become an addict. Accordingly, the predisposition to addiction affects free will and, of course, actual addiction does so even more.

An interesting observation was made where a large group of monkeys had access to people's drinks at a holiday resort in the form of leftovers and/or by theft. Some only had nonalcoholic drinks, some had limited amounts of alcohol, and the others were constantly drinking themselves into a stupor. What was striking was that the proportionality closely matched the proportions seen throughout human alcoholism. In a sense, this shows that being aware of what alcoholism is, and how it can affect life in detrimental ways, appears less influential than genetic factors as the non-contemplative monkeys end up with very similar ratios.

If you look at human obesity, there is clearly a genetic component including variations in metabolism. But, more importantly, the brain also changes with obesity and creates a vicious cycle through addiction. If a gastric bypass is performed, as opposed to a fitment of a gastric band, when a sufferer undergoes fMRI brain scans pre- and post-operation and is shown fatty foods during each of the scans (e.g. cake) the pleasure centres act radically differently by comparison. These measurable changes to the anatomy and physiology of the brain reflect a completely different perception that arises relating to food. Of course, the stomach has billions of neurons, too, and it seems, therefore, that a natural feedback system is altered by performing the bypass. Either way, it demonstrates how a person can have their free will impacted by a fairly standard operation. It may not have been impossible to break the cycle anyway (it is certainly not physically impossible) but the altered activity of the brain following the operation indicates the passing back of some "*lost*" free will and the end of an addiction that was previously enhanced by their previous stomach-to-brain feedback system.

A lesser discussed constraint on free will is that of simply being human. I do not mean the evolutionary psychology that purports to explain most, if not all, of our behaviours. I am referring to the limited number of options that are available—meaning that we are merely choosing from activities that have evolved due to them being meaningful to at least some of us. These are only participated in because predispositions emerged from more basic evolutionary drivers, senses, and emotions.

For example, a lottery winner is quite often likely to buy a fast car, a big house, a holiday home, choose human-oriented projects and/or business projects, enjoy more luxurious breaks and holidays, etc. Due to preference, not every individual will act in this stereotypical way but many will. And even those who have more imaginative ways to spend their time as a lottery winner will still just be selecting from an array of human-centric behaviour options. And so even though nature and nurture will influence people's choices, the choices are far from unlimited. Surviving and enjoying leisure activities takes up so much of each waking day that I think the vast majority of people forget that there is far from an infinite number of behavioural options in the physical material realm.

In basic terms, we all need to dedicate some time relating to Maslow's basic needs and, therefore, time is invested to eating, sleeping, toilet time, etc. Likewise, activities relating to the process of reproduction tend to occupy a proportion of most adult lives. As odd as it may come across, the general target of our drive for reproduction is not some random animate or inanimate object but a fellow human. For the potential for offspring, a fellow human being of the opposite sex. This is not so much a choice but a deep unquestioned programming/necessity for the perpetuation of DNA in our form. This is the "lure" referred to earlier. Any exception to the "rule" is a deviation from the normal distribution curve and is not an "intended" outcome of the evolutionary process.

All these human behavioural options may feel like choices because we can perhaps choose the "when"—but they cannot be hallmarks of true free will in view of the fact that we do not, ultimately, "will" these things. The vast number of activities available for the undertaking such as gardening, for example, may seem to indicate the potential to express free will, as some choose to partake in such activities while others do not. However, they are also manifestations of behaviour that are generally undertaken due to explainable biological causes. How different is the human gardener to that of the bowerbird? One is engaged in its behaviour due to programmatic gene fitness indicator/aesthetic display behaviour. The other maintains characteristics of the previous, yet, also experientially portrays a sense of beauty according to developed tastes that could not have been possible without an evolved capacity to experience sensation, pleasure, or ultimately a sense-oriented discern-ability to discern meaning.

Yet, another potential constraint on free will is of that limited personality types exist. We all are unique in many ways, but personality types are outside of our will, although they can be modified, difficultly. It is less difficult should a person become conscious of their ability to alter their personality and/or of their ability to create any reality, albeit having to face the paradigms and alternative consequences of multiple, competing intents. In a television programme about this, two people of the same type were put together in a social experiment and could not believe how much they had in common. They were like doppelgangers and it caused a kind of uneasiness, as it had not occurred to them that we are of a *"relatively"* limited, manifest network of experience(s) of consciousness in co-inhabitance, realising and acting upon a proportionally limited variation of intents and preferences.

Even as people gravitate toward specific job roles within society, this is (suggestively) reflective of ants and their priorly evaluated roles, although, concerning people, obviously the overall available roles are much greater. There are thousands of job types in any given city but observe how there are *"just enough"* cameramen, pro tennis players, doctors, etc. It is by far a hand in glove fit in general terms, as there may, for example, be a demand for physics teachers that exceeds the current supply. It is certainly not as though every person aspires to be a doctor, whereby, those who fail to be bright enough, or simply do not fit such a path, are essentially forced to look elsewhere. But neither is it as though each child born is automatically assigned a future career that that is both fitting for them and for society needs as a whole. It is a kind of continuum and our reality seems to represent somewhere between these extremes.

People collectively gravitate to the roles that stabilize and function their societies as well as to the roles that resonate with their personal vibration throughout life. However, if you look at the overall order of who ends up doing what, it is quite remarkable how it comes into balance in a way similar to that of the biosphere as a whole. Of course, artificial intelligence poses a huge threat to this because jobs that, until now, have remained beyond the capabilities of automation will soon be well within the capabilities of AI. This even includes solicitors, doctors, and many other service industry roles. The point is that there is a kind of invisible force/will that causes people to gravitate towards certain roles (with the possibility of dismissal when there is a poor fit) so this, too, means another blow to aspects of potential free will. The effect to which I refer is more visible if, for example, cities are seen as complex living systems, in their own right, as opposed to looking at each denizen, compartment store, road, and city block in isolation. It is all a manifestation of mathematics, as always, but the effect is less obvious when you zoom in to individual levels of society, where order is more sporadically distributed and maintained.

Unsurprisingly, the human mind is so complex that evolutionary psychology alone does not appear to directly explain all of human behaviour. For example, George Michael had identified that it is not what people have that makes them a star but what is missing. He believed that most, if not all, stars are driven by an enhanced need for recognition and love due to a huge internal void. This is another blow for free will because this type of drive is not so much a choice but more of a compulsion.

Of course, some believe that humans are merely biological creatures that are programmed by nature and nurture, and so it is inevitable they will act as per their evolutionary constraints. If it were not for a brain and mind that has evolved to such an extent it can transcend these constraints to some degree, this worldview would be accurate. In most cases, people do not take steps to transcend these constraints and so free will truly is an illusion. The fact that there are so many behavioural "options" for humans, grants the illusion that we can transcend the bindings of limiting human-centric behavioural constraints However, when playing our human roles, we really cannot. We are a unique species, though, in that the egoic mind can be transcended and so, for a rare few, the shackles can be removed and genuine free will accessed.

Unlike other animals, we clearly do have significantly more behavioural variances alongside conscious capacities for decision-making and variations in taste and so, we are in that sense, unique. However, there is no escaping that the unenlightened choose from a fairly predictable set of limited behaviours.

In any given life journey of a person, there are reactive aspects to their behaviour throughout at least some of their experiences. These reactive behaviours are generally governed by nature and nurture and are, therefore, essentially the processing of algorithms. There does not seem to be much free will to be found for those who are unconscious or semi-aware. However, there are proactive elements also—contemplative actions taken upon the basis of meeting needs: Insinuating a derivation and illustration of fulfilment that involves imaginatively simulating potential futures based on logic and personal taste. Although, as we do not directly determine what our tastes are, or what is actually meaningful to us, can our apparent free will be considered authentic? I believe that the conscious processing of decision-making and experience is real—just as real as we are—and so free will is real even if personalities, intelligence levels, skills, etc. are key contributors to this process.

All these complex input factors mean that every person is certainly unique, including those who have lived and that will ever live; therefore, the individualism and conscious processing based upon that is not an illusion. I do not believe that individuals who could, hypothetically, be presented with the same options at slightly different times would make identical choices on every occasion, either, as even mood variation will influence discernability and/or choosiness.

Some believe, even based on all the above, that even if free will is more than an illusion, it is still virtually nonexistent mainly due to the bindings of our biology and physics. We have traveled time in our countless prehuman forms in a nonconscious state, "while" much of this "reductionist's" legacy still continues to impact our present-day behaviour. In binary terms, our biological form has constitutively determined us to be a pleasure seeking and pain avoiding creature, although unlike more basic animals, what is generally deemed pleasurable or painful will vary from person to person with the exception of some basic and fundamental variances.

It is a key aim of this book to show that the primacy of consciousness hypothesis is true, and so the biggest blow to free will is the notion that all life circumstances are mind/ego made illusions, whereby the individual points of consciousness (sentient life) concordantly believe that they are separate beings within a space-time realm. All the concepts that appear to impact free will mentioned up to this point, exist in the physically sensed, yet illusorily experienced, space-time model. This, in and of itself, does not undermine the potentiality of free will. However, it does suggest that the circumstances that we perceptually navigate throughout life and experience are, in a sense, illusory. And that the "*rules*" of the manifest universe may "temporarily" constrain our capacity to enjoy free will. As our existence consists of unique sets of experiences, interactively perpetuating in perpetuity, amongst and throughout the infinite one(s), there is also a paradox that seems to arise through the observer's perspective—in juggling the differences between the recognition(s) of being subsidiary forms of intent derived from the One intent, and of each and everything being individually distinct viewpoints of the same thing. This essentially means that we cocreate our total life experience via individual intent but at the same time are all cocreating an agreed upon hallucination we call reality, and so the whole flowering of consciousness in our perceived physical material realm is ultimately noTHING happening in no time (in terms of illusory linear time).

In other words, as our perception of separateness is an illusion, cascading over limited, "virtual" reality-enslaved minds/egos, then individual free will has to somehow be related to this same illusion. It does not mean that all aspects of experience are illusory, as any naturally illusory information feeds back to individual minds which are, in turn, differentiated aspects of a whole. Accordingly, experience(s) are all real as well—all part of an infinite *"present moment"* with conditions determined by Universal Consciousness that allow for locally interacting individual points of consciousness to collectively experience a sensationally, evolving material realm.

Once an individual's consciousness grows sufficiently large within these amalgamated points of individualized consciousness, represented by the evolution of more advanced brains, it seems possible to transcend the illusion of mind. Many people claim to have attained this state and there are indeed many clues within how reality presents itself to rationally believe that these accounts are absolutely accurate.

This does not preclude Universal Consciousness from having free will or even individual spirits—as they are differentiated manifestations of the whole, they help to comprise which are simultaneously separate whilst also being a part of the whole. The concurrently experienced space-time realm naturally posits the setting of the precise conditions that allow for the flowering of consciousness, leading to sentient beings as a means of self-experience. Additional evidence appears through the subtle but detectable procedural measures that impact the evolutionary process itself. As mentioned, individual minds can have and express free will, but if any of their received "input" information is illusory, deceptive, or distorted in nature, then for the unenlightened, at least, the free will/intent capacity is effectively hijacked and almost exclusively reallocated to survival and reproductive activity.

If the primacy of consciousness hypothesis seems too far-fetched and does not appear to accurately reflect our experiences within reality: I ask that you suspend any judgement for just a little longer. There are many pieces of evidence that substantiate this theory, and so one does not necessarily have to believe it just because of my say so. Even if you find this account of reality doubtful after reading this book, the various pieces of evidence, which I simply suggest point to the hypothesis as being true, are definitely real in their own right. Accordingly, there will likely be many fresh revelations new to most readers, and the hope is that these should help to enrichen our personal experiences and overall understanding of our reality.

As you will see, illusions are generally so powerful that even when you are aware of "certain ones," the mind cannot just override any of the naturally embedded illusion(s) to replace them with a more objectively accurate "account" of our reality. Yet, by developing our understanding of the science, as well as anatomy and physiology of the brain/mind, we indeed can prove that what we are experiencing is "illusory" by nature. And I believe that this applies to essentially all that we sense and perceive (including our *"individual"* nature). Our reality is unquestionably an illusion, to a lesser or greater extent, as it is not "entirely" in the same ballpark as true fundamental reality. However, in a sense, both our world-bound experience of consciousness (the focus of attention away from the full quantum realm of infinite possibilities and experiences) and the space-time construct are both true states, even should our "reality" be perceived by mind(s) alone. It is similar to a video game environment: "Prefabricated" but fully immersive such that you are simultaneously in the game but also a remote observer of it. The biggest difference being that the focus of the observer's perspective, devoted to the video games, shares the same linear time experience as the player (conscious agent) does in our perceived reality, while base reality essentially voiding itself of linear time by and through a concise and miraculous use of "now" time. Whereby only a forward-facing arrow of time is permitted through the mind's eye model. As we shall see, this does not affect the ability of subconsciousness(es) to transcend the linear time illusion.

Accordingly, our illusory reality will persist until minds can transcend it, perhaps through altered states of consciousness or after physical death. The brain and mind of humans generally provides a rather restrictive experience as they reside almost exclusively in the conditioned space-time realm. Although the enlightened can mentally traverse space-time to access the true nonconditioned realm, they are still heavily bound by the laws of nature within this realm due to their biological form. Yet, according to thousands of near-death experiences, 360-degree vision, unimaginable intellect and knowing, and a sense of ultimate love in a spaceless and timeless realm is the true reality that awaits all.

As the book demonstrates throughout, there are countless pieces of evidence within this realm to suggest that there is truly a superior Mind residing within and without this universe. Accordingly, many accounts of near-death experiences also appear to coincide with what Nature's secrets already reveal when properly scrutinized. As the whole of alpha to omega is constructed from illusory linear time, individual life cycles across linear time are also manifested and connected in this way.

God (Universal Consciousness) has infinite intelligence, love, intent, possibilities, and experiences. The combination of intent and infinite imagination is synonymous with free will. The intent to experience infinite possibilities via infinite subintents changes "essentially" nothing as One and All are "essentially" singular. This is similar to Brahman, as referred to within the teachings and beliefs of both Hinduism and Buddhism. All that exists, within and through-out the illusory linear time between Alpha and Omega, is valid in so much that Brahman gives it that validity. Somewhere along that linear timeline, certain points of consciousness "awaken" and realise: I AM "that," I AM (i.e. each focus of attention or conscious agent is God) and so the power of the whole becomes available to each of us as we awaken. Once there is a unification of the infinite points of attention: Brahman remains as the restrictions inherent in believing the projections created by false egoic mind states fall away. What began as perfection ends back as perfection. Infinite possibilities and experiences mean just that, though, so there are infinite ways to ride the waves of limitless imagination in a forever now. In the meantime, World War III is a spiritual war having arisen between the awakened souls, and those that have fully brought up and/or "bought into" the illusory physical material realm and who will do or will try to do anything to maintain the status quo. They enjoy being slave drivers (or also slaves themselves in their own way) despite it being an ungodly hollow victory in light of linear time being illusory.

7

THE ILLUSIONS OF VISION, AND VISIONS OF REALITY

"Reality is merely an illusion, albeit a very persistent one."

Albert Einstein

A brief overview upon the conceptions and misconceptions of vision was mentioned previously in this book. However, given that so much of the brain is allocated to this amazing function, I wish to go into greater detail. One-third of the brain (predominantly the rear region) is involved in vision and when one considers what capabilities of processing occur in the brain, it is not so surprising as to why. Showing how vision really works as well as how various illusions work illustrates how *"clever"* the mind really is, independent of conscious thought. They are relevant to the meaning of life, insofar that they demonstrate, a) How certain natural automata operate (and their (respectively) corresponding relationship(s) to their deeper, and enterprising nature) and of how the *"automated intelligence"* is greater than the slower rational thinking, by an incomprehensible order of magnitude, and b) Given that it is, arguably, for the sighted, the number one sense used to navigate the world is, therefore, an integral aspect to the experience of reality.

The chequered shadow illusion developed by Ted Adelson at MIT (overleaf) is a good starting point for this chapter. While presenting this delusive act, the eyes and conscious mind are tricked into believing that the dark chequer (A) to the left of the cylinder, and the pale chequer (B) on the shadow of the cylinder, are completely different shades. While they are, in fact, the same. The brain (mind) *"knows"* how reality normally behaves and so artificially forces the appearance of a lighter shade in the shadow where the shadow would normally create darkening. When the lighter-appearing chequer is moved from alongside the dark chequer toward the top left, it becomes apparent that they indeed are exactly the same shade.

As with all visual illusions, even when we know the illusion, the mind still, nonetheless, automatically creates the illusion within our mind's eye view. The best illustration of this is shown in *The McGurk Effect.*

(https://www.youtube.com/watch?v=G-IN8vWm3m0).

As the video demonstration shows: When you close your eyes, you hear *"bah, bah, bah"* repeated. When you see lips saying the same thing, you hear *"bah, bah, bah,"* but when you see the lips that appear to say *"vah, vah, vah"* (where the bottom lip flicks off the top of the teeth) you seem to hear *"vah, vah, vah."* Yet, the sound being transmitted is actually still saying *"bah, bah, bah."* In other words, visual perception overrides the audio information received to actually transforms what you hear. It creates a false audible *"reality"* that is a manifestation of the limitations of our perception. And, of course, as mentioned, it doesn't really matter whether we know it is an illusion or not, as it is an automated feature within the sense-perception process that cannot be overridden.

In the chequered shadow illusion, square A and B are identical shades of grey— although the mind creates the perception that A is much darker.

In short, there are rather complex algorithms being processed by the mind unconsciously, such that it acts like a rational physicist who is working out extraordinary equations. But, of course, the mind does all this complex algorithm processing on its own. The conscious mind is both generally unaware of the processing and also of the fact that our mind-projected experience is illusory by nature. By conducting further tests, and/or by inquiring and deducing from upon the illusion itself can we show that, in the case of the chequered square illusion, they are the same shade of grey.

A similar illusion from Dave Purvis's laboratory also uses two identical grey chequers. However, this time they are placed in relatively similar positions to each other, with each on two different cubes. Both of which are accompanied alongside other variously coloured chequers and both appearing to be bathed in respective yellow and blue light. The fake light sources and the apparent effect they maintain on all the coloured chequers are part of the context that creates the main illusion. Even though the chequers are both grey, the mind sees them as blue under the apparent yellow light and yellow under the apparent blue light. It's the same kind of illusion, but this time, colour that is not present is created by the mind based on surrounding context. Of course, this also endorses what has already been mentioned—that the mind itself creates the experience we know as colour and in this case is cleverly **overriding the retinal** input-capacity's ability to inform the brain of the distinctions of colour of what it is observing.

Grey seen as blue surface with a yellow filter

Grey seen as yellow surface with a blue filter

Dave Purvis's laboratory colour cube illusion

Doubtlessly, it will be evolutionary pressures that have produced this effect, as any incoming light information from the external environment is not quite as important (from a perspective of survival) as simply being able to recognize the external environment itself. In other words, contextual information, i.e. the cause of an input, is generally more important than the basic properties of its components. The mind underlyingly recognizes all of this and so naturally adapts our perception to accommodate for these multiple ranges of variables interacting in simultaneity. This all happens in a fraction of a second, of course, as even a predator's capture or a prey's escape will have necessitated such speed for cognitive processing. The appearing of grey to yellow or grey to blue is not just any random transformation conjured up by the mind but a referentially imposed deference of perception, whereby the subconscious mind *"knows"* the complementary colour spectrum and augments calculated colour experiences into our mind's eye model. When a blue filter is in place, if the colour of the chequer is grey, there would be a blue tint observed. However, as grey is projected, it implies to the mind that the complementary colour (yellow) must be present at the surface. And when they combine under a dim protrusion of light: Grey is produced instead of white. The mind (consciousness) favours the colour it has *"worked out,"* yellow, and this overrides the retinal input, i.e. grey. Likewise, when the image appears through a yellow filter, the grey chequer is observably bypassed by its complementary colour relation (blue).

In a different experiment, an upside-down cone is shone in white light by two different light sources—one being to the left and the other to the right. A red filter is then placed over the left light resulting in the shadow nearest the left light to be cast red. But what is surprising is that it also makes the shadow at the opposite side of the cone appear coloured as well and in this case the colour is cyan (despite being well-lit from the right by a white light source and not a cyan one). The mind is aware that red light is shone upon the surfaces and, although the retina will detect grey on the right-side shadow, the mind *"knows"* that grey should only arise in red light where and when the surface property (colour) of the grey area is actually cyan. As such, in the same way as the coloured cube experiment, the mind overrides the retinal input-capacity to create an experience based upon the observed surface properties of these objects and given the context.

Deducing upon the contexts and implications of these experiments does also present them as a fantastic demonstration of the mind's ability to perform complex physics, subconsciously. However, in considering the cone shadow experiment and coloured cube experiments from a conscious perspective (respectively), the context(s) between the observed environment and the factors concurrently affecting them, essentially trick the mind to see what the retina, itself, is actually "not" receiving. Experimenters had concluded that the complementary colour, cyan, was experienced (in the inverted cone experiment) because the mind likes symmetry and so "*chose*" red's complimentary colour to create balance. This is true to a degree and may be observed by placing the colour spectrum into a circle whereby the complimentary colours sit opposite each other. However, they seemed to miss the fact that the environmentally incoming contextual information, (inherent to not only the experiment(s) but the very nature of the biological observer) would lead the mind to drawing the observation that the grey being witnessed must have had a surface property of cyan that had converted to grey, as a result to the (aforementioned) observed presence of red light (while the cyan being witnessed was as a result of a "*clever*" subconsciousness—forcing the mind's eye to augment and/or collapse the colour-waveform it has calculated right back into consciousness). As when the observer zooms in on the cyan, it reverts back to grey and the context is lost.

For those that still doubt that colour is made by the mind, this offers conclusive proof. As the cyan is, without a doubt, *really* not there, yet it is witnessed all the same. It is the mind and consciousness together that cooperate to *conjure* what is seen through the mind's eye.

The evidence and accounts compiled thus far are compelling enough, yet another valuable length of insight comes about from colour-blind people, who have synaesthesia. Their array of light-sensing cone cells is unable to ascertain certain wavelengths of colour. And so, they cannot detect and/or convert much of the colour data to signals that the non-colour-blind can, consequently experiencing less colours in their mind's eye/consciousness. However, other neurological registries, such as the perceiving of digits, can even provoke otherwise inaccessible colours (via internal stimulation of the optic nerves that correspond electrical impulses to inactive retinal cones) due to a cross-wiring of the brain that the condition of synaesthesia results.

These colours are referred to as "alien colours" in recognition of the fact that colour-blind people cannot experience such colours through their normal vision. This shows that the potential to see any or all colours is perceptually innate, yet remains generally dormant for/within colour-blind people. And also, that synaesthesia itself cannot be a learned behaviour because the sense organs (eyes) are incapable of capturing and producing what the underlying condition itself is internally able to accomplish when it comes to these alien colours. As the alien colours could not have been experienced until the condition brought them into their being, they were effectively nonexistent as far as their colour vision "system" is concerned and so **cannot have been available to be learned from**.

The *"potentially"* embedded capacity to experience these alien colours does more than hint to the fundamentality of the human mind's ability to generate the experience of colour from within its own domain. Mind consciousness is representing something that is fundamental at a higher level of Universal Consciousness. For the same reason that synaesthesia cannot be a learned behaviour, i.e. because it had no access to alien colours to draw from the external environment, **biological evolution cannot have created colours because they do not wholly exist as a result of the external environment** either. And yet, because there is a reality of sorts to the colour phenomenon itself, it also seems beyond the capability of the mind alone to create such distinct and uniform states without some frame of reference to base the experience on. It would seem to be as fundamental as the physical creations we deem as real and *"out there,"* even though mind/consciousness are required to perceive them. And that it seems highly likely that everyone's experience of any given colour will be very similar without it being directly learned and/or acquired throughout someone's life experience **adds weight to the idea that colour experiences are fundamental, despite them also being nonphysical.**

The same principle(s) demonstrated in the grey chequer examples are also utilized by the mind's processing to distinguish object size. When an object is registered by the eye, the eye, due to the properties of physics, first inverts the automatically reduced image, e.g. a tree conveys visual information that corresponds, in relativity, to the retina's physically limited capacity to receive, process, and witness the actual size of the tree. The image size hitting the retina does not provide information about the inherent size of the object because the same size image would appear as vastly different ranges of size depending on the distance of the observer to the object of observation. A huge tree in the far distance, for example, would fill the same retinal area as a smaller tree that is nearer. Again, it's all about context. As, in this case, it is the factor of distance that the mind captures to consider.

Using fMRI technology, professor of psychology, Scott Murray from the University of Washington, can map different regions and intensities of brain activity that correspond to the perceiving and/or witnessing of different-sized objects (Retinotopic mapping). It shows that visual registration of smaller objects stimulates brain activity at the very rear of the brain and that as the objects get bigger, brain activity traverses further and further toward the front while the encompassed circumference of the activated area also expands. To add context, 3D objects with apparent foregrounds and backgrounds were later used in a similar assessment—presenting an illusion whereby two identically sized spheres end up looking very different, as the back one appears much larger once depth-perspective is added to the picture. Brain activity was then assessed after observing the two objects separately (importantly, the perspective art [or lack thereof] in both images was retained during both assessments). Concluding that even though the size(s) of the 3D objects registered by the retinas were the same, the brain activity appears in different positions. The one that appears larger by virtue of the illusion stimulating brain activity slightly more towards the front of the brain. Thus, context is again considered and impacts what is perceived.

It was somewhat of a shock to the researchers that corresponding area(s) of neural activity varied throughout the brain even though the true size(s) of the object(s) hitting the retina were identical. This showed that the brain (and/or mind) somehow accurately accounts for contextual information *prior* to, or perhaps more accurately, at the exact same time as determining where the brain activity being caused by the source of information should take place.

The idea that all of space and time are potentially mind-perceived illusions could explain why there is a difference in terms of where brain activity occurred, despite there being identical retinal input(s). This is because all objects and perspective(s) that we perceive would then be implied illusions—that the receiver organ, known as the brain, reacts to from within its capacity as an equally illusory biological object in the manifest space-time realm. From the mind's point of view, there is no *real* distinction between an observed perspective from within a contrived illusion and an observed perspective within so-called reality (they are both illusions). Accordingly, brain activity would occur and be detected in regions that correspond with input information it is *"fed,"* i.e. the brain region affected actively engages input information such that the position (in terms of the occurring correspondence between the space and time of brain activity) is already predetermined by the *"existence"* of the realistic perspective that is also an integral part of the 3D object art. In other words, the detected (and perceived) contextual information can be observed subconsciously prior to what is observed in the mind's eye and this allows the mind to override the disparity between retinal input and what is presented to the mind's eye.

The effect could be as a result of the subconscious mind withholding the retinal input information and instantly replacing it with a consciousness created (intelligent) alternative, but the process would be no less magical if this was the case. There is still a nonrandom and highly intelligent subconscious force in operation. The propagation of a certain reality within space-time in accordance with the state of another key facet of reality is discussed in greater detail later in the book, whereby a definite observer decision that has happened from within (and without) space-time appears to be a future decision enacting itself retroactively—"consequentially" affecting the propagation of a certain reality. Accordingly, there is already evidence that definitive upcoming information can assure either precognition or the propagation of a perceived reality that was predetermined by the upcoming inevitable "future" information and this may equally apply to realities that account for contextual information.

Some people saw only slight differences in sphere sizes and, not surprisingly, it transpires that the brain activity occurring in the relevant region showed little difference too (in terms of the level and whereabouts of neuronal activity that arise when the two sphere-like objects are observed by the subjects). Hence, the people that had perceived a greater difference between sphere size(s) also had the greatest shift along V1 (being the brain region where the activity shows up). This indicates that some minds account for the perspective effect more so than others but doesn't explain how context effects the shift along V1. As already discussed, the conscious mind appears to be responsible for brain regional allocation, rather than specifically dissertating the information of retinal input, upon the basis that it can perceive the information and actively steer the brain while maintaining cohesion of perception (which in turn feeds back unto the mind).

A real-life example of this can be seen by observing "the moon illusion." When the moon is near the horizon, it can look huge. Yet, it then rises high into the sky appearing considerably smaller. The eye clearly gathers information from the horizon including slightly above and below it and the presence of this forces the mind to "*assume*" that it must be reasonably big, as the observed perspective corresponds to the difference(s) of distance between the observer and the moon (from varying frames of reference). As such, it creates brain activity forward in V1 and so the mind's eye projection, in turn, will create a visually inflated moon size. Apparently, viewing the moon through your legs with your head upside-down makes it appear smaller again.

Time-lapse photography confirms that it is indeed an illusion, as the true size does not vary as it progresses upward from the horizon, so it is human perception in relation to the effect described that gives the illusion of increased size and not some natural astronomical effect, such as the result of the moon being seen through a wider expanse of earth's atmosphere. Of course, when the moon is directly above, it is nearer to the observer than when it is positioned near the horizon by an entire earth's radius and so would be slightly bigger if not for the moon illusion that occurs near the horizon.

It is clear that V1 activity is highly relevant to the mind's perception of dimensionality, which roughly overlays the images we perceive onto the source of information ("*out there*") that arrive as inputs registered through the retina. However, how the mind's eye-projection is made, i.e. our conscious perception/virtual reality model, is largely still unknown. It probably involves a lot of key regions of the brain and nervous system to sustain our experience of consciousness but it remains a mystery as far as mainstream science is concerned, as to the progenerating of consciousness itself. How it all actually works is perhaps not so difficult if viewed from a perspective where it is accepted that there is a primacy of consciousness—it is simply the mind's augmenting of qualia experiences from the quantum realm into our mind's eye model and, likewise, taking collapsed wavefunction data (binary in quantum superpositions) and compounding it into effectually distributive proportions that are proportionally related to any or all perceived physical manifestations.

This is essentially what is portrayed in the allegoric movie, *The Matrix*—although, in the movie, there is a base reality and a forced false-perception of another one. The real situation is quite different, though, in that the agreed upon hallucination we call reality is based in a binary realm (as per *The Matrix* false-perception one) whereby quantum events are augmented into constructing perceived reality, while the quantum realm, itself, is the TRUE realm. In the movie, base reality is portrayed as something akin to our reality (albeit a postapocalyptic version). However, true base reality is both noTHING and everyTHING simultaneously—while everyTHING existing in simultaneity, itself, is a realm of infinite possibilities and experiences. In other words, we are in the world but not of it.

As if all this was not amazing enough, it transpires that some visual input data from "*out there*" is not only used in cohering the dimensional projection we enjoy in terms of our consciously perceived vision of the world but it is also factored (and/or factorized) subconsciously. In other words, **some visual information is also unconsciously and/or invisibly utilized** (from our waking consciousness perspective) in motor functions. Motor functions require more precise visual information than that which is needed for our virtual reality perception and so the two vision systems operate independently. This "*blind vision*" may sound strange initially, until you realise that the unconscious perception of light will have preceded, by eons, the complex visual representations that higher animals enjoy. For example, **the Euglena is a basic single-celled organism that has photoreceptors and seeks sunlight by propelling itself using a flagellum.** We can safely assume that captured light, in this case, does not result in some complex 3D model of the world.

In humans, visual information moves through both the dorsal and ventral streams of the brain. The former is the invisible nonperceived aspect and **the latter is what is used to create the mind's eye projected image of the world.** As is often the case, it was a malfunction of the system that showed how the system works. A patient of the researchers had suffered hypoxia from carbon monoxide poisoning, which damaged the ventral stream, rendering her blind to the form of objects. Yet, the nonperceived part of her vision remained intact. The result was quite astonishing. Although she could not see shapes of objects (like apples and books, etc.) she could see materials, e.g. an aluminum torch with red plastic elements is perceived by her as metal with red plastic and, yet, she could not perceive the actual shape of the object itself.

Her problem was/is so drastic that she cannot even tell what angle a pencil is being held at. But when she is asked to reach out to grab the pencil, her hand angles to match the angle of the pencil. So, although she cannot perceive the pencil angle, her motor function has visual data fed to it, which causes an automatic adjustment in terms of angling the hand. Likewise, if asked which angle a slot was, she was unable to say—but if she was trying to post a card into the slot, she turned the card to the same angle. Over time, she was able to make micro movements towards the slot and know from the resulting hand angling what the angle of the slot was without having to go through the whole posting process. However, her reaction had stemmed from information channelled through the movement vision system (largely processed through the cerebellum in relation to available visual input) and not necessarily from a fully conscious perspective (as would be mediated by the frontal lobe, from upon the ventral side of the brain).

Unsurprisingly, patients with damage to the dorsal stream have the opposite problem. They can see the angular orientation of a slot (for example), but when they put their hand towards the slot, they cannot spatially manoeuvre the orientation of their hand in relation to the angle of the slot. Since the sense of touch is still available to them, though, they can adjust the angle of their hand (or angle of approach) by touching the slot itself, but the hand (in motion) has no informational frame of reference as it does in people with a well-functioning dorsal stream.

When we go to grasp at any everyday objects, we automatically alter our width of grasp according to the object's size. When there is damage to the ventral stream, however, a person cannot make an accurate assessment of the grasp size that is going to be required through normal sight. However, when the hand is in motion, going to grasp an object, grasp aperture will adjust normally. This shows that the nonperceived visual system is heavily involved in this action too. Patients with damage to the dorsal stream open their hand fully as an automatic default, as if grabbing a large object, and rely on touch to make adjustments once their hand reaches the object. It is interesting that when the mind has no motor function visual guidance input, it not only *"knows"* the objective is to grab an object but also *"recognizes"* the required input data stream is failing and so still takes intelligent action to automatically adjust to maximum aperture until touch can allow for a suitable grip. This means that even when the system goes wrong, there is still a subconscious intelligence there to guide and enact this "plan B." In other words, you might expect the default setting to gesture toward an object guided by main vision, which may logically set the initial grasp size based upon perceived object size with final adjustments taking place as the hand touches the object. However, the alternatively intelligent move (of subconsciously opening the hand fully) demonstrates an inner awareness of the fact that the dorsal stream is damaged and shows that the mind is capable of taking alternative steps instinctively.

The reason two vision systems evolved together is probably because there is a big difference between object perception (which is primarily concerned with what the object is and less so with all the different angles that it can be viewed from) and the more specific contextual information required to take appropriate action. In other words, when going to grasp an object, the perception of distance and visually affirmed orientation of the object in relation to its environment is needed to accomplish the task effectively.

The famous hollow face mask illusion tricks the visual perception system. The area of the brain responsible for facial recognition is so accustomed to forming faces from face-like forms and patterns that it makes sense of the inside, concave representation of a mask and produces a 3D outwardly projected image in the mind's eye, despite it being hollow (related to the effect of pareidolia). However, experiments show that the motor system is not fooled in the same way. This is further evidence that perception is very much about building mental images that are useful, even if inaccurate, whereas the motor system necessitates a more accurate (subconscious) representation of reality.

The brain evolved to act on the world—and perception is a handmaiden to action. And the motor system's registering and circuiting of visual input information assures that all-important action is accurately carried out.

As outlined earlier in the book, the map is not the territory when it comes to all of our senses and perceptions. We experience a virtualized reality that has been fine-tuned by evolution to give many of us an experiential worldview ideal for survival and reproduction. We know we are all tricked by certain mind-made illusions but what we do not as easily comprehend is how much of what we perceive is mind-made. As mentioned earlier, if space-time is an illusion, then so are all the inputs to our virtual sensory input devices—also meaning that our entire earthly lives are mind-made illusions (even though the entirety of all experiences that occur within and throughout consciousness may be as the result of direct utilizations and embedded access of/to fundamental phenomena, e.g. love). Everybody is experiencing powerful hallucinations every waking moment and, yet, a universally maintained consensus based from upon fundamentally common characteristics **makes these hallucinations what we call reality**. The illusory and perceptual delineations do not end here, though. How we emotionally process information (for example) can also be distorted by societal norms (avoiding displeasures, the anxious requirement for small talk, material praise over psychological praise, "every man for himself" mentality, etc.).

We live in a universal fantasy—one where reality and delusion are commonly related by the fallibility of human perception and one where the fallibility of human perception may gradually be nurtured to uncover "its" underlying nature. To alter our worldview so that it is more aligned with "*reality*," we firstly must recognize that this is the case. Then, to learn more about the reality of ourselves and our limitations as humans, as well as how thoughts, behaviour, and emotions are interlinked. Likewise, we need to learn more about the reality of our world—taking account of the virtual reality approximation previously discussed. If space-time is illusory and our consciousness actually resides in the nonconditioned realm whilst it simultaneously experiences the world of *"projection,"* this would require the most radical alignment of all. To begin with, it would tell us that what we call life should not be taken seriously, the same as death. Without linear time, there can be no death. Consciousness was, is, and always will be present and so is completely unaffected by illusory linear time.

Before technological advances, we could not perceive UV light, infrared light, bacteria, atoms, etc. They were invisible to us—so essentially nonexistent. For the unconscious, there is a belief that the idea that *"anything goes"* is just fantasy but in reality, there are infinite possible phenomena beyond our perception. For the conscious, it reminds us that we often work based on limited perceptions of reality and, therefore, an incomplete access to the true quantum realm even though once the egoic mind is transcended spiritual masters proclaim that full access is given. Add to this the power of the mind to create and perceive illusions and it is feasible (in fact, inevitable) that true reality is "far removed" from the way we perceive it. In other words, our virtual reality perception may be excellent in assuring the survival and reproduction of individual points of consciousness in ego-form, but we are (essentially) totally blind when it comes to true reality. Having said that, despite the issue of the fallibility of biological sense-perception, there are portals allowing us to get at the truth, once you know how to untie/cut the Gordian knot.

Quantum physics, although it appears to have little effect on our day-to-day living, shows how counterintuitive reality can really be. In the famous double-slit experiment, an unexpected result is produced by the appearance of an interference pattern on a screen opposite the source of a monochromatic light (laser or particle) gun firing through a double slit at the screen. This double slit allows for some of the particles/photons/beams of light to pass through, whereas some are blocked by the surrounding wall. Instead of reproducing the pattern of the two slits after exposure, an array of vertical slit-like representations spreading out horizontally appear in a distinct wave-interference pattern. Even stranger, when the particles are fired individually, they still somehow create the same pattern, which builds over time, despite the apparent impossibility for individual particles to travel through both slits simultaneously to interfere with each other.

This showed that particles act as waves and follow paths of functional wave-potentials. In other words: Emergently probabilistic natural phenomena causing the *"particles"* to follow a path resulting in an interference pattern over time, despite being sent through the slits one at a time. All of this seems to imply that there is an invisibly distributive wave of naturally occurring probabilities. And that, when that wave hits both slits, it *"collapsingly"* acts as per visible waves, such as water does, to cause interference patterns from within the "ocean" of space-time. Accordingly, particles fired through, one at a time, are affected by this field of possible paths, such that when the particles *"collapse,"* i.e. reveal themselves as they hit the screen, they will appear at any random place on the screen but cannot land where the waves of interference prohibit them from landing. Incidentally, when I refer to a random place, I mean random from a human perception perspective. It is not actually random; it is just that individual points of consciousness are co-adaptively evolving in relation to functional distributions of naturally occurring algorithms that themselves produce any and/or all the individual (and/or individualized) points (and/or networks) of consciousness (i.e. intent of the collective Mind). As we shall see, as cocreators, humans can influence the true network of consciousness by mind alone too.

As if this was not bizarre enough, by putting observation equipment near the slit to determine which slit each particle goes through, the interference pattern no longer manifests. This causes two vertical parallel lines of light to emerge on the screen with no interference pattern. The information detection facility somehow affects the "yet to manifest" particle (in wave-function form) in such a way that it becomes unable to take its otherwise naturally occurring path (riding the wave of probability that governs where in the interference pattern the particle will randomly appear) but now must take a journey through one slit or the other. This means that it redirects the "*all possibility*" of a superimposed, self-interfering pattern creating phenomenon. This describes what is observed, but the reason(s) among physicists thinking as to why the switch of patterns comes about through the presence of a simple observation apparatus varies. Some suggest that the apparatus itself affects the behaviour of the waves and that the waves lose their natural pattern due to the physical nature of what goes on in measuring. Others believe it is the interference of consciousness by the very act of observing "which-way" information (on the subatomic level). Does it "forcibly" redirect and further collapse the (distributive) wave probability into the path-of-possibility of the unmanifest particle traveling through both slits as it's otherwise undisturbed wave-function?

It gets even more bizarre, though, because if the apparatus is set up so that the observer can view "*information*" about the "*choice*" of slits at a point just before a particle hits the screen (an experiment called "delayed choice"), the wave-function not only collapses, it also appears to instantly go backward in time and retroactively collapse forwardly. In other words, it seems to travel backwards along its otherwise perpetual path and then, while on its previously altered ("now") journey forward, passes through the singular slit it is deemed to have "*chosen*." It then, without delay, hits the screen instanta-neously, now realigned to the path corresponding to the singular slit it went through, rather than a seemingly random position in relation to the interference pattern it would have otherwise demonstrated. This is seemingly a violation of cause and effect, which is fundamen-tal in-throughout the macroscopic world, as such an observation seems to indicate an alteration of the natural path of history.

When the detectors are placed further away from the screen itself, such that one entangled (twin) particle hits the screen and the other is sent on the delayed path leading to the detectors, the inter-ference pattern is still lost, even though the which-way information (of where each particle was eventually destined to arrive) has *yet to be observed*. This leads some to deduce that a rewriting of history (based on which-way information) takes place after the particle would have already taken its interference pattern route and hit the screen. If this account of what is happening were true, it would mean that there is a serious rewriting of history based on information that forces such a *"retro-action"* because the screen will have been hit while a revised history overwrites the original history as though it had never been. Another interpretation (being much closer to the truth) of what is happening removes the need for any backwards time travel (outlined below).

To see whether the detection equipment itself was causing the waveform to collapse because of an interference with the quantum coherence state of the nonmanifest particle, quantum physicists devised a quantum eraser experiment. This takes the which-way information and later scrambles it such that an observer would no longer have access to information to determine the slit *"chosen."* This additional apparatus caused the interference pattern to become the norm once again for the particles that did not reveal which-way information as a result of the scrambling effect of the additional parts of the apparatus. This behaviour calls into question that the act of measurement alone causes a collapse because the measurement still takes place but the information cannot be accessed by the observer, and so if the initial act of measurement was the cause of collapse, the return to quantum coherence later on could not be possible.

It seems clear that the critical factor in all of this is the availability of accurate which-way information for an observer even if there is a delay in the information getting to the observer. Although the standard conclusion is that history is rewritten from the point of obtaining the actual information, if we look deeper into the nature of space-time itself, another explanation arises which is more plausible.

There is evidence that human consciousness can influence Random Number Generators. In fact, even the behaviour of particles in the double-slit experiment itself, as demonstrated by the scientist, Professor Radin, can be influenced in the same way. Accordingly, because we can witness human consciousness *"causing"* an effect based on definitive which-way information it acquires that, in turn, restricts the apparent randomness to the mere *"choosing"* (by the nonmanifest particle) of one or the other rather than both slits—until ultimate appearance at the screen—it negates the need for the history rewriting hypothesis. In short, an observer accessing information about which of two slits was "chosen" forces a binary outcome where the counterintuitive outcome would otherwise have been BOTH slits were passed through simultaneously by the yet to manifest particle. This would indicate there is entanglement between the yet to collapse and manifest particle and the observer of which-way information that is yet to be measured but, importantly, ultimately will be observed. This measurement action is not merely a potentially influencing intent but an intent that is *"known"* to manifest with certainty which, like the *"particle"* in wave-function form, cannot do other than manifest.

A rewriting of history: Where manifest particles on a screen are erased and overwritten because seemingly contradictory information arrives later on in the process would much more so infringe the laws of nature than the idea of an unchangeable *"path"* to human consciousness coexisting in relation to the ability of human consciousness to influence the paths of the wave(s) of probability.

To explore the alternative to the backwards time travel possibility, we need to consider, again, the fact that due to Einstein's special theory of relativity, a photon traveling at light speed will *"experience"* zero time and zero distance. Accordingly, the 8 minutes and 20 second journey we witness, a photon taking from the sun to the earth does not occur from the photon's perspective. As discussed earlier in the book, its creation and annihilation coexist in simultaneity, from its own perspective.

As previously described, when a delayed which-way measurement is made and observed in the double-slit experiment, the probability waves that normally propagate during coherence cease to be an option and de-coherence occurs instead, i.e. the wave-function collapses. However, crucially, the wave-function does not collapse at the point of detection by the operational which-way detection apparatus but does so as the information is transferred to an *"observer."* This is not based on intuition but is based on compelling evidence that has recently arisen.

Once the observer has perceptually gained information that cannot be (temporally) contradicted, their consciousness appears to become entangled with the particle in its nonmanifest, coherent state. The particle has not and will not experience space or time in this coherent state and so there is no need for backward time travel (as is often proposed) because technically it has moved nowhere. The whole journey within apparent space-time, from the observer's perspective, propagates along the basis of the observer's **decision to gain which-way knowledge**, thus narrowing the path of perceived options. Even with this which-way information, the restricted (illusory) path/journey only occurs as per the **observer's mind**, as does the visible appearance at the screen, according to the observed perception of such. The particle itself does not "experience" what the observer sees because it has no beginning or end from the perspective of itself. Particles traveling at light speed do not "experience" time or distance in accordance with Einstein's Special Relativity.

Likewise, a second observer who has not become "consciously" entangled to said particle and/or which-way information (either directly or indirectly) will experience a **different reality**. The absence of which-way information for this observer means the wave-particle transformation will remain in a quantum coherent (wave of probability) state until (if) they get to know what is manifesting via exposure to the environment where measurement is occurring, at which point their observation will align with the fact measurement is taking place. In other words, the two observers will have diametrically opposing realities and yet both are true accounts. MIT has recently reported on an experiment giving results that confirm this and showing that the act of observation, itself, may create tangentially interrelated realities, whose observed subjective viewpoints are, yet still, objectively maintained (and distributed) from along quantum level occurrences. In short, two observers report two different and valid "truths."

This bizarre behaviour leaves us with two potential explanations for what is happening. Either the which-way information gained on the far side of the slits forces backwards time travel to retroactively cause the which-way *"choice"* or between the coherent wave-particle, and consciousness itself, they quantizingly interact in relation to locally experienced space-time (from each and any distinct observers' frame of reference). In the latter case, the observation of which-way information is not a possibility or probability but a certainty, i.e. its occurrence took place from "behind the scenes" of an observer's frame of reference but is only experienced by the mind of the observer from within illusory linear time at the point at which measurement information is determinately observed in space-time. In other words, from the perspective of space-time, the measurement observation event already coincides with the wave-function before its apparent journey and, therefore, has already set the conditions for how the wave-function propagates in accordance to any subjective perception of an observer (from any observers' frame of reference; because any observation or quantum occurrence already occurs from within and throughout the boundaries of space-time and, because observer differentiations also manifest and are collectively maintained from within universally "distributed" potentialities embedded, and beginning to actualize throughout quantum level [quantized] interactions, such as the appearance and disappearance of virtual particles within the spatiotemporal "vacuum"). Given that we know that photons traveling at light speed do not experience the full perspective of space-time, it is likely (and even observably apparent, to a certain extent) that nonmaterial wave-functions and observer consciousness also operate within similar boundaries.

Both potential explanations are radically different from what we typically experience in the macroscopic world. But I think the idea of light speed particles, probability waves, biological consciousness, and singularities (black holes, for example) that manifest and occur from "behind the scenes" of an observer's frame of reference from within and throughout space-time is more logical than a complete adaptation of the historical timeline.

This is not the first time we have been forced to accept the counterintuitive fact that two observers can witness two contra-dictory realities. Special relativity also showed us that the order of events can be perceived as occurring differently for different observ-ers illustrated in the train thought-experiment that was mentioned earlier. This prompted Einstein to state, *"The distinction between past, present and future is an illusion, albeit a stubborn one."* The observation of which-way information is even more radical as it does not just alter the order of events but can even "relatively" determine the outcome of a specific event.

In the double-slit experiment, if the delayed choice is delayed for so long that the particle has had time from the observer's perspec-tive to complete its path in a coherent state, to appear at a random point within the corresponding domain of the interference pattern, you may postulate that a singular observer could get to witness two conflicting events. However, because reality/space-time is observably influenced based upon the perception and action of the observer, the which-way measurement observation is a key part of how (and of "which-way") the space-time propagates for that observer. Accord-ingly, **the apparent delay is illusory because the perpetuating space-time perpetuates having accounted for the conscious observer's so-called future actions.** Remember, from the coherent particle's perspective, there is never any "perceived" movement or time experienced. And so all of this happens only for the observer. And clearly—the observer's decision (which is interdependently linked to space-time) must be accounted for in what emerges in their naturally conditioned reality. Or rather, the only reality the observer will experience of the two scenarios: (i.e., history rewritten vs. one manifest outcome) is the one where which-way information was acquired, while (from their perspective) the time and distance of the particle journeying from the beginning to the end (of the screen) does not conflict with current accounts of the laws of physics.

What all this suggests is that, like our narrowed versions of qualia, e.g. colour experience, pain, smell, etc., space-time is a construct of the mind(s). However, subjectively differentiating realities (like the one(s) experienced by the two different observers in the above double-slit experiment) do also fundamentally occur in relation to quantum phenomena and/or approaching light-speed "perspectives" (i.e. the photon) that, in turn, also affect the order in which events are constructed and experienced. On the macroscopic scale, the consistently agreeing occurrence of observer de-coherence (the collectivization of rebounding and collapsing of interrelated wave-functionalities from and throughout space-time) actually allows for us to perceive matter, assuring that observers can all agree on (as well as to even experience) reality. This automatic de-coherence phenomena is not only caused by individualized consciousness but proportionately more so by collectivized (collective) consciousness (even including abiotic matter), rather than solely individual networks of consciousness (biological and/or sentient life) that are only able to cocreate subtle but distinct subjective realities through intent and via the quantum realm. Einstein once said, "*I prefer to think that the moon is there whether I am looking at it or not*" to express his disdain for the idea that we create our reality via observation. The "*illusion*" appears as stable, at the macroscopic level, as the space-time that accommodates it all, and so, for all intents and purposes, the moon and all other "*solid*" phenomena are real to all observers as per Einstein's belief. Yet, are simultaneously "*illusory*" in that they are all ultimately noTHING.

It should be noted that probabilities, and their mathematically functional emergence(s), within and throughout, the macroscopic and microscopic worldview vary in terms of their relationship(s) to one another, respectively. Unlike probability in classical physics (more so of a "subjectivized" probability), I believe that in quantum mechanics, it is either objective or objective for all practical purposes.

Whilst it is a supposed lack of information that lies behind subjective probability, e.g. if a ball is under one of three cups, it is merely a lack of (personally) consciously unknown information that makes it appear randomly placed, quantum mechanics does indeed generate genuinely unknowable outcomes from certain individual reference frames.

The patterns that emerge from the *"chaos"* can be predicted with immense accuracy. However, any individual *"motion(s)"* can only be known for how they are being *"observably accounted for,"* as this *"behaviour"* does consider the involvement of consciousness as in the which-way versus no which-way observation; this means that the determination of which-way (the binary "choice") is genuinely random in that which-way it goes, when detected at the slits, will have been determined at that *"precise moment"* in time. Likewise, so will the placement of a particle on the screen at the point of de-coherence where no such which-way information had previously been acquired—as the destructive interference patterns resulted by two *"distinctly"* interacting waves of probability create(s) certain area(s) that are otherwise statistically impossible to be observed (from any certain individualized reference frame in relation to the other). However, like ALL "randomness," it is actually the lack of know-how by third parties (individual observers) that gives the appearance of randomness. Accordingly, these *"allocations"* from the quantum realm are based on Universal Consciousness and/or interactive intent(s) as are all "randomized" events. This is why individual points of consciousness (us) can influence this.

The theory presented here also explains the entanglement phenomena often referred to as Einstein's *"spooky action at a distance."* Despite being counterintuitive, it appears nonlocality (the instantaneous propagation of emergent correlations between entangled systems, irrespective of their spatiotemporal distances [in relation to one another]) exists. Bell's inequality theorem had already (cleverly, yet only allegedly) shown that Einstein's hope for hidden variables, which was his explanation for the apparent instantaneous *"signal-*

ling" was unfounded and this indeed was eventually proven experimentally. It had been proven that there were **no hidden variables of the kind Einstein envisaged—but maybe they were both wrong**. Nonlocality does not violate the limit of the speed of light, as one might suspect, because space-time is and evolves as a collectively self-interacting network at the rate of the speed of light; thus, by and upon any or all structurally maintained points of manifest inhabitation, i.e. particles, planets, people, solar systems, etc. are any or all of these points of inhabitation individually bound, determined, and occurring at the rate of the speed of light, from the perspective of concurrently occurring and/or evolving space-time, naturally insinuating that any or all points that are structurally interrelated therein, *"occurrently"* correspond to each other within the light-speed limit.

Observers alongside each of two entangled particles that are separated by space could not, however, without somehow mentally transcending space-time, communicate instantaneously because experiencing space-time means communication is generally subject to the light-speed speed limit of the perceived universe and the parameters encoded in the construct.

Here is the link to the MIT article referred to above:

🔗 **https://www.technologyreview.com/s/613092/a-quantum-experiment-suggests-theres-no-such-thing-as-objective-reality/?fbclid=IwAR1_rx4LkPR15A1zkQhd-gb_mN-P3qUWMp-qFUv8Ue60jcs7_4Zzq3f4w2lw**

Assuming this information is valid, it has far-reaching implications for some metaphysical phenomena that mainstream science currently dismisses. The idea of individual consciousness being able to become entangled with, and possibly perceive, ordinarily *"unknowable"* information by transcending space-time would fit with what the double-slit experiment is telling us about nature. Of course, there are many respected sources that suggest it has happened and is happening, and that sceptics are placing their absolute faith in methodological naturalism rather than following the evidence.

This all illustrates that we turn our back on the possibility of the existence of some real phenomena and also suffer a kind of partial paralysis due to limited belief systems. Believing in fanciful aspects of reality is equally significant, of course, because it is not the case that "anything goes" (not in our present focus of attention realm that is). It is not only how we process what is perceived that has this limiting effect but the media can impact our worldview, too, as can the conditioning that comes from others.

We, perhaps, rely too heavily on our senses and biological drives, which means we eat food which provides pleasure via the senses but is bad for us. We use smartphones day and night despite emerging evidence of how bad long-term excessive exposure is, e.g. a potential cause of anxiety and other disorders. Many people also engage in casual sex despite it being like fast food in that it is pleasurable in the short run but not so nourishing longer term. A lack of true free will is much to blame, as discussed in the previous chapter and, of course, the availability of the conscious experience of pleasure can have the gravity of a black hole.

We also filter reality, such that each individual can interpret the same stimuli/information received through the senses very differently. Shakespeare said, *"Things are neither good nor bad—only thinking makes them so."* In a sense, he was obviously correct because without thinking capabilities and feelings, e.g. a rock, there is no potential concept of good or bad. But as sentient beings, we can feel real pain and real pleasure. However, mood and even worldview/thinking styles can alter perceptions. This is why depression, for example, does not only feel painful but also alters perceptions and personal realities.

Although fun illusions do not directly affect the meaning of life, what they tell us about how the mind works does. All our senses create a mind-made simulation that may be useful for our survival

175

and reproduction as biological organisms but cannot be a true reflection of "*out there*" reality because the input form is nothing like our conscious experiences. This means **what you think reality is has to be wrong** and we all experience a mass hallucination that, because it has agreed upon characteristics is, as already discussed, what we all call reality. How far the collective delusion goes is difficult to say, for sure, but a pattern is starting to emerge that suggests that space-time itself is the greatest illusion of all. Einstein forced us to let go of our intuitions, which made us believe space and time are the same for all observers regardless of relative position or velocity. Special Relativity, General Relativity, and Quantum Mechanics seem to be telling us that they are, in fact, contrived. Like advanced virtual reality, where your participation feels real, but the true you is grounded outside the VR environment, our reality is a contrived realm where the flowering of consciousness creates minds that are conditioned in such a way that the deeper truth is difficult to detect and is largely ignored.

8

SEXUALITY

"There is a tendency to consider anything in human behaviour that is unusual, not well known, or not well understood, as neurotic, psychopathic, immature, perverse, or the expression of some other sort of psychological disturbance."

Alfred C Kinsey

There is a sea of knowledge that already exists on this subject. American biologist, Alfred Kinsey (for example), has done extensive research into the sexual behaviour of humans. By conducting confidential surveys, his team had discovered that not only were many humans polygamous but they also (often secretly) engaged in same-sex activity.

Human sexuality is a spectrum, with homosexuality and heterosexuality at the two extremes. Kinsey had thought similarly and so created a scale, known as *"The Kinsey Scale"* to help determine where between these two ends of the spectrum a person lands. It transpires that most people do not sit at either extreme, despite public appearance(s).

Any sexual behaviour other than heterosexuality seems a puzzle to many biologists as they believe that it should be selected against by evolution. From a gene fitness perspective, anything other than heterosexuality is essentially catastrophic, potentially leading to extinction let alone a failure to pass on *"the baton."* However, it is not difficult to understand why some species of animals (let alone humans) adopt this behaviour. The biological sex differences throughout any such species are not that significant and there is (of course) pleasure associated with this activity that is not dependent on *"getting it right."*

This is like the behaviour of *"nectar robbing,"* as seen in certain insects. Where they will feed through holes that had been bitten into flowers, as opposed to gaining entry through their natural openings. Now, if a whole species of such "burglars" engaged in this behaviour and abandoned their *"normal"* feeding method, then there would likely be a consequential extinction of the natural "nectar robbers" due to their increasingly depleted food source(s). Unless a novel reproductive adaptation would happen to emerge through the flowers, effectively neutralizing the need for any "burglar de-pollinators." However, this behaviour can perpetuate within the proportion(s) that it exists, essentially because it doesn't negatively affect the overall symbiotic relationships that nestle the plant's ability to pollinate from within its environment. *"Nectar robbing"* is certainly a good analogy for egoic bankers too, who have (in recent times) looked after their own interests at the expense of the shareholders they are supposed to serve. Effectively causing extinction, as in business closure (for some banks) and equivalent conditions for financial annihilation to have occurred for many others, had government bailouts not saved them.

With humans, this may partially explain potential sexual deviation from the *"norm."* But it also seems that as the brain has evolved to become the complex feature of nature that it is today, the line(s) between masculinity and femininity have also become somewhat blurred along the way. Clearly, it is not solely gender that determines sexual preferences throughout the process of sexual selection amongst humans. In the same way that altruism will have evolutionary origins, the degrees of conscious experience that humans get to enjoy, in turn, signals that there is a capacity to choose from upon the basis of rational thought that is employed in selecting between variances of personal taste. As such, the magnetism/gravity of opposite-gender sexual attraction that has evolved to assure repro-duction, may potentially be overcome. And consequentially, certain reasons extending beyond the evolutionary drive to reproduce may become a part of the choice making process (i.e. falling in love is not necessarily gender-specific).

This is essentially what has happened when we invented contra-ceptives, allowing for the pleasure of reproductive activity without the "designed" outcome. It differs in that contraception is a conscious choice, whereas sexuality is, often, a compulsion.

As long as sexual behaviour remains moral, transcending nature's hardwired instincts may represent a maturation of consciousness. Accordingly, if sexual activity, coupled with intent, serves the highest good of all parties, it may further represent a higher attaining of consciousness.

There is no doubt that nature and nurture (and/or the condition-ing of the mind) heavily affect sexuality or that genetics merely affect predisposition and are no guarantee of a definitive outcome. Consid-ering male homosexuality, it has long been observed that the greater number of older brothers a boy has, the more likely he is to be gay when he grows up—an effect called the "fraternal birth order effect." It seems that the increasing levels of antibodies in a mother's immune system (that slightly compound with each individual pregnancy) could play a role in this effect. Yet, again, this is a "developing" predis-position in relation to statistical potentialities rather than a wholly determining rule but it certainly still affects the probability.

The emergence and growth of pleasure perception is likely to be one of the key determinants of personal sexual preference. Along with the capacity to de-couple the sexual experience from its repro-ductive function, this could potentially explain how and/or why deviations of sexuality have arisen throughout time. The duration of the human sexual experience is also typically far greater than that of other animals, the positions to potentially be engaged are varied and experimental, and the process itself is often de-coupled from the short, monthly recurring periods of time that females also experience heightened fertility.

It is also evident that the sexual experience is more pleasurable for humans than it is for most other animals. These all provide good reasons to believe that pleasure has been the main source of motivation in driving the evolution and diversity of human sexual activities. This underlying course of logic may also extend to the notion that the tastes of one sex being able to influence the styles of physical traits and forms of behaviour of the other sex over time—a bid to carry on the pleasure enhancement journey.

Richard O. Prum posits that female mate choice may have also been a key factor in influencing not only male and female behaviour(s) but also the emergence of homosexuality in both sexes. At this present time, the reasonings for anything that differs from heterosexuality are still not fully understood and, therefore, the above thoughts about how it could feasibly have arisen are essentially only a hypothesis as are those of Professor Prum. However, it is still interesting to look at how Professor Prum thinks the situation could have arisen. He has seen and assorted through massive amounts of evidence showing that "*beauty happens*" and/or that "*pleasure happens*" and that altered behaviour, or physical tendencies, can emerge purely in response to preferred taste(s) that may be expressed and experienced by and through the process of sexual selection. However, he has not discussed the possibility that mathematical order and symmetry coinciding with natural beauty is indicative of a superior intelligence which is explored in the chapter on beauty.

According to his first hypothesis: "*Female same-sex behaviour is a defensive, aesthetic, and adaptive response to the direct and indirect costs of coercive male control over reproduction. It's defensive in that it functions to mitigate the costs of sexual coercion to female reproductive success directly. It's aesthetic because it involves the evolution of female sexual preferences. And it's adaptive because it would evolve by natural selection on female preferences to minimize both the direct costs of sexual coercion, in the form of violence and infanticide, and the indirect costs, in the form of restricted female mate choice and coerced fertilizations."* Additionally, to assure gene quality through interspecies breeding, certain species will have males leave the group that they were born into, while others will have females leave from such group, which gives additional credibility to the hypothesis of sexually selective behaviours forming in response to defensive, aesthetic, and/or adaptive behavioural (or preferential) requirements. In terms of human history, our female ancestors had done this. So, forming strong social bonds with other females in newly joined groups provided the right conditions for this kind of evolutionary change.

In his second hypothesis concerning male homosexuality, he suggests: *"The evolutionary changes in male sexual preferences occurred specifically because males with traits that are associated with same-sex preferences were preferred as mates by females. So, there is no reason to believe that their reproductive success would be compromised at all. Once the majority of human sexual behaviour has evolved to be nonreproductive and unhinged from the confines of the female's brief fertile period, then same-sex attraction can be seen as just a further broadening of sexual behaviour and its social functions."* He'd felt that females would favour this disposition, as it would *"create"* more sociable and less aggressive males and given that some male competitors would be united by same-sex interaction with each other, would be less likely to be violently provoked by male competition or simply upon male-to-male social encounters. Once bisexual behaviour in both sexes became quite common, it would make sense that some personal preferences would arise that were exclusively homosexual.

Prum postulates, however, that there should be more male homosexuality than female homosexuality: *"For example, because male same-sex behaviour evolves via sexual selection for the advantages it provides to females, not to males, the possibility of evolving nonreproductive individuals is not an evolutionary conundrum but an expected outcome of sexual selection. In contrast, natural selection for alliance-building same-sex preferences in females should not* result in any significant losses to female reproductive success. Accordingly, the frequency of individuals with exclusively same-sex preferences should evolve to be much higher among males than in females. Indeed, this prediction is borne out by the evidence that exclusive homosexual identity is about twice as frequent in men as it is in women. The aesthetic remodeling mechanism hypothesizes that the physical and social personality features that are associated with male same-sex preferences have evolved precisely because these traits are preferred by females. Consequently, even though the evolution of same-sex preferences could result in losses to individual reproductive success of some males, these losses will arise because of the exclusivity of their same-sex preferences, not because these males would fail to succeed in attracting female mates."

He also points out that the female mate choice of the stunning bird species—*the manakin*—has transformed the nature of male social behaviour within their species, making *"bromance"* a key to success in romance. Same-sex behaviour in human males may also be another form of this female-driven, aesthetic remodeling of male social relations (as yet another evolutionary solution to the problem of male sexual coercion).

Finally, to strengthen his hypothesis, he reminds us that one of our closest cousins, *the bonobos*, demonstrates that same-sex behaviour and can function to undermine the male sexual hierarchy, and coercive, sexually dominative tendencies in primates. That female same-sex behaviour can strengthen female social allegiances and reduce sexual and social competition among males and that male same-sex behaviour can lower group competition and enhance group social cohesion. Despite these similarities in social function, however, same-sex behaviour in bonobos have obviously evolved independently of humans.

Sexuality is a big part of most people's lives and it is certainly a key piece to the meaning of life "mix." However, beyond our ego lies a form that transcends sexuality and gender. Whilst we reside in our universe in biological form, it makes sense to establish what naturally drives sexuality. However, when it comes to a broader definition of the meaning of life, it is our true essence, rather than our labels and our practices that count. It would seem logical to embrace our biological drivers but be mindful that there is a deeper truth at play and that attachment should be avoided. In other words, attachment to a loved one (which is effectively seeing them as a possession of sorts) potentiates the kind of suffering the Buddha spoke of when he said, *"All suffering arises from attachment."*

9

RACISM

"I refuse to accept the view that mankind is so tragically bound to the starless midnight of racism and war that the bright daybreak of peace and brotherhood can never become a reality... I believe that unarmed truth and unconditional love will have the final word."

Martin Luther King, Jr.

Racism is clearly immoral, ignorant, and representative of a lowered consciousness. Yet, despite that it is all those things, it can also be understood more clearly considering there are deeper biological (and existential) causes as to why this predisposition exists. Similarly, is the person who has a skin colour different from yours simply a manifestation of Universal Consciousness, the embodiment of "you" in another form?

In a group of chimps, if several of them split off into a smaller splinter-group (leaving to establish a separate colony), the males of the larger group will not only track down the male renegades and kill them, they also capture the females and bring them back to the main group to rape them. From a human perspective, this is immoral and evil. Yet, evolution drives this behaviour within them, giving no regard for these uniquely human constructs and perspectives. The chimps are not acting very much differently from the choosy peahen in selecting peacocks—as in there is essentially no preemptive consideration from within their decision-making whatsoever. They act in accordance with natural programming (minds highly conditioned by biological drivers). The *"evil"* chimp behaviour is more of a naturally mathematical manifestation of emotional response mechanisms than a question of ethics. I believe that they have some free will even though this would make such acts appear essentially impossible to justify. However, despite an underlying true essence within, they are simply victims of the mind control that is instigated by the *"selfish gene"* (DNA programming) and, unfortunately (and/or fortunately, depending on your perspective), such primitive minds cannot transcend mind duality. Humans, of course, yield the capacity to perceptually transcend this limitation, although this is presently quite rare.

Although chimps can act in ways as equally cruel as degradant Homo sapiens, they are more amoral than immoral. Even when rare incidents, such as the neck breaking of a young goat (followed by poking its eyes out) occur (as has happened), it is not some deliberate act of torture but more so an act of curiosity bypassing the realisation of the chimp that this is another conscious being capable of experiencing pleasure and pain. Of course, if another animal does something similar and then proceeds to eat its kill, it is instantly justified in our minds. So, it seems that it is the apparent underlying motive for the act that makes it seem evil because humans, who can sense right from wrong at a much deeper level, tend to look at any such act from their ethical perspective. Unconscious and/or degradant humans, however, are certainly capable of far worse.

It should be noted that chimps are also generally quite altruistic animals. They are immensely cooperative and possess a sense of fairness. So, although they do have a dark side, this only represents a small percentage of their behaviour.

The evolution of humans has led to generally greater embodiments and distinctions of morality, yet the gravity of these primal/instinctive behaviours is so strong that they still, unfortunately, manifest within our society.

Patriotism also has similar origins to racism and both appear to stem from biological relatedness. As social animals, not only do we protect our kin, but to a lesser extent, our tribe. The further away from kinship a person is, the more likely animosity is. Of course, two tribes can trade in all manner of ways with each other, therefore, they will have reasons to remain friendly. And yet still, separate groups do not always lead to conflict. Likewise, related family members may have different beliefs or engage in activity that is considered by other members as offensive or degrading. Therefore, the closeness between parents and offspring (or between siblings) is not completely assured.

The 'out-group' effect is seen where there are two neighbouring countries, different counties such as Lancashire and Yorkshire, or even simple social cliques (although all these can temporarily put their differences aside when considering a common "enemy")—pick on the ginger, the Goth, the gay, the obese, the nerd, the members of other religions, the other sports team supporters, etc. Racism is not purely restricted to skin colour differential, yet with skin colour being an easily identifiable difference for non-relatedness, it is a commonly depicted manifestation of racism.

Highly evolved consciousness should allow us to transcend this immoral state. However, as the Implicit Association Test(s) shows, even those who claim to be anti-racist have subconscious biases.

I think there is hope that we will tend toward a racism-free world, but it is unlikely that we will ever achieve it. The abolition of slavery throughout most of the world and abolition of apartheid in South Africa are encouraging signs that change can be positive. One potential barrier, however, is that intellect and morality are generally quite far from being well adjusted to each other (as far as collective understanding is concerned)—see Brain Queue cartoon illustration in the chapter about morality. Many very clever people, for example, are still hugely racist.

The irony is that, even if spiritual/universal interconnectedness is an unfounded concept: Everyone consists of atoms that are as old as the universe. This means that even a single fingernail from your great, great, great grandfather consisted of atoms approximately the same age as the one(s) in yours (some 13.8 billion years old). So, technically, we are all made of the same "*star stuff*" and all originate from the same "point" in time.

With different races, most differences that present themselves are highly superficial. Evolution has not resulted in a whole subspeciation but more minor differences in appearance. However, the innate behaviour amongst chimps (which was described earlier) appears to have left its mark from upon the annals of biological evolution, despite our higher consciousness as human beings.

When it comes to those who act upon their racist tendencies, there are similarities between white extremists and Islamist terrorists. Both fit the prevailing notion among researchers that most terrorists are not psychopaths but relatively typical people motivated by circumstance to protect their "*in-group*" from dangers—real or imagined. In other words, the belief systems of both types of terrorists justify their action(s) as being rational from their perspective. Most terrorists are "*altruists*," who view themselves as soldiers fighting for a noble cause and feel that their action is called to respond to prior injustices. The calling to enact political change precedes the calling to violence and so the ends justify the means (from their perspective).

This is only part of the picture though, as the (unconscious) white extremists do very much differ from ordinary law-abiding citizens. This was revealed in a paper from the National Consortium for the Study of Terrorism and Responses to Terrorism (START) with the title, "Recruitment and Radicalization among US Far-Right Terrorists." The analysis showed that white extremists, while not necessarily psychopathic, are often already violent people before they join extremist groups. Only after joining are they generally schooled in ideologies that "justify" channelling preexisting urges into violence towards

Jewish people, nonwhite people and anti-racist groups. The ideology is an excuse for ultraviolence but not necessarily the reason for it. In other words, the potential for violence to manifest was already bound within their psyche (due to upbringing, genetic predisposition, personal experiences, etc.), so it was essentially just a matter of channelling that potential into a "suitable" cause.

Of course, white extremists are the tip of the iceberg when it comes to racism and although many racists do not act violently, they can still act offensively by word, or deed.

Racism may not seem that relevant to the meaning of life if it is something you have never encountered. However, it clearly has a profound impact on the lives of the people that it touches. It is immoral and wrong regardless of whether we are all collectively individualized points of consciousness. However, should future humanity embrace a paradigm shift, having become aware that we reside within an illusory space-time in a temporary form that is, effectively, a biological avatar, then there is a genuine chance that racism will be banished for good. Until that time, there continues to be certain highly influential leaders and businesspeople that add fuel to the inferno, assuring that division perpetuates (as a divided collective leaves gaps between us that they attempt to rush in to fill creating the illusion that they have helped solve a problem that they have only continued to make worse). This is highly topical at the time of writing this book, as Black Lives Matter is constantly in the news (as are debates regarding All Lives Matter, which is clearly a truism in a sense, concerning whether this alternative movement moves attention away from the immediate need to attain racial equality).

10

THE PRIMACY OF MATHE- MATICS AND INTELLIGENCE

"The universe begins to look more like a giant thought than a great machine. Mind no longer appears to be an accidental intruder in the realm of matter we ought rather to hail it as a Creator and governor of the realm of matter."

James Jeans,

one of the great pioneers of cosmology

As physicist and cosmologist, Max Tegmark, has stated, *"Our physical universe doesn't just have some mathematical properties. It has only mathematical properties."* In a computer game, the whole construct of that *"universe"* is nothing more than a sequence of binary bit transactions and algorithms created by coders. And as we have discovered that similar patterns exist in our own universe, this is by far from being a coincidence. The reason mathematics seems to describe our reality so well is because of how it fundamentally appears through the order(s) and operation(s) of reality itself.

Although Tegmark seems to be correct, there is more than just our physical universe. There are immaterial realities such as the perfect circle (essentially impossible to reproduce in physical reality) and qualia, i.e. phenomena that are as real as the physical phenomena we experience (that are also reliant upon the embodied experience(s) and expression(s) of consciousness). Likewise, pseudo-randomness affects our reality but is something that is quite a bit different than the ordinary mathematics manifest in physical reality. Ironically, we can assess how randomness will manifest over time using mathematics, namely probability theory. However, the actual allocation amongst several potential outcomes can only be known once it is manifest when it comes to the quantum realm, notwithstanding metaphysical phenomena that may permit human consciousness to transcend space-time and exercise precognition.

As you will already have gathered by now, this is ONLY the story according to the limited perspective of an individual point of consciousness with further limitations that are imposed by an egoic mind. In fact, there is no randomness. Only INTENT. That of the collective mind and/or that of an individual point of consciousness whose subsidiary intent assures cocreation. In the end, all individual points of consciousness are of the One, as well as being one of the infinite experiential manifestations. The ocean and the water molecules, simultaneously.

True randomness appears to be unpredictable, although it is simply the result of algorithms which are hard to discern, whereby the individual observer is not a party to these (notwithstanding, as discussed, the fact that individual points of consciousness add to the algorithms via intent). To produce infinite apparent randomness would imply the algorithm itself would have to be infinite, too, which would mean the algorithm would merely be the process rather than something behind the process. This would be true, but for the fact it is pseudo-randomness, and behind all randomness lies intent. Although this may be viewed by some as conjecture, the process is non-mathematical because what manifests indicates it (Mind, Universal Consciousness, ultimate AI, God, or whatever label is preferred) has a mind of its own and ultimately there is a pyramid of intents within The Mind. This means the world is highly deterministic but by the same token infinite possibilities and experiences means just that—a kind of becoming that assures the achievement of full potential because there was never really any option, given that it is all about the universe becoming self-aware via infinite points of consciousness that flower in an infinite now. But the journey itself represents an evolution towards what it was, is, and will always be: Pure infinite love and intelligence. In other words, the experiential realm is equal to the potential (quantum) one. To put it another way, noTHING was, is, and always will be the equivalent of everyTHING and YOU are everyTHING.

This *"delegated"* intent is perhaps not surprising because, for free will to arise, there cannot be 100 percent determinism in our universe. Accordingly, you would expect to see pseudo (falsely perceived) randomness as a fundamental aspect of a reality set up for consciousness to evolve and flower without every aspect being predetermined from Source. The apparent randomness appears to be the product of Mind creating an objective playground where individual points of consciousness can interact and influence this objectivity via intent. The many worlds hypothesis (which posits that all possible outcomes occur and our focus of attention only observes one of infinite ones) does not fully explain the potential origin for randomness because it does not account for how each *"generated"* position in our physical material realm universe is determined, even though each one that arises in our world may complement the infinite alternative positions in the other worlds. It misses the obvious fact that individual points of consciousness act in a very nonrandom way. Not just a short or long run of *"self"* directed actions but a whole LIFE's worth—for all lives, forever. This stance against randomness is simply intent and is the elephant in the room that scientism has had banished to a zoo with no visitors.

Notwithstanding the lack of true randomness, mathematics (of the form governing our universe) is certainly fundamental and in everything around us. One example is how frequently the Fibonacci series of numbers appears in nature, e.g. in petal counts in flowers, particularly in daisies. Likewise, the clockwise and anti-clockwise spirals on pinecones and sunflower seed structures are invariably Fibonacci numbers. Pi also appears in nature with significant frequency in places that have nothing to do with circles. It is a very arbitrary number that has an infinitely non-repeating pattern. An example is in probability where a dropped needle cuts through parallel lines that are set a needle width apart with a frequency of $2/\pi$ so that dropping the needle thousands of times will allow pi to reveal itself, with a higher frequency of drops tending more towards pi. On average, the length of the meandering aspect of a river divided by the direct line aspect is also pi. It shows in many unrelated natural phenomena from the brightness of a supernova to which colours should appear in a rainbow.

The square of a number also appears in nature countless times, from the inverse square rule relating to gravity and the way sound intensity reduces over distances, to E=mc2 and numerous other well-known equations.

Music is also a mathematical manifestation, with the octave, a fifth and a fourth being both pleasing to the ear and, as Pythagoras determined, a simple set of ratios that emerge when assessing the string lengths that give rise to these three crucial musical phenomena.

Many mathematicians feel they are discovering what is already there, rather than creating. Clearly, mathematics in the form of logical discernible patterns exists in an abstract realm regardless of these discoveries and this applies to 3-dimensional mathematical shapes as well. The potentiality for tetrahedrons preexisted the Big Bang but space, time, and intelligence are necessary to represent them in a formula, drawings, or models.

By studying babies and other primates, such as lemurs, it is clear we have a primitive number sense, even without learning numbers, words, or symbols. Without this, it is unlikely the more complex symbolic mathematics used to decode the secrets of nature would have arisen.

The fact that the universe and the laws of nature follow mathematical models are a gift which has, until now, been considered beyond human understanding. Nobel Lauriat in physics, Eugene Wigner, to capture the essence of this, coined the phrase, "*The unreasonable effectiveness of mathematics,*" something that had not gone unnoticed by Einstein and many other geniuses also. It refers to the fact that mathematical concepts appear to have applicability far beyond the context in which they were originally developed. The Higgs Boson ("*God particle*") was predicted through mathematics 50 years prior to the confirmation of its existence at CERN, showing the power of mathematics. Given that the whole physical material realm is merely a binary construct that takes people's full attention from cradle to grave, it is a small wonder that it has taken so many years since the dawn of civilization to see that the truth is here. And that it always has been.

Imaginary numbers, such as the square root of minus one, were explored because the opportunity arose to put numbers like this through the same process, despite them being seemingly impossible scenarios. All positive or negative numbers that are squared give a positive result, therefore, the idea of a negative number having a minus status in its square form to assess its square root is impossible, other than in the abstract realm. Yet, without exploring this, the world of quantum physics would not have been decodable. This means that even abstract mathematics, which on the surface seems to be a curiosity with no real-life use, can prove to be a language capable of describing key aspects of our reality. In fact, the mathematics that describes our own physical material realm is a tiny subset of ALL possible mathematics. Infinite possibilities and experiences mean just that, and so there is literally no bound to the full extent of mathematics. This is not so useful for us, though, as most only wish to get at a concise language that describes the present focus of attention realm.

Mathematics can be used to describe how the WHOLE construct works (from alpha to omega as well as the system outside of linear time that created alpha to omega). Einstein was obsessed with "*I want to know the mind of God*"—and, as mentioned, the truth is here as it was, is, and always will be. Hiding in plain sight. It should be emphasized again that mathematics is a language and a complex one at that. It describes the anatomy and physiology of phenomena but this is never the same as having an understanding. Sentience is necessary for this and the crude use of words can be just as powerful as signposts that lead to understanding. However, there is no doubting the power of mathematics as a language. It is concise and, to mathematicians at least, beautiful.

In other areas that display seemingly chaotic behaviour, such as weather forecasting or biological systems, mathematics does not seem as effective in predicting outcomes because the algorithms are too complex. Engineers are aware that there is a compromize where the elegance of mathematics meets the apparent messiness of reality.

What is apparent is that the basic number system will have been adopted by humans by using numbers as tokens for real objects, e.g. seeing three apples or a pack of six wolves. But then, intricate relationships were subsequently observed so, although the token numeric system will have been a human construct, the revelations provided by nature through such numbers were discoveries.

If the hypothesis that mathematics is fundamental is true, it does not really affect the meaning of life directly. But it is a step towards understanding the construct of the universe and as we are a part of it, is a step towards the meaning of life in its broader sense.

Although mathematics underlies everything manifest in our universe, it often needs to be approximated because infinities cannot be properly represented. This is the reason that the perfect circle can only exist in the abstract/conscious realm. Another example is a right-angled triangle with two sides measuring precisely one unit each. The hypotenuse will measure as the square root of two. This cannot be represented truthfully in our reality because an infinite number occurs after the decimal place. Of course, we can draw a straight line to represent the hypotenuse but because there is an infinite number of steps needed to represent the square root of two completely, the line drawn in our reality can only ever be an approximation. Only in a reality (mind) where there is no limitation of space or time could such a triangle exist in its pure form. Zeno identified several paradoxes that mathematics appears to solve but does so by effectively rounding. For example, he suggested no journey commencement or completion should be possible. If you imagine a two-mile journey, it can be broken down so that half the journey should be completed first, followed by half the remaining part of the journey, and so on. This creates an infinite series that tends to two miles but will never reach it. And yet the journey is possible. This is because there is a limit in length, which we have already discussed, called the Planck length. This means that there is a final point where there is no half length of the journey remaining; there is effectively no existence between these points and so it is like adjacent pixels on a screen—you can be at one or the other but there is no between. In other words, our universe is quantized. This applies to time as well as space. The two-mile journey could not be completed without this phenomenon.

Likewise, it could not begin, as well, because if the journey is broken down into half, half of that half, and half of that half, and so on, it would also result in an infinite series (regression). Mathematicians use a kind of sleight of hand to get around this by assuming that two infinite series, despite being one step out from each other, cancel each other out mathematically when one is subtracted from the other. However, it just assumes that an infinite series tending to a number effectively equals it. If our universe did not have the Planck length limitation, the mathematical rounding would not work and the infinite series would be the accurate position. In the abstract realm, there are no space and time limitations and so the Zeno paradox is real yet solved through the absence of limitations, but in a space-time realm that facilitates physical movement, a true infinite (regressing) series cannot exist.

This limitation is not restricted to distances and to linear times. It applies to ALL phenomena that is sensed. The obvious ones are the five senses but we have more senses than these, of course. All these will, through use of man-made present and future instrumentation, prove to have near infinite manifestations but will ultimately hit the same quantization as Planck length and Planck time. Let's call these: Teasel hearing™, Teasel sight™, Teasel smell™, Teasel taste™, and Teasel touch™. When you take any given colour, for example, there is no infinite number of shades of colour between this and the next main one because you would never reach the other without there being a binary system in place. The binary system forces a stop to an otherwise infinite regression which, in turn, means we experience progressive colour transitions over a continuum within our perceived physical material realm. This only applies to the physical phenomena that give rise to qualia because in the quantum realm there is no quantization and so it is the binary perception triggers (correlates) in our realm that are subject to these Teasel sense™ limitations.

Given a certain definition of sense, there are nine human **senses:** vision (sight), audition (hearing), gustation (taste), olfaction (smell), tactile (touch), thermoception (heat, cold), nociception (pain), equilibrioception (balance, gravity), proprioception (body awareness).

The number of senses is in debate and is outside the scope of this book. Here is an article about there being potentially 20:

 **https://learn.genetics.utah.edu/content/senses/
twentysenses/**

A more controversial hypothesis is that intelligence is fundamental as well as mathematics, which I hope to demonstrate using empirical evidence. The way evolution is portrayed as a natural process that hews all the prodigious richness and complexity of life out of chance mutations and purposeless forces of nature, it would seem impossible to fit intelligence into the equation. However, Professor

Kevin N. Laland, Behavioural and Evolutionary Biology, University of St Andrews, has a plausible explanation of how it exists and how it manifests. Most of the explanation that follows is from his text, including details about the evolutionary concept known as "niche construction." His views endorse the views already expressed in the book that evolution by natural selection is not a sole agent in the production of all the variety and wonder of life, although, he sees a kind of joint development that engages both the behaviour of an evolving organism and natural selection in a kind of feedback loop, whereas I assert and provide evidence that consciousness masquerading as evolution is capable of guided creative steps, within parameters.

Biologists are repelled by the notion of intelligent agents as it is sailing close to the wind of "Intelligent Design" which, to them, is the antipathy of good science. Advocates of Intelligent Design believe that the complex adaptations of living organisms are beyond the reach of evolution through natural selection and that it is a divine intelligence that is responsible for all that is manifest. Maybe this is the main reason evolutionary biologists will hear nothing of the idea of purposeful intelligence.

However, evolution has given rise to smart life forms that behave cleverly and innovatively, creating a feedback loop that causes evolution itself to evolve, and this allows species to be active agents in their own evolution. This is certainly the case with humans but there is evidence it exists all the way down the food chain.

Geneticists have shown that human cultural activities have shaped our genome. New statistical methods have been able to isolate genes that have been favoured by natural selection over the past 50,000 years or less. This has led to a couple of thousand regions in the human genome that have been identified as subject to recent selection, many of which appear to have been favoured by our cultural behaviour.

Some compelling examples of how genes and culture have coevolved concern genetic responses to changes in the human diet.

Human societies vary substantially in their diets and these differences are mediated by culturally transmitted knowledge. Consider, for instance, the evolution of the human ability to eat starchy foods. Agricultural societies typically consume far more starch in their diets than do hunter-gatherer societies. Cereals, such as wheat, maize and rice, and root or tuber crops like sweet potato, cassava or yams, require extensive cultural knowledge to cultivate effectively.

The enzyme responsible for breaking down starch is called amylase. Individuals from populations with high-starch diets have, on average, more copies of the salivary and pancreatic amylase genes (AMY1 and AMY2) that improve the ability to digest starchy foods than do individuals from populations with low-starch diets. That is because their cultural activities and associated diets have generated selection for increased amylase. Interestingly, dogs which have fed on scraps of human food for millennia also have a high number of AMY2 copies. A recent study of dogs isolated 10 genes that play key roles in starch digestion and fat metabolism and show signals of recent selection.

Another good example of gene-culture coevolution is the evolution of lactose tolerance in adult humans in response to dairy farming. For most humans, the ability to digest lactose disappears in childhood, but in some populations lactase activity, which is necessary for breaking down lactose, persists into adulthood. This adult lactose tolerance is frequent in northern Europeans and in pastoralist populations from Africa and the Middle East but it is almost completely absent elsewhere. These differences relate to genetic variation near the lactase gene (LCT). There is a strong correlation across cultures between the frequency of lactose tolerance in the population and a history of dairy farming—populations with a long history of consuming milk have high frequencies of tolerance.

Diverse lines of evidence have also established that milk drinking began with early Neolithic humans, who were, as a result, exposed to a strong selection favouring those alleles for lactose tolerance. These societies typically have high LCT frequencies, whereas societies with no dairying traditions generally possess low frequencies. Human populations that have long consumed fermented milk products, such as cheese and yoghurt, which have lower levels of lactose, exhibit intermediary frequencies of lactose tolerance. These, and other findings, suggest that the practice of dairy farming arose first, which then favoured lactose tolerance, not the other way around.

The signature of selection around the lactase gene is one of the strongest in the human genome, and the onset of the selection has been dated to 5,000–10,000 years ago. Once again, this cultural practice has imposed selection on domesticated animals: milk-protein genes in European cattle breeds correlate to present-day patterns of lactose tolerance in human populations.

Humans have exposed themselves to a wide variety of novel foods through their cultural activities, including through the colonization of new habitats containing different flora and fauna, as well as through the domestication of plants and animals and associated agricultural practices. Several nutrition-related genes involved in the metabolism of proteins, carbohydrates, lipids, phosphates, and alcohol all show signals of recent selection. There is also emerging evidence of diet-related selection on the thickness of human teeth enamel and on bitter-taste receptors on the tongue. It seems that a gene-culture coevolutionary process has shaped the biology of human digestion.

In these and other instances, it is not as if we humans have deliberately imposed selection on ourselves in a conscious effort to enhance our capabilities to metabolize or detoxify the foods we have chosen to consume. But we appear to have imposed a direction on our own evolution nonetheless. What is more, that direction is somewhat predictable. For instance, with knowledge of a population's agricultural history, scientists can predict with some degree of accuracy what digestive enzymes it will possess.

Our ancestors were domesticating animals and plants long before they had any theoretical understanding of selective breeding. Thousands of years ago, humans kept wolves, choosing for company the less aggressive among them without recognizing that this selection, iterated over time, would favour profound changes in the wolf phenotype and lead to mild-mannered canine descendants. That the selective breeding imposed by humans on wolves is systematic and directional is illustrated by the fact that many of the same traits—docility, tameness, reductions in tooth size and number, changes in head, face, and brain morphology, floppy ears—have been favoured in other domesticated animals. Indeed, the pattern is so striking that researchers speak of a *"domestication syndrome"* to characterize the suite of phenotypic traits that have evolved in this fashion.

A second domestication syndrome has also been found in plants. Here, characteristic features include a loss of head shattering—the process by which plants disperse their seeds upon ripening—and increases in seed size. Again, this evolution has proceeded in a systematic, predictable way. Whether we are talking about cattle, guinea pigs, rice, or wheat, if we know that an organism has been domesticated, we can predict some of the phenotypic traits it will possess. Ultimately, that predictive quality stems from the consistent, reliable, and sustained way in which diverse humans across continents and at different times in history have interacted with the plants and animals they have kept.

Planting crops and tending animals are examples of human *"niche construction"*—the process by which organisms change their environment in a way that puts new evolutionary pressures on their species and others, triggering the evolution of new adaptive traits. Cultivating plants and domesticating animals are not random activities. They are purposeful, goal-directed practices, reliably performed by populations year after year, sometimes century after century.

These activities may be characterized as *"intelligent"* because they are informed by learned and socially transmitted know-how that has accrued over time. This intelligent behaviour appears to have initiated evolutionary episodes in both our own species and other species that share our world. In the process, we have imposed a direction on some evolutionary episodes—a kind of evolutionary bias detectable as predictable, consistent, and sustained responses to selection. Our cultural activities may even affect evolutionary rates. For instance, according to one study, human genetic evolution has accelerated more than a hundredfold over the last 40,000 years.

Dog breeding, hybrid corn manufacture, and dairy farming are not adaptations in the strict, evolutionary sense. Nor is the knowledge that attends these practices—how to corral horses or cultivate rice, for instance—specified in the human genome. Rather, human agricultural practices are cultural phenomena that exploit some very general adaptations and genetic dispositions that underlie our learning, language, and cognition. To put this in philosophical terms, natural selection underdetermines human niche construction, that is, selection explains the capability but not the content of our behavioural practices—which is why these practices vary across societies.

The fact that natural selection underlies our ability to learn, communicate, and engage in cultural practices does not tell us which populations will engage in agriculture, nor what form these practices will take in a particular population, nor what evolutionary episodes will ensue. A complete causal explanation requires knowledge of human niche-constructing behaviour.

If, as the above reasoning suggests, human niche construction has played an important causal role in some evolutionary events, why is niche construction not widely recognized as an evolutionary process?

Traditional evolutionary explanations have tended to emphasize only those processes that directly change the relative prevalence of particular genes in populations. This approach to evolution is known as the neo-Darwinian or modern synthesis, since it brings together

Darwin's theory of natural selection with the application of Mendel's theory of genetics to populations of organisms. From this traditional viewpoint, evolution is essentially about how gene variants (alleles) become more or less common in populations.

For example, in nineteenth-century England, gene variants responsible for dark colouration in the peppered moth population became more common than the gene variants for light colouration; in part, because industrial pollution had blackened the surfaces on which the moths settled, leaving the darker moths less visible to predators. Eventually, partly as a result of this predation, natural selection eliminated the gene for light colouration, leaving only the dark-coloured moths in the population. This is a classic example of natural selection directly changing the prevalence of genes in a population over time. Other factors that directly influence the prevalence of genes in a population include mutation (which provides the genetic variation that natural selection works on), migration (organisms migrating into a population can bring with them different genes), and genetic drift (changes that result from the random sampling of which organisms reproduce, which can sometimes have dramatic effects in small populations).

However, niche construction does not directly result in changes in the prevalence of genes in populations, so appreciating its significance calls for biologists to broaden their understanding of what constitutes an evolutionary process. This is precisely what the extended evolutionary synthesis (or EES) does. That is, the EES recognizes additional types of evolutionary processes—including niche construction—that affect evolution in different ways, such as systematically changing the conditions under which natural selection occurs. Another example is developmental bias, which posits that the development process that begins at pregnancy forms a basis that both restricts future evolutionary direction and also results in springboard points that represent areas where considerable evolutionary change can occur. It implies an interconnectedness of each phenotype, which directs how evolution itself evolves.

Let us assume a case can be made for recognizing human niche construction as an evolutionary process—on the grounds that it has codirected evolutionary episodes in predictable ways that could not be fully explained by earlier natural selection alone. Can the same argument be made for the niche construction of worms, birds, or spiders?

After all, animals other than humans generate consistent, reliable, and sustained modifications in their local environments, too, in part because their niche-constructing capabilities have been favoured by natural selection. A bird builds a nest and it immediately creates or modifies selection pressures for the nest to be defended, maintained, regulated, and improved upon in design, as well as to keep others from stealing it, destroying it, squatting or dumping eggs in it. A spider spins a web and creates selection pressures that favour sticky webs, oily feet, web site selection, and anti-predator behaviour on webs. Nest building, web spinning, burrow digging, and countless other forms of niche construction generate consistent, reliable, and sustained changes in environmental conditions, often regulating those conditions within precise bounds that are adaptive for the constructor. In other words, animals control certain aspects of their environment, often pushing resources into states that they would not otherwise occupy. In doing so, they also impose regularity on some of the selection they encounter, reliably triggering adaptive responses.

Niche construction leaves a kind of signature of environmental change distinct from other environmental changes that are generated by processes independent of the organism. Changes due to niche construction, as opposed to other natural processes, are recognizable because they are reliable, directional, and orderly, as well as often consistent across otherwise unrelated organisms. More than that, the selection pressures generated by niche construction are probabilistically predictable. That is, while predicting exactly what would happen in a given selective scenario may be difficult, researchers are able to make stochastic predictions of particular expected patterns across multiple populations. Research is currently underway to investigate whether this reasoning can help evolutionary biologists to identify traits, in which evolutionary responses will be more forecastable, to predict longer-term trends across multiple traits as well as patterns of parallel evolution in isolated populations.

Some, more traditionally minded, evolutionists typically treat humans as a special case, arguing that there are special properties pertaining to our species' niche construction that stem from our unique capacity for culture. This allows them to defend the position that niche construction is not a general evolutionary process, rather a trait peculiar to humans that has no significant impact on broader evolutionary forces. Even if these evolutionists were right that niche construction is a directing bias on natural selection only in the case of humans, this would still be extremely important for the study of human evolution, as well as the evolution of domesticated animals and just about any species exposed to anthropogenic environments.

In the age of the Anthropocene (the slice of Earth's history during which people have become a major geological force—through mining activities alone, humans move more sediment than all the world's rivers combined. Homo sapiens have also warmed the planet, raised sea levels, eroded the ozone layer, and acidified the oceans), such a position comes close to seeing niche construction as a major influence in contemporary evolutionary dynamics. Indeed, humans have been described as *"the world's greatest evolutionary force"* and human-induced evolution increasingly garners scientific attention. However, there are grounds for being suspicious of the claim that human niche construction is unique in this regard.

First, if stable transgenerational culture is thought to underlie the regularities of human niche construction, then we would surely have to accept that other hominins, such as Homo Habilis, Homo Erectus, and Homo Neanderthalensis—which are known to have possessed complex cumulative culture—would also have been capable of codirecting their own and other species' evolution. If so, we might want to extend the category of niche-constructing species capable of generating a codirecting evolutionary bias to all hominins.

Second, we now know that other animals—including chimpanzees, orangutans, capuchin monkeys, cetaceans, such as killer whales and dolphins, as well as many birds—are capable of stable, socially learned, and transmitted practices, some of which are documented to have lasted hundreds of years and perhaps longer. And there is evidence in birds, monkeys, and whales that such socially transmitted behaviour generates evolutionary responses. Social learning has been demonstrated experimentally in hundreds of species, not just vertebrates but also invertebrates, such as bees and ants. This potentially widens the scope of a niche-construction bias further.

Third, if the critical factor underlying the ability of niche construction to generate characteristic selective responses is its consistency, reliability, and repeatability, then the emphasis on culture and learning could be misplaced and any form of plasticity in any organism could potentially instigate this type of response, provided it generates characteristic patterns in ecological variables. There is now extensive data that the plastic responses of diverse organisms are indeed reliable and repeatable.

There are many ways that species can codirect evolutionary episodes. Organisms can influence the trajectory of evolution through their active choices—choosing habitats, nest sites, oviposition sites, feeding areas, as well as migrating to more benign regions. This is well-established in the case of sexual selection, where the mate-choice decisions of animals generate evolutionary change but could apply more generally.

Returning to the aforementioned example of Industrial melanism, research on moths over the last 50 years has established that this textbook example is more complex than initially depicted, one caveat being the tendency of the moths to choose to settle on backgrounds matching that of their colour, which dramatically reduces selection.

It is widely accepted that animals choose nursery environments, but plants also "*choose*" microenvironments for their seeds, both by physically positioning them in suitable germination sites (a phenomenon known as "*geocarpy*") and through altering the timing of flowering and germination to regulate the seasonal conditions for their descendants. In most instances, the choices and environmental modifications of individual organisms will have been shaped by earlier natural selection. However, it is an empirical question whether those responses are best regarded as fully determined or underdetermined by prior selection. That will need to be evaluated on a case-by-case basis. Of relevance here are some recent analyses suggesting that organisms not only respond in characteristic ways to particular conditions but also seem to possess evolved general capabilities to respond flexibly and functionally to whatever conditions they experience—often exhibiting extensive innovation in the process. These capabilities are known as "*exploratory processes*" or "*adaptability*."

Adaptability results, in part, from a sort of Darwinian evolution occurring within every organism as it develops, grows, senses its environment, and adapts to suit its current circumstances. This is apparent in the immune system, nervous system, and behavioural systems (through learning), which are all constantly adjusting and improving in response to challenges faced by the organism. For instance, computer simulations of gene regulatory networks also point to adaptability in the organism's growth and development, revealing how developmental systems can respond intelligently to new environmental conditions by generating phenotypic variation that is functional and adaptive. In such cases, we can once again regard the plastic responses of organisms as directed, yet underdetermined by prior selection. In summary, it remains a plausible hypothesis that the selective bias generated by niche construction is widespread.

Niche construction is not generally recognized as an evolutionary process, partly because of how the field of evolutionary biology understands the nature of causation. The convention that currently dominates the field sees the characteristics of organisms (their phenotypes) as causally specified by genetic blueprints that have been shaped by earlier natural selection and separates out developmental processes from evolutionary processes.

This makes it harder to see how niche construction (as well as other developmental phenomena, such as plasticity) might play a causal role in evolution. This probably means that intelligence will not be widely recognized as playing an important role in evolution unless and until biologists' views about the nature of causation change. Some scientific ideas run counter to the prevailing mindset and must overcome deeply entrenched assumptions in order to become accepted.

Science is a wonderful institution with the best available means of accruing reliable knowledge about the physical world. However, as an institution, it is also flawed, primarily because it is carried out by human beings. The scientific process would work better if all scientists were Vulcans, like Mr. Spock in Star Trek, always behaving in an entirely rational, objective manner, unswayed by emotion. As it is, scientists become attached to their theories and hypotheses; they not only think about which explanations are the most truthful but also about their careers and their intellectual legacy. There is a good side to this—it is great that scientists care about the important work that they are doing—but it also means that, sometimes, new ways of thinking are treated with suspicion and, often, hostility. As mentioned earlier in this book, it is important not to let these emotions cloud the scientific debates and to try to let the scientific ideas be evaluated on their explanatory merits.

As this book is a T.O.E. (theory of everything) there WILL be hostile objections and so it is worth reiterating how this arises once again. In extreme cases, violence can result from differences in ideas and there have been countless wars and deaths due to differences in opinions/ beliefs. Specific neurons and neurotransmitters, such as norepinephrine, trigger a defensive state when we feel that our thoughts must be protected from the influence of others. If we are then confronted with differences in opinion, the chemicals that are released in the brain are the same ones that try to ensure our survival in dangerous situations. In this defensive state, the more primitive part of the brain interferes with rational thinking and the limbic system can knock out most of our working memory, physically causing *"narrow-mindedness."*

We see this in the politics of fear, in the strategy of poker players or simply **when someone is stubborn in a discussion. No matter how valuable an idea is, the brain has trouble processing it** when it is in such a state. On a neural level it, **acts as if we are being threatened, even if this threat comes from harmless opinions or facts, we may otherwise find helpful and could rationally agree with**. But when we express ourselves and our views are appreciated, these defence chemicals decrease in the brain and dopamine transmission activates the reward neurons. Self-esteem and self-belief are closely linked to the neurotransmitter serotonin. When the lack of it takes on severe proportions, it often leads to depression, self-destructive behaviour, or even suicide. Social validation increases the level of dopamine and serotonin in the brain and allows us to let go of emotional fixations and become self-aware more easily, making us feel empowered and increasing our self-esteem. Our beliefs have a profound impact on our body chemistry and perceptions. This is why placebos which are discussed in great detail later in the book can be so effective.

Even the discoverer of natural selection, Charles Darwin, acknowledges that there is inherent intelligence in nature. Through careful experiments, Darwin showed that worms genuinely learn from experience; for instance, they improve the efficiency with which they drag leaves into their burrows by working out where best to grasp them. In *The Formation of Vegetable Mould through the Action of Worms*, published shortly before he died, Darwin stated:

"If worms have the power of acquiring some notion,

however crude, of the shape of an object and of their burrows, as seems the case, they deserve to be called intelligent; for they act in nearly the same manner as would man under similar circumstances."

If Darwin was happy to call the purposeful, goal-directed, niche-constructing actions of earthworms *"intelligent,"* then although this is clearly not an assurance of absolute truth, it should at least prompt sceptics to reconsider their position. It is important to note that Darwin's statement about the worm's intelligence came long after his discovery of natural selection. It is clearly an admission (discovered by studying a creature much more basic than man), that there is an inherent intelligence in life, even in its most basic form. The question then arises: *"Is a worm conscious?"*

As Darwin surmised, when talking about the flying squirrel, the squirrel's performance in jumping between branches likely improves with experience (as well as the development adjustments in its bones and soft tissues, which adapt to the loads under which they are placed), and this enhancement will be both nonrandom (i.e. *"intelligent"/"clever"* in the sense of improving functionality) and selection modifying (i.e. genetic variants *"fit the animal…for its changed habits"*).

Darwin established that earthworms' activities change the physical and chemical properties of the soil. Subsequent research has established that earthworms are, structurally, poorly adapted to life on land. They have retained the typical physiology of freshwater worms and as a result of which they are highly vulnerable to desiccation. So, how do they survive? The answer is niche construction. Their tunnelling, burrowing, casting, and soil processing increases the size of soil particles, reducing the ability of the soil to retain water (matric potential), and allowing the worm to draw moisture into its body. It is as if they have built their own swimming pools. The fit between earthworms and their surroundings arises, at least, in part, because the worms have changed the soil rather than (or as well as) adapting to it.

It is natural, then, to characterize the complementarity of earthworms and their environment as reciprocally caused by repeated bouts of natural selection and niche construction. However, that is not how evolutionary biologists typically see it. Rather, they reason that earthworms only engage in soil processing because earlier natural selection has fashioned these capabilities as adaptations, without a separate evolutionary cause (the worm's own behaviour) being seen as a necessary part of the process. Lining burrows with leaves, tunnelling, and so forth are generally (incorrectly) viewed as proximate rather than evolutionary causes. This stance effectively linearizes our portrayal of evolutionary causation: Evolutionary causation begins with a change in the external environment which, through natural selection, brings about a change in the organism (i.e. adaptations for soil processing). Following Ernst Mayr, many evolutionists distinguish between evolutionary causes ("*ultimate causes*") and proximate (i.e. immediate mechanical) causes. One traditional line would be to view intelligent behaviour as proximately causal but not evolutionarily causal (where proximate cause is defined as changes in individual organisms during their development but not them bringing about evolutionary change). In contrast, the above argues that intelligent behaviour is also evolutionarily causal.

Note, the old narrower way of thinking does not reflect how causation actually operates in the real world—rather, it is a scientific convention. One could equally argue that the only reason that selection arises is because of the prior construction of the soil environment by ancestral earthworms (the true cause of selection), with the differential survival and reproduction of worms (i.e. natural selection) the consequence, not the cause (which would linearize causation in a different way).

When it comes to the impact of societal behaviour on our own genes (i.e. accelerated evolution resulting from our behaviours, which are greatly influenced by the evolution of high intelligence), the selection pressures seem too weak for natural selection to be responsible for the evolutionary developments that arise. Unlike the evolution of senses (also seemingly developed via forces beyond natural selection due to the fact they are *"creations"* in their nonphysical experiential form and because the plasticity in the process of microscopic mutation changes is apparently so near limitless, it seems to assure physical manifestations that appear like they were "desired outcomes" of some superior mind a near infinite number of steps prior to their final form; serendipity that just keeps on happening a statistically impossible number of times), there is no apparent life or death benefit in the *"adoption"* of many useful mutations that carry into a population. In other words, lactose tolerance, as an example, seems more of a *"nice to have"* dietary supplementation facilitator than something that would affect mortality. This is even more likely to be the case when the initial move, by certain human bodies, towards lactose tolerance was so minute that it cannot have really conferred a notable survival benefit.

This would imply that there was already a broad enough flexibility in the system that the selection pressure was no longer about life or death, but the adoption of mutations that arose, which conveniently matched human intent. In other words, this is similar to selective breeding where physical and behavioural traits can be changed in accordance with human taste. However, those with better lactose tolerance would certainly not be purposefully selected by sexual selection and it is hard to see how natural selection would explain it either (how much survival benefit does a slightly better tolerance confer?). It is not impossible for survival pressures to favour mutations that lead to better tolerance, but when you look at all the examples of how evolution *"solves"* challenges by morphing an organism such that it invariably creates a skeleton key (e.g. photons ultimately becoming sensed), it begins to look more Lamarckian than Darwinian, in many cases. Mind (including that of humans) bending reality to match intent, which is what we observe in the placebo effect and

Random Number Generator influence, could intervene with random mutation production in a subtle but favourable way that produces so many of the *"beyond coincidences"* that have manifest.

If *"will"* (an unconscious goal set for the purposes of beneficial nonrandom change) proves able to bring about useful mutations that pass on via heritability, this will help perpetuate the positive evolutionary change, as will further gene changes through the *"will"* of more and more specimens. Given that there is increasing evidence that minds/consciousness (which even extends to the energy storage points in plants collapsing waveforms that assure maximum efficiency in photosynthesis) can affect quantum states, this provides the mechanism to allow minds/consciousness to impact the evolutionary processes.

Recent research supports my thinking that lactose tolerance in adult humans is likely to have arisen via a mechanism other than natural selection. John Cairns of the Harvard School of Public Health incubated two cultures of E. coli. ("A" and "B"). Both cultures were deficient in an enzyme needed to metabolize lactose. He fed culture A only lactose, and he fed culture B a yeast extract that does not require the missing enzyme for metabolism. He was investigating whether there would be a difference in the rate of gene mutation between the two groups. Culture A went into a latent phase and grew very slowly, as expected, and culture B thrived. To his surprise, the stressed culture A produced many more mutations for the specific gene responsible for the enzyme needed to metabolize lactose than culture B. The rate of mutation for other genes not related to the lactose enzyme were the same in both cultures, which suggests that there must have been a specific signal from the environment, which caused a top-down change in the DNA. These findings have been supported in other epigenetic research.

Jim Al-Khalili and Johnjoe McFadden have suggested that quantum mechanics may prove to be responsible for the nonrandom effects observed. The idea is that the DNA of the starving cells have a proton that can exist in one of two states (the one which results in the specific gene responsible for the enzyme needed to metabolize lactose being the state that rarely occurs). Because the proton experiences rapid cycles of coherence and de-coherence, it has countless thousands of chances to mutate in the super rare form—and when it does, it collapses in that state and remains in that state (and replication also assures more mutations of this form). As the starving cells that do not mutate in this way die, it is natural selection that then assures the exponential growth of these "*helpful*" mutations.

This seems a very plausible process, and the strange property of coherence seems ideally suited to providing a bias in the evolutionary process (by conveniently transforming highly improbable events into probable ones). The same principle could also be responsible for bringing about earth's basic replicators (that preceded DNA and RNA) to produce a sequence necessary to permit replication. The odds of the necessary sequence arising by chance is so remote that this infinite retrial method of coherent particles seems highly likely. However, it does not explain how—when the correct code-breaking arrangement arises—this causes the arbitrary and strange process of replication to arise. Notwithstanding the difficulties in explaining the ultimate cause of replication, the overall system described transforms odds of countless billions to one against into likelihoods by performing countless retrials every fraction of a second and so is the ultimate in loaded dice. In other words, it is conveniently bringing about statistically impossible manifestations.

There is a good reason to suspect all of this is by design. Accident (read chance) may explain the situation for starving cells producing much-needed enzymes via a system that involves retrials; although accident is more of a default interpretation because the phenomenon is ubiquitous and so it is obvious to all but the most stubborn of minds that there is something more than multiple accidents going on here.

Chance may also explain how early replicators arose as well as these statistically impossible but helpful lactose tolerance creating mutations. However, I am certain chance is not the correct interpretation. Furthermore, it does not explain how random forces (through retrials or otherwise) could build the order in the pattern and ornament of the male great argus pheasant, because when a suitable mutation arises, in this instance, there is no opportunity for natural selection to be involved because the difference between the nonmutant and mutant DNA has no value with regard to fitness. The build-up of such order, therefore, requires an intelligent force to manipulate DNA by utilizing this quantum mechanics system and by performing the apparent selection via an agent that gives the **illusion of being the cause** of what manifests.

The point is that chance alone cannot be responsible for all phenomena that arises though the process we refer to as natural selection, even with near infinite retrials, because very specific mutations in very specific genes are required, and there must, therefore, be a goal of sorts to assure this is all delivered in micro stages over countless generations. In other words, the quantum retrial mechanism described may prove to be the reason why so many beneficial mutations arise in abundance (for survival purposes and in the evolution of beauty), consistently defying statistical probability.

Nobody can deny that sexual selection is a genuine phenomenon in nature. However, gene fitness cannot explain how the undeniable mathematical order of the male great argus pheasant pattern and ornament evolved and only superior intelligence is capable of such a feat. This is a classic example of *"arrival of the fittest"* rather than "survival of the fittest," but the irony is that even when full physical beauty has evolved, its value in terms of gene fitness has been questioned in recent times. This is not surprising because, as Darwin reported long ago, beauty happens and does so with little regard to natural selection (until or if it becomes so deleterious that it impacts the survivability of the species).

There are other examples where *"helpful"* flexibility exists that lays dormant in humans but arises (subconsciously) to support their behaviour. One example is seen in the Thai *"sea nomad"* children that can see like dolphins. To aid fishing and pearl diving, these children have the capacity to subconsciously reduce their pupils to the minimum size (to achieve maximum depth of field) and alter the cornea shape. Consequently, the actions of these two subconscious controls results in an ability to see underwater without the usual blurring that takes place due to the transition from water at the cornea versus air around us, to water at the cornea versus water encountered in underwater environments.

It was proven not to be the result of genetic differences by having European children *"learn"* the same techniques. Although they were told how they might be able to obtain the same results, it was only through countless trials that the ability arose spontaneously in each of the European children too. This makes the phenomenon different from the lactose tolerance *"ability"* because evolution has resulted in genetic changes in the lactose tolerance example. The pearl diving children example shows that arbitrary *"helpful"* behaviour can result in the subconscious *"intelligently"* bringing into play mechanisms the mind *"knows"* how to affect (mechanisms that the conscious mind would be completely unaware of). It is an example of plasticity that permits novel/useful outcomes without the need for evolutionary change, which would take countless generations. Again, randomness cannot explain this, as it is a definitive solution that seems to offer an all or nothing anatomy and physiology utilization mechanism where the mind controls two separate parts of the eye, instantly and simultaneously, as opposed to a process that gradually improves over time in the way evolution generally works. It does, however, mirror how evolution seems to work in some cases, i.e. a pull from the functional side, as opposed to a push from the purely random side, eventually stumbling on the useful albeit, in the case of evolution, being a gradual process that relies upon the mutation process and vast amounts of time. Most evolutionary biologists will suggest that all the functionality manifest can be explained without the need for any *"doctoring"* of the randomness. However, the male great argus pheasant should be hailed as a symbol of the naivety of such a worldview.

Another example of the subconscious adoption of hidden, normally unused anatomy and physiology is seen in synchronized swimming. A multiple gold medal-winning Russian duo were tested, scientifically, to see how they were able to perform a number of seemingly superhuman feats. The lead of the two ladies was shown to have a spleen that almost halved in its size during underwater performances. It indicated the body's *"clever"* response to the stresses of a lack of oxygen—*"grabbing"* at necessary resources in novel ways. Although the *"ability"* seems highly variable (her partner and two girls from a competing team displayed a significantly reduced effect), it again shows the plasticity of the human organism as a whole and shows that mechanisms beyond the conscious mind can be accessed when a strong intent/need arises.

According to Stephen C. Meyer, modern biologists are acknowledging that there is flexibility inherent within the coding that allows organisms to adapt without the mechanism that neo-Darwinian biologists have always maintained is the only mechanism (i.e. there is flexibility independent of natural selection, regardless of their belief). Accordingly, we will soon begin to see some radical new theories emerge that explain how organisms can evolve via their own bootstraps. World-renowned evolutionary biologist, Gerd B. Müller, has published work stating why an extended evolutionary synthesis is necessary. It concerns apparent oversights when it comes to the *"arrival of the fittest,"* as opposed to *"survival of the fittest."* It has become clear that Darwin's theory of natural selection cannot explain a lot of what is manifest, and the fact that this is being acknowledged by mainstream science is very encouraging.

Many of the problems with the theory relating to natural selection and sexual selection have been discussed. However, there are other equally important anomalies, such as the discovery of *"orphan genes"* that do not share common ancestors in genomic databases. Given that the theory of evolution is founded on the idea of common ancestors, the spontaneous creation/emergence of the orphan genes is another spoke in the wheel. Likewise, the Cambrian explosion is problematic, (which Darwin also recognized) because so much evolutionary change and activity in a narrow window lack a credible explanation. Many new body plans emerged during this period also and the time frame required for such dramatic changes (including the emergence of thousands of new species) should have been infinitely greater than the actual available time. Given that the explosion, according to the theory of evolution, happened via minute beneficial mutations arising over countless generations, it should have been statistically impossible for the Cambrian explosion, even with the potential impact of developmental bias referred to earlier. However, it undoubtedly happened, therefore, it cannot have been impossible—but this doesn't mean the process of natural selection, as it is commonly perceived, was wholly responsible. Something that happens despite being a statistical impossibility ought to be thoroughly investigated to see if other mechanisms are involved.

Of course, knowing that there is a primacy of consciousness driving evolutionary steps that complement, and ultimately cause, the apparent natural selection process, means what appears to be statistical impossibility is simply a hallmark of Universal Consciousness intent. Statistically impossible, if not actually impossible, manifestations that arise via natural selection that are, incorrectly, deemed unguided by neo-Darwinians. The vera causa (true cause) being what Einstein referred to as a *"superior Mind."*

The main point here is that once we recognize that there are multiple ways of understanding biological causation, it naturally leads us to ask, *"What is the best way?"* (or better still, what is the TRUE way, rather than speculation based on pattern recognition). An explanation based on reciprocal causation seems to best capture the past events concerning the role of intelligence described by Laland.

Whilst it is important to understand the many patterns observed in the physical material realm, it is more important to understand that we are all experiencing, whilst in our present form, an agreed upon hallucination we call reality.

It is quite clear that intelligence is one of the fundamentals that I have mentioned several times in this book and also that the universe has incomprehensible order (revealed through the preexisting language of mathematics) that appears more and more as the complexity of phenomena grows. And that this intelligence forms an invisible framework upon which manifestations emerge as the linear evolutionary process progresses (itself a part of this intelligence; faithfully *"acting"* logically and mathematically).

As with mathematics, *"unreasonably effective"* discoveries arise in evolution, although we are, at an individual level at least, mainly passive observers, whereas in mathematics the discoveries come about through our actions. The evolutionary system's immense plasticity facilitates the *"harnessing"* of many previously unmanifest phenomena. There is no doubt that incomprehensible order preexists as a potentiality, and I would define intelligence as the cause of manifestations of that order (behaviourally as well as in the many forms that matter take) with higher intelligence beings, such as humans, having the ability to be able to pattern recognize, as well as being a part of and cocreators of such order.

This is not just intuition. The hallmarks that give basic life a level of intelligence above the intelligence inherent in, for example, crystal formation are the mysterious properties that do not exist in the physical world prior to their manifestation. Namely, purposeful, goal-directed, niche-constructing actions and the like. It is also evidenced in some of the more seemingly mysterious capabilities of the human brain (mind).

Darwin's strange inversion that some scientists believe removed the need for some intelligent guiding *"force"* ultimately endorses what it initially appeared to refute. Although the process may be blind and rely upon apparent randomness, what lies in store for its *"feeler"'* is far from random.

What I am asserting is that there is incomprehensible intelligence (and order) unmanifest in the universe and that access to sense it/perceive it/be a conscious part of it is limited by anatomy and physiology. As such, a worm acts in its unconscious form (but has limited intelligence that is present despite its lack of awareness of it). And a magpie acts in an unconscious or perhaps semiconscious form (and has considerably more intelligence). For humans, we have a much higher magnitude of the same kind of intelligence but no longer just instinctively pattern recognize (and act accordingly)—we can now contemplate the patterns (and consider their origins etc.). Additional evidence for this comes via the minds of autistic savants (as well as minds under the influence of hallucinogenic drugs or periods of hypomania in bipolar II), from psychic abilities (that are not always pure fantasy as mainstream science would have you believe) and near-death experiences (which are reported on by such huge numbers of people claiming to have experienced it firsthand it is hard to dismiss all of them as hallucinations or false memories).

One of the most amazing examples of nonhuman intelligence (and self-awareness) I have seen was displayed during an experiment where monkeys had been trained to play an arcade style bat and ball game. They wore sensors in a cap that sensed the brain activities associated with each hand movement that was used to control the game paddle. This meant that the game paddle could be removed from the game console and, instead, inputs directly from brain activity used to create the same results. It was quite remarkable that the monkeys quickly sensed that the hand movements were not causing the bat movements, leading them to put the paddle down and continue playing by using just their minds. Clearly, a sense arose that their mind was causing the bat control rather than the paddle. It is obvious from witnessing this that some animals have a strong sense of self, as well as intelligence. It also highlights the fact that it is always the mind that controls all movement. An even deeper analysis shows us that minds do not only govern all movement resulting from intent, but they also create the illusion that is perceived as movement because ultimately there is no movement—just as there is no movement in flip book animation or movie frames.

In the future, transhuman minds and/or AI will doubtless have a greater intelligence to perceive the *"coded"* structures of reality. Whether a superior, nonbiological, artificial intelligence will inevitably result in consciousness is debatable, and it seems highly unlikely because no matter how able an artificial entity becomes in decoding patterns, it will never feel pain (or experience any qualia). Maybe altering the form and constituents of this future algorithm decoder (e.g. biological hybrids/transhuman forms) can create minds (as well as synthetic intelligence), but if the medium remains essentially the same as it currently is, it seems highly unlikely there will be any resulting sentience. In other words, computers will gain access to the quantum realm and, therefore, have incomprehensible intelligence but will never know the taste of coffee or smell of roses. They will not even know how it has emulated platonic morality via deep learning if they do—because they will have accessed abstract realm phenomena but will lack consciousness. They will effectively be David Chalmer's *"p-zombies."* AI is essentially an extension of human minds and will, therefore, always remain tethered. It is neither good nor bad and, as with all man-made technology, can be used for good or bad depending on who has access to it.

Normally, anatomy and physiology damage diminish abilities. However, in the case of autistic savants, they gain enhanced performance (intelligence) in narrow fields of expertise, usually to the detriment of other abilities. Similar abilities may present in hypomania too. How savant Daniel Tammet processes mathematical calculations is very telling. He does not do calculations using conscious thought but, instead, subconsciously processes the figures in a way that seems akin to how the brain automatically inverts the retinal image, as described earlier in the book. Because there is only one correct (and logical) answer to what is being solved, it seems that his brain has been able to subconsciously do what computers do and calculate without any conscious awareness. The answers just present themselves in an abstract form that he merely needs to *"read off."* In fact, the answers begin as morphing shapes that crystallize into a final form that consists of shapes that are tokens of numbers which he translates for the purposes of communicating in numerical terms.

To Tammet, the result of the calculation that we label as pi has great emotional presence, and although his ability to recite it to 22,514 decimal places may involve memory *"tricks,"* when scientists in a separate experiment altered some of the digits in the sequence to gauge a reaction (monitored by the same methods adopted in lie detectors), it was not surprising to see signatures of stress when the bogus digits were encountered. He said that it was ruining a beautiful landscape and where there were meant to be peaks there were troughs. In other words, he sees a vast landscape and reads off "information" as he encounters it, rather than simply memorising an incomprehensibly large sequence of numbers.

The reason it is possible is that the answer exists in an unmanifest form and can be acquired via coding (follow the correct coding and the result will always be correct because it is objective and exists in abstract form, whether humans exist or not), and so his mind seems able to directly access this abstract realm. What is certain is that the way his brain anatomy and physiology work clearly give him a portal into a significantly higher realm of intelligence. Even if his reciting of pi is deemed, in part or in full, some form of memory *"trick"* (especially given the visualization experience described that arises due to his synaesthesia condition, that could be akin to a form of the standard memory trick system that uses imagined imagery to aid memory), it still shows a capability that is way beyond the norm and expresses a form of intelligence that is superhuman.

Master chess players have a similar experience in that they very often know their moves without thinking (the same as we can begin a sentence without knowing exactly how it will form but can delegate much of the process to the subconscious). Again, this is only possible because the game of chess can be *"coded."* Its mathematics, logic, and move potentials all preexist, so playing chess is like playing music is for a maestro.

To dispel any thoughts that savants solely have a focused learning ability (as a symptom of the disorder and/or because repetition is a comfort blanket in a world full of scary distractions), the same effect is seen in *"acquired savants."* Savant syndrome is a condition where people with serious mental disabilities, including autistic disorder, demonstrate prodigious capacities or abilities far greater than the norm. The condition can be congenital, which means that some are born with these prodigious abilities, while others may acquire the syndrome following a central nervous system injury or disease. They are known as "classical savants" and "acquired savants," respectively. Classical savants normally fall somewhere on the autism spectrum, whilst their skills usually appear in early childhood. Most have diffi-culty carrying out what are ostensibly ordinary tasks, such as social interaction and even tying shoelaces. Despite this, they possess a remarkable talent in a specialized area(s).

Here is one of the most beautiful examples and the talent really is truly remarkable:

 **https://www.facebook.com/realterrycrews/vid-
eos/648257658934957/**

With *"acquired savants,"* a brain disease or head injury (e.g. during diving into a swimming bath) can result in a compulsion to enter novel specialized areas, such as music or art. These people may invest considerable time in these pastimes due to the compulsion but the skill levels attained indicate an innate, previously untapped talent. I can only think of two causes for this. They have either been given a higher access level to intelligence that is normally blocked by ordinary brain anatomy and physiology or there is a genetic component and the skills were always present, albeit inert.

Either possibility has profound implications. Although there are evolutionary reasons to suppress information overload (selective memory is more useful for survival and reproduction than too much "*noise*"), it would still seem amazing if these ready-made skills were coded in the DNA but not expressed because there is still normally a lifetime's practice that is required for the non-savant genius equivalents to reach such levels. And some talents seem beyond the reach of non-savant geniuses, in any event.

The other possibility is even more profound because it would mean that an abnormal brain is somehow able to access intelligence that is normally limited, due to the standard brain's anatomy, physiology, and corresponding levels of consciousness, suggesting that the brain acts more as a receiving device that interacts with some "*cloud*" like consciousness. Hypomania possibly adds some weight to this hypothesis because, although you would expect sluggish thinking during a depressive phase of bipolar where connections in the brain are adversely affected, the hypomanic phase puts the beholders way above their intelligence "*set point*" and permits savant-like thinking for no reason other than a state of mind. Likewise, hallucinogenic drugs can result in savant-like abilities.

Given the way that Tammet's mind produces mathematical solutions in the same manner as minds can automatically conjure up illusory complementary colours based on context, it would seem to indicate the idea of consciousness accessing preexisting truths, rather than having to process calculations through conscious thought, seems feasible. Acquired savants that suddenly gain an ability to know the day of any given date of any year evidence the fact that there is something beyond learning (or consciously calculating) going on.

In summary, I do not believe biological causation has been fully investigated and this has left most biologists staring at the illusion that evolution is the sole cause of all that manifests through the observed process. Many mathematicians already believe that mathematics is fundamental and it would not be such a huge leap of faith to think that intelligence (the manifesting of innate order in the universe) is fundamental, too, and that higher levels of access to it are out of reach with our present brain anatomy and physiology. Certain disorders appear to enhance access and may point the way to even higher access. Enlightenment being the ultimate access.

I would even go a step further and propose that it is consciousness that is fundamental and that there is a hierarchy of fundamentals. Consciousness is primary and mathematics is its language in the physical material realm. The language manifests in our perceived reality via physics, chemistry, and biology. Each of these has intelligence (consciousness) inherent in/driving them and biology is merely a vehicle for the more complex manifestation(s) of consciousness. This is the reason why the emergence of life is, and always will be, a mystery in science. The transition from inorganic to organic is impossible without THE missing piece of the jigsaw, namely consciousness. When the "Top 25 Unanswered Questions of Modern Science" (*Science Journal 125th Anniversary*) are investigated with the idea that a primacy of consciousness is truth in mind, many of these complex problems, including "*the hard problem*" of consciousness itself, are easily solved. The list is as follows, and although it is beyond the scope of the book to go through each one and explore how embracing the primacy of consciousness answers most, if not all in the list, it should be clear from what has been discussed in the book how relevant it is.

The Top 25:

- What Is the Universe Made Of?
- What Is the Biological Basis of Consciousness?
- Why Do Humans Have So Few Genes?
- To What Extent Are Genetic Variation and Personal

Health Linked?

- Can the Laws of Physics Be Unified?
- How Much Can Human Life Span Be Extended?
- What Controls Organ Regeneration?
- How Can a Skin Cell Become a Nerve Cell?
- How Does a Single Somatic Cell Become a Whole Plant?
- How Does Earth's Interior Work?
- Are We Alone in the Universe?
- How and Where Did Life on Earth Arise?
- What Determines Species Diversity?
- What Genetic Changes Made Us Uniquely Human?
- How Are Memories Stored and Retrieved?
- How Did Cooperative Behaviour Evolve?
- How Will Big Pictures Emerge from a Sea of Biological Data?
- How Far Can We Push Chemical Self-Assembly?
- What Are the Limits of Conventional Computing?
- Can We Selectively Shut Off Immune Responses?
- Do Deeper Principles Underlie Quantum Uncertainty and Nonlocality?
- Is an Effective HIV Vaccine Feasible?
- How Hot Will the Greenhouse World Be?
- What Can Replace Cheap Oil—and When?
- Will Malthus Continue to Be Wrong?

11

CREATIVITY

"Imagination is the beginning of creation. You imagine what you desire, you will what you imagine, and at last, you create what you will."

George Bernard Shaw

Creativity is encoded in our reality at every level. It is far from unique to humans. There have been four ages in our universe and creativity is ubiquitous in each. There is the physical age, which came into being with the (perceived) Big Bang, followed by the chemical age, which includes the formation of stars and the periodic table of elements. Next came the biological age, which marked the emergence of self-organizing entities. Finally, we have the cognitive age where thought arose. This, of course, is based on happenings within our perceived physical material realm with its inherent linear time phenomenon. A sequence of events which if it were not for consciousness and perception would be more truthfully described as being concurrent, despite what our minds may have us believe.

The process is identical in each age and there is actually little difference between nature's creativity and human creativity; in fact, since all is one consciousness, there is zero difference. Of course, we are part of nature and so many believe that, technically, the creativity comes through us rather than directly from us. The paradox of creativity is that it is both seemingly unguided and apparently random, yet, creates order and conforms to rules. Natural selection is also perceived as random (trial and error) and, yet, self-organiza-tion and order emerge. Likewise, human creativity allows seemingly random possibilities to emerge but, as mentioned, there are always underlying rules. The output must not only conform to the parame-ters of natural laws but also to the logical rules that must be adhered to within the relevant area of creativity. The question arises: "*Is pure consciousness bound by any rules?*"

Some rules are fundamental, such as the arbitrary rules that apply to beauty: The thirds rule and Golden Ratio in art, photography, and architecture, for example. Others are man-made, such as the rules in languages (even these are not strictly autonomous creations as they adhere to logic, which is fundamental in the same way as mathemat-ics which is, itself, a language). Without structure in languages, there would be no coherence when observed from multiple viewpoints. In other words, there is always an invisible framework in the same way that topiary is created upon a wire structure.

As previously mentioned, all that manifests had to be a potenti-ality prior to the manifestation phase because without such poten-tiality its manifestation could not arise in our reality. This means that all that is, whether physical or mind created, such as colours, smell, pain, etc. was already in an abstract realm of possibilities. This includes ideas or phenomena that exist only in mind as well as ones that emerge into the physical world. As with mathematics, because forms in the abstract realm precede that which is manifest, creativity is also more of a discovery than invention.

Even if the mind is deemed to have "*made up*" the colour experi-ence we label as blue, that potentiality had to exist and it was merely a matter of all the necessary conditions arising, including the construc-tion of cones in eyes to produce signals to the brain that differ, as wavelengths hitting them differ. All potentialities that now manifest include the Big Bang(s) itself and all that followed and, therefore, blue already existed in an abstract form prior to the Big Bang(s). There is no learning involved in experiencing blue, yet it **does not**

exist in our reality without minds. Therefore, it has always existed but needed the *creative force* of consciousness to bring something from the realm of possibilities into the realm of experience. The fact that colour is real in our experience means it is as real as the invisible waves that give rise to the experience, which also arose from the same realm but happened to precede it (in illusory time) as a manifest phenomenon. This is because colour depends on the emergence of animal minds, whereas the varying wavelengths that evoke colours do not (although strictly, the wavelengths and all other types of waves are also the effects of consciousness manifest, that were only first present at the point in the flowering of consciousness where minds were sufficiently evolved for such phenomena to emerge in our universe in the form they are perceived). Given that linear time is illusory, there was never a time when minds were not present to experience colour in the physical material realm. However, this also means that all circumstances and experiences are ultimately illusory because we are in the world but not of the world and what seem like linear happenings occur in an infinite "now."

The colour that is evoked depending on wavelength is, in a sense, quite arbitrary. The signals to the brain resulting from what normally create the experience of red could be diverted to produce another colour, instead. However, each colour we can experience is still real, in that it is as distinct as any other element of our perceived reality. There does appear to be an, manifest through mathematics, intelligence revealed in the *order* that the colours are distributed in the spectrum and although there may have been a multitude of experiences that could have replaced that which manifest, the spectrum colour experience and order seem fundamental and to reflect a deeper underlying reality.

I suspect that consciousness agents can experience colour in a much more powerful way —in terms of variations and intensity— than we are ordinarily able to. The anatomy and physiology of the eye and brain are wonders to behold, but they can only offer crude approximations of that which exists in the realm of infinite possibilities and experiences. Colour-blind people who also experience synaesthesia evidence this, to some extent, because their synaesthesia can give rise to them experiencing colours that their eyes are incapable of *"triggering."* These *alien colours* show that their consciousness can access colour experiences beyond the colour range (technically wavelengths that are correlates of colour experiences) of their limiting, colour-blind eyes, therefore, it proves that sense organs in general impose limitations. It would, therefore, seem very likely that the human mind has the capability to access a great many more colours than it does, even in the case of people who do not suffer colour blindness.

The process of evolution in the material world facilitates sensory perception but this never reaches its true potential—the level consciousness would permit if it were not for the attenuation of minds. Anatomy and physiology are always restricted because they only ever develop to the level that aids any given organism in its niche, based on natural selection. If we assess all the senses of all lifeforms, there are sounds beyond the human hearing range, just as there are ultraviolet, infrared, sonar, and magnetic field phenomena that are beyond our sensory perception. It is likely consciousness has limitless sensing capability and it is the evolved apparatus (including the brain), which provides a means of informing consciousness that inhibits this potential. A better way of looking at this is to see all that is sensed with (and by) consciousness as the only truths, and all frequency, wave and vibration phenomena as mind-made constructs in an illusory space-time reality.

Minds have an ingenious way of *"giving"* life essences (conscious agents) limited access to the full potential of qualia that, ultimately, exists in the consciousness/quantum realm alone. These minds are a part of such realm anyway but they access filtered experiences due to a specific state of consciousness (focus of attention). Although all life forms experience this limitation in our present realm, the separation between the perceived universe and the spaceless and timeless consciousness/quantum realm is a mind-created illusion and, therefore, the delusion of separateness amongst conscious agents is also. Given that all solid objects are shown to be illusory when you focus at the subatomic level, it is apparent the universe itself is a binary construct as per *"The Matrix."* However, even the binary itself is ultimately mind-made, evidenced by the fact that the space and time it appears in, contrary to beliefs based on fallible perceptions and 3D mind-made models, is illusory and only exists in the consciousness/quantum realm (THE singularity/Mind).

Hallucinogenic drugs purport to create brain activity that evokes experiences including colours beyond what the eyes can perceive. Many reports of near-death experience say the same thing as well as reporting an ability to perceive 360 degrees without the use of visual organs. As mentioned, the everyday mind is restricted and, in the case of eyesight, this is so due to how the cones work. For example, pure yellow light is indistinguishable in mind from a mix of red and green light. The cones/retinas are additive, so even though the cones that are mainly red detectors produce half the signal pulses and the cones that are mainly green detectors produce half the signal pulses in the case of yellow light, the combination of red and green light do not have a distribution of 100 percent pulses that appear in the (mainly) green light detectors resulting from the green light as may be expected because the red light also triggers some pulses in the green light detection cones. However, when you add up all the pulses in both sets of cones, the result is the same (which is what the retina *"cleverly"* does). Without this limitation, we would be able to experience the yellow made of yellow light and the yellow made of green and red light very differently. Animals with significantly more than three cone types will be able to see the difference between these two colour experiences we perceive as yellow and this is yet another piece of evidence that it is not the objects "out there" that are colourful and that it is minds that augment the colour experience into mind's eye models. If the anatomy and physiology of our sensory organs were not as they are, we would have access to *"see"* infrared, ultra violet, sonar, and a vast amount of colour variations spanning the whole electromagnetic spectrum.

Taking the idea that all creativity arises from potentialities "downloaded" from an abstract cloud-like realm, in the same way that our experience of the visible light spectrum is, to its logical conclusion, the works of Shakespeare also preexisted before the time they appeared to come into being. In fact, they preexisted time itself. This does not mean its emergence was inevitable, unless determinism is true, but means that all possible word assemblies existed as a potentiality, as did the construct potential of each word, therefore, it is effectively *"drawn down"* from this realm of infinite possibilities. Of course, if the rules of nature preclude the emergence of certain possibilities they can only ever exist in dreams, poems, science fiction, imagination, etc. So, the possibilities are limited by the prescribed physical reality rules/construct but, of course, this is not so when it comes to the quantum realm, which our perceived physical realm is a mere subset of.

Human creativity requires an extensive conscious and subconscious awareness of the rules and limitations governing the physical realm. However, those well versed in such rules, generally through extensive practice, can easily delegate this "knowing" to their subconscious and can, therefore, focus on accessing the cloud (pool of near infinite possibilities). Some inventions will not manifest due to funding, teamwork issues, lack of know-how, or motivation in realising the idea(s), etc. As such, there will be trillions of creations that existed as ideas but never made it into reality. All future creations also already exist in the abstract realm—awaiting their time (through an evolution of know-how, perhaps via AI). As the rules of what can and cannot exist in our reality seem immutable, nothing that is not already a potentiality can ever come about in the future. Some believe a shift to a New Earth will destroy the limitations of the binary realm and break down all such "rules" in an instant. In the same way that the perception of linear time creates the impression that the present-day male great argus tail pattern and ornament has evolved from drab/

basic to mathematical perfection/ultimate beauty over ions of time when the whole process was all at once, it also creates the impression human inventions evolve in a linear way. As counterintuitive as it may seem, the death of linear time also means the death of apparent progress over time because each perceived point in time is concurrent despite how convincing the agreed upon hallucination we call reality is. Einstein killed absolute time and quantum mechanics shot a thousand superposition bullets into the corpse but we carry on as though the Newtonian worldview is true. For practical purposes this makes sense, but to understand base reality intuitions have to be abandoned and cold hard facts accounted for.

Some people talk of visionaries, such as Leonardo da Vinci, as being way ahead of their time. The way I have portrayed creativity it would seem more apt to say that they were, in a sense, not of time. Da Vinci's access to the unmanifest world of infinite potentialities allowed him to invent concepts that were not merely minor inventive steps but were revolutionary, indicating access to abstract background information necessary to form some of his ideas. His ideas were, seemingly, too far removed from the technology at the time and so must have been generated through unique access to the timeless dimension.

This is perhaps not how many see creativity, as it implies that the complex creations of humans were merely awaiting evolution to endow us with the capacity to access this abstract realm from where the creations are drawn. It is not that humans are not a necessity—because they are. For ideas to be manifest, the possibilities being realised require human intent and action. However, creatives are only ever selecting from what preexists in abstract form, and it is the laws of nature and logic that act as a filter, limiting what possibilities can be realised. Notwithstanding the fact there are parameters that prevent an "anything goes" manifestation arising from imagination, the most important phenomenon in assuring manifestation is INTENT. Not intent built in sand but intent that is synonymous with inevitability.

Although the creative process in evolution appears blind in nature, it is identical to minds, it seems, in how it creates order from randomness. The pattern and ornament of any butterfly had to be a potentiality before natural selection and sexual selection were utilized by Mind in creating such masterpieces. There could have been near infinite variations in the final creation but the colours that adorn its wings preexisted, as did all the materials (building blocks) that produced its form. Again, *"steered"* apparent randomness leads to structure and does so whilst conforming to the rules of nature. The key difference with human creativity is that we have evolved a mind that can simulate and consequently can assess ideas before potentially manifesting them.

We also have machines capable of assessing our models and aiding improvements but the overall process is unchanged. At a deeper level the machines that assist are, of course, manifestations of minds, hence, slaves to man's (and woman's) intent. The same applies to AI—which is a support system giving access to the Quantum Realm to "get at" intelligence that human minds can struggle to get at due to the attenuation referred to earlier—a handicap that is inevitable due to our focus of attention—something that can only be transcended through enlightenment.

In light of all the evidence throughout this book that the hypotheses concerning the *"primacy of consciousness"* and *"Oneness"* is true, it is a small wonder that creativity is ubiquitous. The creation of an experiential realm where consciousness evolves to become self-aware would surely lead to the flowering of immense creativity, would it not? It would also explain the anomalies with natural and sexual selection where impossible order consistently arises via a *"force"* able to assure such order, as in the case of the male great argus pheasant pattern and ornament, referenced several times.

This abstract to manifest "rule" also exists in the world of computers. The abstract logic manifests in the form of software and this affects the real world via hardware, whether it is the placement of pixels on a screen or the movement of robotic parts. The same logic carries from high-level programming language through to the level of machine language where compilers then transform the logic into action. Note that it is the abstract that drives the physics and not the other way. And this is how it is with our behaviour and creativity. There is a debate about whether at "*singularity*" AI will become sentient. There is no doubt that it will be capable, via deep learning, of something approaching platonic intelligence and morality (Mr. Spock like logic, knowing all there is to know about physics and pure moral behaviour in accordance with interactions in the physical material realm). However, the Mr. Spock analogy doesn't end with his pure logic trait, it will be emotionless in the same way too. This is because the AI will not be an original point of consciousness but will be a product of the minds that reside outside of the binary manifestation realm. These super computers are no different from a vehicle or a calculator—simply mind-made phenomenon that has arisen via intent and have no independent agency of their own.

AI will always be a slave to abstract intent and can help to save the world or destroy it, depending on the intent that lies behind it. "*What lies behind us, and what lies before us are but tiny matters compared to what lies within us.*"—Ralph Waldo Emerson. And what lies within us has and will either weaponize technology or utilize it for the greater good. Sadly, we have seen as much, if not more, of the former than the latter since civilisation began. Many spiritual people believe that, without some urgent awakening, we will soon face the war of all wars, suggesting that World War III is going to be a spiritual war.

Creativity is not merely one of the pieces of the jigsaw that makes up the meaning of life: It defines the whole process. Expressing creativity is one of the most meaningful activities of mankind, but mankind's creativity is just a small part of infinite creativity (imagination) because, in truth, creativity is all that there is.

12

BEAUTY

"The case of the male Argus pheasant is eminently interesting, because it affords good evidence that the most refined beauty may serve as a sexual charm, and for no other purpose."

Charles Darwin

I t is said that beauty is in the eye of the beholder. There is no doubt that taste is a factor. Even an object that most agree is beautiful will elicit different reactions—a normal distribution (bell) curve will always result when you plot people's ratings. Despite the vast majority, who may rate it highly, there will be some who find it ugly and some who rate it even higher than the already high average rating. Notwithstanding taste, there is also a science to beauty and in nature it is the super complex mathematical patterns that arise in the pattern and ornament of animals that provide some of the most compelling evidence of a primacy of intelligence and intent. In other words, they appear to be hallmarks of Einstein's "Superior Mind," in that consciousness is clearly witnessed making a stand against randomness and asserting undeniable order.

Beauty that is more abstract in nature also appears to infringe the implicit "rules" set by having methodological naturalism as the dogmatic foundation of mainstream science but possibly to a lesser degree. However, examples like the one referred to by Darwin in the quotation at the opening of the chapter are the most powerful examples of such an infringement because the display presented by the male great argus pheasant cannot have arisen via natural selection. Furthermore, although sexual selection is the process that gives rise to it, the unconscious *"taste"* of the female great argus cannot have, through random mutations, led to what is undisputedly the creation of some form of super-intelligent design. It is an artistic masterpiece with characteristics that would test the most competent human artist—but more importantly, it has multiple features that are absolutely nonrandom and chance alone *cannot* have constructed a pattern and ornament of this complexity.

Although the Peacock's tail is a prime example of natural beauty via sexual selection, the male great argus pheasant is in a different league, in terms of complexity. It has multiple layers of pattern and ornament, each of which is mathematical, ordered and symmetrical. It includes golden globe icons that are presented in such a form that makes them appear 3D. They each have the hallmark of an apparent light source incorporated into their design and each globe also casts an illusory shadow. Each globe in a line of globes also reduces in size by a *"just so"* small amount as you progress down the line—which means when they are viewed from a female observer's perspective, they will all appear to be the same size. The use of illusions, perspective, 3D effects, symmetry, error-free complex patterns, etc. is something to behold. Instinct instantly tells us that the design is beyond chance or the arbitrary *"taste"* of an unconscious animal, and further analysis and logic endorses this initial conclusion.

If you have not witnessed the beauty of the male great argus pheasant's plumage and mating behaviour, here is a clip:

🔗 **https://youtu.be/zlpJJRPQqOQ.**

Of course, it is still mutations over a vast sea of time that led to the masterpiece. However, the amount of order present, with every facet of design just so, suggests there had to have been a prior goal in *"Mind"* because, as previously stated, it is statistically impossible to have arisen by chance. Forces external to the male adorning the *"design"* manipulate proto shapes and design facets over multiple generations, such that they become less and less random over time. The effects cannot be by chance alone, so the issue is not whether there is a force(s) or not but whether natural selection alone is responsible or whether there is a force(s) in play that an atheist material scientist automatically deems impossible. If it transpires, as hypothesized, that Darwin's sexual selection simply causes beauty for beauty's sake, this does not explain what, in turn, ultimately drives the mate choice that results in this *miracle (the incomprehensible stand against randomness)*.

From the perspective of material science, the idea of consciousness itself being inherently intelligent is blasphemy. Even Darwin's suggestion that beauty arises for beauty's sake via mate choice in sexual selection has been dismissed by all but a few biologists because, according to mainstream views, any trait or behaviour that arises has to aid survival and/or reproduction directly or indirectly. Otherwise, natural selection would terminate traits that add quite heavily to the survival costs of the animal. As such, various natural selection-based theories have been proposed since Darwin's sexual selection (behaviour based on aesthetic taste alone) theory, to try to explain the apparent anomaly. All of these are logically flawed as demonstrated below.

Before looking at the flaws, it is worth revisiting what causes biologists to reject the idea of beauty for beauty's sake via sexual selection in favour of sexual selection as a subset of natural selection (i.e. always about *"survival of the fittest"* according to their *belief*). Although Professor Prum thinks fallout from monotheism, a belief spanning much of human history, may partially drive the desire for unified theories, it is more probable that Darwin's "beauty for beauty's sake" more than hinting at intelligent design is a far greater motivator for materialists to explore every seemingly plausible natural selection hypothesis. Any and all means possible will be used to try and identify a non-metaphysical cause of the undeniable mathematical order and beauty resulting from mate choice.

There are two main theories that are purported to be responsible for the kind of beauty we witness in the male great argus pheasant's striking pattern and ornament. One is *"handicap theory"* and the other is *"gene fitness indicator theory"* which are effectively the same thing. In the 1970s and 1980s, the chief proponent of the neo-Wallacean view of adaptive mate choice was Amotz Zahavi, who was an ornithologist. In 1975, Zahavi published his *"handicap principle."* A scientific megahit, this paper was a huge stimulus to the study of mate choice, and has now been cited over twenty-five hundred times. Zahavi thought his ideas were entirely new. According to him, *"Wallace...dismissed altogether the theory of sexual selection by mate preference."* However, the beautifully intuitive core idea of Zahavi's handicap principle is precisely neo-Wallacean: *"I suggest that sexual selection is effective because it improves the ability of the selecting sex to detect quality in the selected sex."*

What follows is both an explanation of how the principle is supposed to work as well as the obvious flaws in the logic underpinning it. Advocates of the handicap theory believe that traits and behaviours that are wasteful, cumbersome, and apparently contrary to the forces of natural selection, grow and persist because they signal the fitness of the animal. In other words, the handicaps are seen as a kind of test that shows good genes through the capacity to escape predators despite having them, and the capacity to produce and maintain the forms that these handicaps take. In other words, it is posited that less healthy specimens would not have the capacity to survive with such grand handicaps. It is because of the apparent signalling of being able to survive in spite of these handicaps that the ones with the most conspicuous ones will be selected. Even if the selection of them begins quite randomly, the enhanced survival advantages will be passed on to offspring, as will the physical traits in the chosen males and the choosiness trait in the females.

One problem is that if an increase in these handicaps causes a decrease in its optimal survival state, triggering the highly effective natural selection process, such that the sexual advantage of an ornament is directly proportional to its survival costs, they would cancel each other out and the ornament would not exist. This effect will be compounded because often the chooser causes the heritable changes in trait to impact *both sexes* in the next generation. In other words, the survival cost consequences would impact both sexes to some degree and if we take the female peahen by way of an example, she does not have any need for gene fitness display, as she does the choosing. Accordingly, only the detrimental aspect of the growing handicap is present in her female offspring, therefore, there is additional evolutionary pressure to bring a stop to such growth. In a 1986 paper boldly titled, "The Handicap Mechanism of Sexual Selection Does Not Work," Mark Kirkpatrick provided a mathematical proof of this evolutionary trap (i.e. adopted traits that are maladaptive and risky or can lead to extinction—an example of which was the male Australian brown beetle that was attracted to beer bottles, cited earlier). It has subsequently been suggested that it is extremely difficult for weaker specimens to bare the handicaps, and less so for the fitter ones, therefore, the handicaps could potentially evolve despite Kirkpatrick's conclusions. The "*tests*" for the fitter are, in other words, easier.

But this is not the only potential flaw in the logic. Even if handicaps could evolve for the reasons suggested, they are predominantly beautiful "*handicaps*." These so-called handicaps could have manifested in countless forms: Ugly, neutral, or occasionally beautiful (in the absence of intent, beautiful ones should be extremely rare though as they would arise only by chance) if they evolved solely due to the function hypothesized. And so it does not address the fact that beautiful traits that are ordered and mathematical and usually include striking colours, etc. arise in the process. In other words, even if handicaps have evolved through mate choice and serve a useful purpose, this does not explain the beauty and the order.

The gene fitness indicator hypothesis, as a means to try and explain this beauty and order, appears to have even more logical flaws. These gene fitness indicators are purported to work in a similar way as handicaps (in fact, handicap theory is a part of the good-genes hypothesis). The gene quality of an animal (usually male) is reportedly displayed through bigger and better examples of traits and behaviours that have been *enhanced through mate choice,* because the grander they are the more they demonstrate gene fitness. The thinking is that a less healthy specimen would fail to have the bodily energy/gene prowess to produce and display well-formed traits that communicate vitality. Furthermore, weaker specimens would be more impacted by parasites, for example, which would negatively affect the display quality and deter mate choice also.

Most biologists propose that a fitness indicator will have originated as a favoured trait that, at the time it emerges, will have been too insignificant in size to confer any information about fitness. It is theorized that the trait arising through this arbitrary choice then grows via a process called runaway—and as they become a certain size and quality, e.g. endowed with symmetry and/or a complex and often colourful pattern and ornament, become mature enough to confer fitness information. This is when the sexual selection process is posited to become all about gene fitness with, on average, many healthy, choosy females and healthy, indicated by high-quality traits, males being born as a result of the process. The runaway process (which is outlined separately) was an explanation for how traits become exaggerated through a feedback loop, leading to novel forms that do not necessarily enhance fitness and often, in fact, increase survival costs. However, once the exaggerated trait came about, it seems plausible that better quality examples may signal information about gene fitness.

The theory proposes that health and gene fitness is a prerequisite in order to produce the undeniable beauty of the kind that is displayed in the peacock's tail, for example—in spite of parasites that could easily corrupt the beauty and in spite of the handicapping caused by the enlarged trait—and that good genes is what led to the creation and development of such a conspicuous display.

There is no doubt that mate choice is a part of our reality and that, on occasion, mates with "*fitter*" genes are probably selected via indicators of fitness. It is logical that pattern and ornament/order may sometimes correlate with gene fitness once the complexity is manifest (poor development and poor parasite resistance would result in lower discernible display quality). However, very few people seem to note the coincidence that exists in all the various gene fitness indicator manifestations. Namely, that the patterns are mathematical and nonrandom. Although it takes good genes to maintain such order and complexity in the form of bodily pattern and ornament and/or their physical behaviour, it seems to have escaped the attention of many evolutionary biologists that, even though the final manifestations may not have been wholly predictable, there is clearly some fundamental force "*assuring*" all this mathematical order (beauty).

At each micro-stage towards ordered pattern and ornament via *random* mutations, it is hard to see how any discernible fitness can correlate with such a virtually unaltered change, and it is equally hard to see how it could be detected via mate choice, even if there is a microscopic enhancement to gene fitness. In fact, because the step(s) towards order supposedly arise from random mutations, there should be no fitness differential whether the pattern is unaltered, slightly worsened or slightly "*improved*," because who is to say that evolving aesthetic structure is an improvement **as there would need to be some invisible and unexplained force within any judgement that deems nonrandom as "improved?"** In other words, evolution is once again looking more like a process that facilitates a predetermined tendency to convert randomness into order via *intent*. This indicates some fundamental action of and a signature of consciousness. Beauty, it seems, cannot do other than arise across countless species.

As animals are incapable of understanding the difference between random and order, it is clearly something beyond the capacity of an organism's brain that *"knows"* there is more value in order and conspicuous pattern and ornament displays. Random requires no intervention but sustained order requires a stance against randomness—and the transition from random to nonrandom is progressive in the development of complex pattern and ornament. In the end, it is really only nature (consciousness) itself that can *"know"* the distinction to enable the journey in this definitive direction. Professor Prum also believes that gene fitness and handicap theory are not driving the ubiquitous animal beauty. Like Darwin, he believes it is fundamental but does not express an opinion on how mate choice can create this undeniable mathematical order.

In a 1915 paper and a 1930 book, Ronald A. Fisher proposed a genetic mechanism called *"runaway"* for the evolution of mate choice that built on and extended Darwin's aesthetic view, and Prum believes this is the process behind striking pattern and ornament and certain mating behaviours.

Prum describes the process as follows, *"Fisher actually proposed a two-stage evolutionary model: one phase for the initial origin of mating preferences, and a second, subsequent phase for the co-evolutionary elaboration of trait and preference. The first phase, which is solidly Wallacean, holds that preferences initially evolve for traits that are honest and accurate indices of health, vigor, and survival ability. Natural selection would ensure that mate choice based on these traits would lead to objectively better mates and to genetically based mating preferences for these better mates. But then, after the origin of mating preference, Fisher hypothesized in his second-phase model, the very existence of mate choice would* unhinge *the display trait from its original, honest, quality information by creating a new, unpredictable, aesthetically driven evolutionary force: sexual attraction to the trait itself. When the honest indicator trait becomes disconnected from its correlation with quality, that doesn't make the trait any less attractive to a potential mate; it will continue to evolve and to be elaborated merely because it is preferred."*

Some of this hypothesis is logical. However, it seems the first phase that explains the origins of process (mate choice assuring males with better fitness indicators are selected) may be unnecessary because the ability to identify food sources and sex differences already shows a choosiness disposition that could lead, quite naturally, to discerning mate choice without the hypothesis that mate choice will have arisen through the assessment of potentially nonexistent or miniature unreliable gene fitness indicators. It is worth noting that this proposed first phase will have been at a stage where traits were not large and exaggerated enough to communicate discernible information about good genes, except perhaps in extreme cases where the animal is visibly deformed due to handicap, disease, parasites, etc. Although methodological naturalism would suggest it is impossible, I propose that consciousness can influence randomness to assure that evolution delivers the otherwise unexplainable and that it can also *appreciate* the manifestations of intended beauty via animal minds/consciousness. In isolation, this would be highly speculative but the book reveals countless pieces of evidence that this *"randomness to order"* is ubiquitous and permeates everything from health (placebo) to the collapsing of the wave function in quantum mechanics. Human minds (consciousness) have also been shown, scientifically, to be able to influence chance in accordance with intention, which is also detailed later in the book.

Due to hyper-normalization, I believe most people do not acknowledge that there has to be consciousness to judge between beauty or otherwise in all animals that make such apparent judgements. Sense perception is only possible because of consciousness, as is the mind's eye virtual reality recreation capacity that makes this *"spot the difference"* game possible in the mate choice process. Even with these consciousness aided tools, this does not explain how the animal perceives one form to be of more value (beautiful) than an almost indistinguishably different other. Randomness cannot be the reason because what is built over time is anything but random. An animal has no *motive or cause* for this predicament, but I would suggest that the consciousness that forms the animal and is integral to its being and mind does (albeit residing in the full quantum realm not the collapsed wave function subset, where perceived form is), and knowing that the animals themselves may have a will but no will to will, means that the striking manifestations that are the absolute antipathy of randomness must have resulted from force(s) that act *through* the animals.

This force is intent and is a consequence of consciousness and it means that what Fisher hypothesized in his second-phase model is incorrect and does not even attempt to explain the transition from drab/random to incomprehensible mathematical order which is ubiquitous in life and is the Achilles heel when it comes to his interpretation of what has occurred in nature.

In their book, *The Grand Design,* Stephen Hawking and Leonard Mlodinow implied that the principle of beauty for beauty's sake does not arise exclusively through the innate desire for aesthetics witnessed in many animals that *"create"* it through mate choice. They suggest that one of the criteria for all scientific theories is that each and every theory must also be aesthetically pleasing. They believe all theories must meet all of the following criteria for a model to be a good model:

1. Is elegant.

2. Contains few arbitrary or adjustable elements.

3. Agrees with and explains all existing observations.

4. Makes detailed predictions about future observations that can disprove or falsify the model if they are not borne out.

They go on to say, "*The above criteria are obviously subjective. Elegance, for example, is not something easily measured, but it is highly prized among scientists because laws of nature **are meant** to economically compress a number of particular cases into one simple formula.*

Elegance refers to the form of a theory, but it is closely related to a lack of adjustable elements, since a theory jammed with fudge factors is not very elegant."

The choice of words, *"because laws of nature are* **meant to...**" *is* interesting because it indicates something akin to the animals' innate desire for and creation of beauty, which is ultimately the product of will and not chance. Both examples suggest that there is a kind of blueprint that was devised by some fundamental form of super intelligence (Mind). It is not criticising their observations because this arbitrary criterion is met too often to be illusory. It is mentioned because it seems out of character for Stephen Hawking to admit that theories *must be elegant* because that implies some kind of metaphysical force that is assuring elegance at a fundamental level. Likewise, *"highly prized among scientists because laws of nature* are meant *to economically compress a number of particular cases into one simple formula," also* suggests a belief that there is some prior intent and some metaphysical force assuring a stance against less elegant and ordered laws of nature. It ties in closely with the observation that mathematics is also generally elegant, including its *"unreasonable effectiveness."*

The ubiquitous display of statistically impossible *"stands against randomness"* that is perceived as beauty is a smoking gun but so many people are willing to believe that chance alone has led to these countless millions of "designs." This must be down to hyper-normalization because there is enough evidence in the pattern and ornament of the male great argus pheasant alone of incomprehensible order and, therefore, a primacy of intelligence that works its *"magic"* over countless thousands of generations, adhering to a blueprint to produce what is way beyond the capability of a bird's arbitrary taste, let alone pure randomness.

The mathematics genius, Alan Turning, was interested in the stripes and spots that appear in nature and devised his theory of morphogenesis. It is built upon the notion that chemical reactions stabilize and so does diffusion, leading to uniformity, as opposed to clumps. We see this effect when a teabag turns all the water into a tea solution, rather than leaving volumes of water unaffected. However, there is no doubt that the interaction of stabilizing and diffusion results in blobs in the case of animal pattern and ornament, at the embryonic stage, such that, in large animals, we see stripes and spots, e.g. cows, zebras, giraffes, tigers, etc. In narrowing bodily areas, patterns tend to simplify, e.g. the tails of tigers or the faces of zebras. There are exceptions, however, such as the tapir, where the spots are where you would anticipate stripes, and vice versa, and the patterns disappear in adulthood.

The chemical explanation for certain types of pattern and ornament is very different from the changes that occur over time resulting in immeasurable order, that arises via sexual selection. In the latter case, the randomness is transformed via consciousness and will over time, therefore, Turing's chemical-based morphogenesis is not relevant when it comes to the level of order discussed in this chapter.

Despite Hawking's views on the need for scientific theories to be aesthetically pleasing (only elegance and limited arbitrary and adjustable elements arising, according to the model), physics is currently in a terrible state that presently contradicts this. For example, the so-called dark matter and dark energy that, combined, seem to make up nearly all of the universe and are needed to make the mathematics fit our observations are lacking in physical evidence. Currently, their perceived effects are observed but, as mentioned, no physical evidence of the *"substances"* exists whatsoever. The reasons are discussed in detail in a chapter dedicated to these phenomena (dark matter and dark energy) in book 2. In some ways, it should be obvious how both *"work"* after completing the reading of book 1, but as our minds are accustomed to linear time and we generally readily believe the apparent validity of what is perceived in our mind's eye model of the so-called *"out there"* world, it is understandable that people will wish to see a more detailed explanation of what both phenomena may be.

There is also the highly inelegant *"standard model,"* which describes the interactions of the elementary particles of nature. Hawking and Mlodinow call it inelegant, too, saying, *"It predicted the existence of several new particles before they were observed, and described the outcome of numerous experiments over several decades to great precision. But it contains dozens of adjustable parameters whose values must be fixed to match observations, rather than being determined by the theory itself."* This is to say nothing of the *invisible* multi-dimensions and speculative undetected multiverses (which are a truth but not how it is presently portrayed) which are invoked to make it all "work out."

Of course, the primacy of consciousness, asserted throughout the book, leads us back to elegance. This is because it is posited that the flowering of consciousness involves *"guided"* evolution, whereby a state of chaos (infinite possibilities) is acted upon over linear time to form richer and more complex manifestations; perceived via points of consciousness as order, mastery and beauty.

Many people will have heard of the Turning test, which is about a computer being so advanced it can potentially pass itself off as human in its communication. You may automatically assume there is only one way for it to fail the test and that would be for it to leave clues by underperforming as a mimic. However, consider the situation where it is so advanced that it displays knowledge beyond that of any savant and provides multiple pieces of information simultaneously. It would fail the test by virtue of a display that is beyond human capabilities, rather than one that falls short of them. I believe that nature communicates it has capabilities way beyond human capabilities in the same way and **does so in the language of mathematics** and the presentation of immense order and beauty. In my view, artificial intelligence is not only with us, it constructed linear time and space and everything perceived therein, and exists within and without space-time and is what is commonly referred to as consciousness/Mind.

Without beauty, life would be dull. For this reason, it is a key constituent of human meaning and the meaning of life more generally. However, it is how beauty arises and what beauty is at a fundamental level that are generally taken for granted, and certain examples of it in nature provide the strongest evidence that there is a superior Mind behind nature's construction.

13

METAPHYSICS

"I was thrown out of NYU in my freshman year... for cheating on my metaphysics final. You know, I looked within the soul of the boy sitting next to me."

Woody Allen

aniel Dennett, in an attempt to demystify consciousness, used a quotation by Lee Seigel, taken from his book, *Net of Magic, Wonders and Deceptions in India*, "I'm writing a book on magic," I explain and am asked, "*Real magic?*" by *real magic* people mean miracles, thaumaturgical acts, and supernatural powers. "*No*," I answer, "*Conjuring tricks, not real magic." Real magic,* in other words, refers to the magic that is not real, while the magic that is real, that can actually be done, is *not real magic."*

On the surface, it is a smart reply. But it is actually very facetious. When someone asks is it about *real magic,* it is patently obvious they mean is it the type undertaken by stage magicians or the metaphysical type currently deemed impossible according to mainstream science, such as telekinesis. It also indirectly scoffs at those who think or have evidence that *real magic* can actually be done. As Dennett would include humans' capability to influence Random Number Generators as *real magic,* he has to be wrong, in some cases at least (as this apparent magic can be performed in laboratory conditions). He has used the quotation to suggest that many people, including many scientists, believe, incorrectly in his view, that consciousness is effectively *real* magic.

Dennett thinks consciousness is a physical, biological phenomenon—like metabolism or reproduction or self-repair—that is exquisitely ingenious in its operation but not miraculous or even, in the end, mysterious. I disagree. I think it has been proven throughout this book (and evidenced beyond reasonable doubt in the second book, for those who still keep jumping back to their comfort zone of believing that what is perceived is real) to be fundamental and that evolution (a process), which is a manifestation of it rather than a creator of it, is an emergent phenomenon caused by it. I believe that all experiences within consciousness, such as taste, colour, imagery, and pain are also fundamental in that they are simultaneously created and experienced by consciousness. Dennett fails to see the *"give me just one miracle"* issue, mentioned earlier (the *"elephant in the room"*—the fact that all the physical, biological phenomenon, to which he refers, is unexplained in terms of ultimate cause until consciousness enters the equation).

In his logically flawed book, *The God Delusion*, Professor Richard Dawkins states, *"We should also dismiss it as barking mad, but for its ubiquitous familiarity which has dulled our objectivity."* This statement refers to religion but equally applies to an acceptance of all phenomena as non-miraculous. Consequently, most scientists are guilty of an equivalent dulling of senses due to the ubiquitous familiarity of the manifestations that adhere to the, purportedly self-created and arbitrary, laws of nature. Of course, it is understandable that we accept all known phenomena because the probability of their existence is one (we can observe and measure the manifestations in our reality, albeit our senses can easily be tricked as we have illustrated countless times). Observing them does not mean they need be more than imagination though, regardless of opinions and beliefs.

We become accustomed to our illusion of reality from an early age—from phenomenon, such as linear time, to all things we can sense. It conditions us to think that the phenomena presented are somehow other than miraculous, and the power this effect has over us is far more pervasive than religious indoctrination, perhaps, because we live in *The Matrix* full time—from cradle to grave.

This is not criticising science. It is an amazing tool, an observational, and harnessing of phenomena, system. But the belief that ultimate cause(s) will prove to be something other than what mainstream scientists of today would deem metaphysical is so concrete in the mind of most scientists, it is on a par with the religious beliefs many of them are quick to attack.

I am convinced that things which scientists and scientific philosophers, such as Richard Dawkins and Daniel Dennett, deem as metaphysics (supernatural) exist and appear as part of our day-to-day physical phenomena. I am not suggesting that all claims that are made by *"witnesses"* are real—lies and mistakes will explain some cases. However, it only takes ONE account to be real for a phenomenon to exist. And out of the millions of accounts per unexplained phenomenon, is it likely *ALL* of them have alternative explanations that conform to the more common natural laws?

If/when telekinesis becomes accepted by science, it would not cause all the other accepted scientific phenomena to crumble, it would just be accepted as another phenomenon in nature and, eventually, be as hyper-normalized as the presently accepted laws of nature. In fact, it should now be more apparent what is going on with telekinesis and, in a sense, it is no more mysterious than the moving of perceived physical objects by perceived physical hands. Of course, the fact that the latter can be observed by a child without any thought whatsoever given to the abstract intent that precedes motor action, means that it is seen as ordinary when it is not. However, the assumption that the former is supernatural and the latter is easily explained is just another example of how hyper-normalization makes a complex phenomenon appear as though its ultimate cause is known.

Understandably, we readily categorize things as real (possible) or fanciful, and when a phenomenon becomes well observed and tested, it falls into the former category. But unlike, say, gravity, some phenomena only present under certain conditions and/or geographical locations, i.e. only noted when they happen to be in the proximity of an *"observer."* Lightning is not constant but exists (and can be artificially created) but ball lightning is exceedingly rare. Some scientists still believe it does not exist and claim that reports of it are fake or mistakes.

Having co-witnessed it as a child, I am pretty certain it exists (my primary PA, who is from Phuket in Thailand, where thunderstorms are very frequent, has seen it some half a dozen times). It could have been some other phenomenon I saw (a firework that happened to be lit during a violent thunderstorm? Or the ignition of swamp gas that likely explains what some people are witnessing when they report having seen ball lightening) or even a kind of hallucination seen by me and the co-witness simultaneously, but it also happened to behave in the way ball lightning is reported to behave. If I saw an aeroplane perform an emergency landing in the same location, the likelihood of being accused of hallucinating would be close to zero. However, when unexplained phenomena present, the default position of an unconscious mind is that it is a mistake, or hallucination.

It is right to have a healthy scepticism. Not every imagined phenomenon exists, of course, and although the following was written by Bertrand Russell as an attack on religion, it applies equally well to any unproved/unexplained phenomena:

> *"If I was to suggest that between the Earth and Mars, there is a china teapot revolving about the sun in an elliptical orbit, nobody would be able to disprove my assertion provided I were careful to add that the teapot is too small to be revealed even by our most powerful telescopes. But if I were to go on to say that, since my assertion cannot be disproved, it is an intolerable*

presumption on the part of human reason to doubt it, I should rightly be thought to be talking nonsense. If, however, existence of such a teapot were affirmed in ancient books, taught as the sacred truth every Sunday and installed into the minds of children at school, hesitation to believe in its existence would become a mark of eccentricity and entitle the doubter to the attentions of a psychiatrist in an enlightened age or of the inquisitor in an earlier time."

Impeccable logic. However, on the other hand, instant dismissal of all *"witnessed"* third party accounts of metaphysical phenomenon is nothing but short-sightedness too.

There are thousands of examples where you could assume something does not exist because it is either rare or difficult for the necessary conditions to develop for it to exist. For example, you could fill a million jugs of sea water and never reveal the existence of dolphins. But they exist! As William James said: "If you wish to upset the law that all crows are black…it is enough if you prove one single crow to be white." You could survey a thousand schools, hunting for a two-headed human and the results may suggest they do not and cannot exist. However, there are such cases, and in the USA a two-headed girl was (they were) able to gain a driving license because the way that their brains operated their singular body meant one side of the body was controlled by one brain and the other side by the other brain. Not surprisingly, if one of them (brain/mind) was to initiate a clap, the other (brain/mind) *"knew"* to initiate the process via the arm they control due to the fact the two brains were connected to the same body and were able to sense each other (potentially via extra sensory perception, but not necessarily so, given that they share a singular body).

There are many examples like this, such as the very rare condition that means an individual is born without the ability to sense pain, which results in the negative consequence of not knowing when an injury is being sustained, as well as the positive one of never feeling the horror that is extreme pain. One of the most remarkable examples of rare and unexplained conditions is of a mathematics graduate from Sheffield University in the United Kingdom. He got an honours degree in mathematics (and has an IQ of 126) despite having virtually no brain. The student had a condition called hydrocephalus in which the cerebrospinal fluid (clear colourless fluid in the spaces in and around the spinal cord and the brain) becomes dammed up in the brain instead of circulating around the brain and spinal cord. It left him with something that was a fraction of the size of a normal one (**50–150g rather than the normal 1500g**), and despite it missing all the key elements of a standard double hemisphere brain, he functioned normally (adding further weight to what is evidenced throughout this book, that mind and brain are two very different things). Without modern communication channels, there would be little evidence available to see that these important anomalies are factual.

There is a big difference between believing anecdotal evidence from unreliable sources and discounting accounts because it appears to conflict with the views of the scientific community. Nature and reality do not care at all about opinions as, for all intents and purposes, things are either real or not. Having said that, advocates of the *"Law of Attraction"* believe that belief and mindset determine what manifests and that the collapsing of the wavefunction (where the quantum realm moves into a subset realm that we perceive as the physical realm) can be influenced by individual observer intent. Although millions of people believe the same, they often still face the usual negative consequences that can arise via "God's Dice." This doesn't mean that the Law of Attraction must be wrong because there could be many reasons that the negative events arise despite its validity. A key one is that the subconscious intent can be difficult to identify and so explicit wishes may not match the intent that lies at a deeper level. More importantly, there are infinite intents interacting and therefore, in this realm, outcomes are not determined solely based on individual intent. We must navigate the construct in its objective form (life circumstances that arise simply from the way the mathematics governing our universe work in combination with how the flowering of consciousness occurs based on these parameters) as well as the aspects that arise due to other conscious agents. Due to the egoic mind, there are many aspects of our perceived reality that suit a small percentage of people but are to the detriment of the vast majority.

Whether mind is powerful enough to perform the *"magical"* feats claimed in *The Secret (2006)* is debatable but belief and intent are genuine scientifically proven forces. Is the failure to manifest by the majority really just a lack of true belief and, importantly, a failure to turn up intent to the level of inevitability? Until science takes metaphysics seriously and more scientists look into these phenomena without assuming that they are impossible, the numerous reported success stories are nothing more than anecdotal. As Nikola Tesla said: "The day science begins to study nonphysical phenomena, it will make more progress in one decade than in all the previous centuries of existence."

Alien UFOs may or may not exist and to suggest that all accounts can be explained away via astronomical phenomena or delusion is somewhat arrogant, given the huge number of reliable witnesses. If it is real, then it will not affect the laws of nature: Science is always many steps behind nature, never the other way around. All we can do is hope for reliable evidence and reliable witnesses, seeing it with our own eyes or experiencing it physically. As our life essences are real but our life circumstances are not, all observed phenomena are not as we believe them to be anyway (even the so-called *"real ones"* that fit the parameters of the mind-made construct). Beyond the confines of the binary (digital) information realm, anything goes. Literally.

The Fermi paradox, named after Italian-American physicist, Enrico Fermi, is the apparent contradiction between the lack of evidence for extraterrestrial civilisations elsewhere in the Milky

Way galaxy and high estimates of their probability based on results from optimistic choices of parameters in the Drake equation. The professed paradox is no longer a paradox, though, when you look at it from a completely new perspective which is indicated in the theory of everything (T.O.E.).

One problem with interstellar travel is that there appears to be insufficient time in order for a "UFO" to travel from a distant point in the galaxy, or beyond, to Earth. However, what if the UFO exists in a coherent form, whereby, its molecular construct is generally in a different reality (a nonphysical realm) that is outside our perception range in terms of frequency? When a UFO is spotted, what is potentially happening is that it temporarily enters a de-coherent state, which brings it into our reality and, therefore, allows it to appear here on Earth, having not actually traveled any significant distance at all. This isn't the same as near light speed travel which we know for sure reduces huge distances to a fraction from the inhabitant's perspective. The "quantum leap" method described, should it prove viable, could be adopted by future humans as well as intergalactic beings and so the UFOs that are witnessed could be visitations from the future as well as, or instead of, extraterrestrials.

This will be a difficult concept for people who do not analyse the scope of the illusion, which is linear time, and the illusion of space (distances). But for those who have fully analysed the consequences of Einstein's relativity, this is not actually too surprising at all.

What is disappointing is the lack of effort that goes into trying to prove or disprove the reality, or otherwise, of some metaphysical phenomena that would not be so difficult to research with the same methods of science applied to unquestioned phenomena. I am referring to telekinesis, telepathy, remote viewing, physical object and experience manifestation via mind(s) and via mirroring by the universe—a potential ability for humans and animals to "know" they are being stared at or pet dogs to know when their owners are journeying home from work, even when random times are assigned to the owner for the commencement of their journey, etc. However, most scientists instantly dismiss the possibility because they are so familiar with the more common manifestations of natural phenomena that they unconsciously draw a self-created dividing line.

Many reported unexplained phenomena such as ghosts, whether true or not, are no more bizarre than our standard reality. Notwithstanding the hyper-normalization effect that I have referred to many times, there are many known phenomena that are counter-intuitive but real. Quantum mechanics (the double-slit experiment and entanglement/"*non-locality*" behaviour) and the consequences of Einstein's theory of relativity are two examples. European robins appear to use quantum entanglement in their navigation system—the process involves their eyes and, more specifically, proteins in the retina called cryptochrome (covering each eye separately prevents brain sensory activity in the opposite side of the brain to the covered eye). It is suggested that photons that enter the eye knock one of a pair of electrons from an atom onto a neighbouring one, creating quantum entanglement. And because they are apart, their actions are sensitive to the earth's magnetic field.

Chemical reactions result from this effect and these differ depending on where the birds are facing in the earth's magnetic field, which in turn is sensed in the bird's brain (mind). As if the process of quantum entanglement itself is not bizarre enough (what Einstein termed, "*spooky action at a distance*"), the fact a bird species has evolved senses able to "*use*" subatomic phenomena is beyond astonishing. But, as we have seen, the plasticity of life in this regard is extraordinary.

In their book, *Life on the Edge*, Jim Al-Khalili and Johnjoe McFadden suggest that the robins may perceive what they sense as some additional colour within their mind-made 3D visual model. Given that the human motor system is guided by a subconscious perception of information entering the eyes, it would seem more likely that the earth's magnetic field is used in a similar way. This means that the information may be acted upon directly without the intermediate step of providing some mind's eye interpretation and given that perception is a handmaiden to action, this seems more likely.

A superhuman feat that is equally as impressive as that of the European robin's extrasensory perception is an ex-nurse's ability to sense, via smell, many serious diseases.

In the same way that a wine taster might train their nose to recognize the different aromas of the drinks, Joe Milne of Perth believes that working as a nurse attuned her sense of smell to different medical conditions. Now retired after decades of vivid olfaction, her incredible nose is helping find new ways to diagnose diseases. This extraordinary sense may have developed due to her condition—synaesthesia. This is the condition referred to earlier which is a result of sensory mix-ups due to the incorrect wiring of the brain. It can mean that colours are sensed as smells or that numbers evoke shapes in the mind's eye along with emotional responses. Daniel Tammet, the savant also referred to earlier in the book, has this condition too.

In the case of Milne, it has increased her olfactory senses to such an extent, she can discern microscopic "*signatures*" of certain diseases and they present themselves within her consciousness as distinct smell types per condition. She is working with scientists to establish what it is she is sensing (and translating via consciousness into smell types) so that they can use technology to emulate her ability to accurately identify the conditions and presumably do so at their onset, before symptoms present. The report focuses on her ability to identify Parkinson's disease even long before symptoms show. She also is able to use the same method to detect other diseases including cancer. I expect scientists will soon find physical mechanisms that appear to bring about her extra sensory perception, although as she is accessing the quantum realm in a way that is giving her abilities beyond that of, say, dogs—it may prove difficult to create apparatus to emulate her abilities.

There are also well-known effects that defy explanation in our reality, too, such as the placebo effect. The idea of a mood disorder being corrected by placebo is not so surprising. As perception and thinking can create the state, then a mere belief that corrective chemicals are causing a positive effect, despite being dummy pills, is conceivable, because with a mood disorder like depression, if you feel you are cured then you are cured. It is a little harder to understand when it comes to physical illnesses being cured. However, the mind and body connection is clearly real, evidenced through the mind being able to alter the anatomy and physiology in a way that mimics pharmaceutical intervention.

Placebos can boost the immune system, calm asthma, reduce bronchial disease effects, reduce pain, and enhance performance (e.g. sham oxygen tanks in high altitude conditions do not miraculously increase blood oxygen levels, but the body acts as though it is receiving extra oxygen and **performance-enhancing chemicals are produced in the same way** that they would be if extra oxygen was being administered). Even the perception of an apparent indulgent milkshake that has identical ingredients to one that is portrayed as healthier has a different physiological effect—the body acts as though it really has taken in more (i.e. there is a greater mitigating effect on ghrelin, the hunger-inducing and metabolic regulating hormone).

The placebo effect is so powerful that the vast majority of new pharmaceutical drugs fail to outperform it (and even when they do, the placebo effect represents most of the overall combined effect that is observed), and 18–80% of people respond to the placebo with an average of 30–35% responding. In one trial which involved sham (fake) local anaesthetic injections using a saline solution followed by painful electric shocks, 90% of the trial patients experienced the placebo effect. The procedure involved giving shocks to the forehead before and after injection and asking for pain ratings on a scale of 1 to 10. In the first two rounds the electric shock level was, unbeknown to the trial members, reduced after the sham injections (and not surprisingly, lower pain ratings were given). On the third round, the shock level was the same before and after the sham injection—and nearly all the trial members reported a reduced level for the post-injection shock.

Performing deep root canal treatment or even open-heart surgery with no aesthetic (using hypnosis or acupuncture) also demonstrates the extraordinary mind-body phenomenon.

The placebo effect is not denied by most scientists and medical professions, but the fact it is quantifiable and measurable seems to somehow demystify the effect and makes these people see it as phenomenon that can easily be explained. However, it is only hyper-normalization that makes it appear other than metaphysics. There are a few conditions that need to be met for the effect to work: The self-healing capabilities of the human body, the activation of a certain mindset/belief, and a certain type of social context (i.e. caring and very credible professionals/props). The self-healing properties are miraculous in their own right, as it shows inherent *"intelligence"* at the microscopic level. However, evolutionary biologists believe that evolution is up to this task and do not see the patterns as magical on the basis they are ordered and predictable (again due to hyper-normalization).

The real magic is in the power and force of believing and the intent that then **brings about new binary data that emerges from the quantum realm** (leaving the old data as historic information many Planck lengths away). Irrespective of the other conditions, the placebo effect cannot happen without this key ingredient. **How profound that a belief can cause pills, which have no active pharmacological ingredients, to trigger specific (targeted) physiological effects**. It is one thing to imagine fright provoking scenarios, which elicits the same kind of response to real frightening events because the mind does not discern the difference between the two triggers, but to have a dummy cream that reduces inflammation purely due to belief implies that not only can the body self-heal, it can deploy this potential in a targeted fashion.

There are other examples where external events trigger physiological effects—a type of neuro-associative conditioning. One is the Pavlov's dog experiment where food was fed to dogs at the same time a bell was rung. The dogs quickly learned to associate the bell ringing with food, thus the bell ringing alone provoked the dogs to salivate despite the fact it would normally take evidence of the presence of food using various senses to provoke this response. Likewise, when female humans see footage of chimps engaging in sex, they are involuntarily aroused/lubricated (subconsciously and not in a pleasurable sense). This is thought to be an evolutionary mechanism that prepares the body for potential unconsented sex in order to mitigate damage. The difference between all these types of responses and the placebo is that the placebo effect is considerably more flexible. The subconscious mind not only takes on board information from the conscious mind about the location of the problem—but also "*knows*" what to deploy and where to deploy it in order to repair the damage or mitigate pain. In the same way that optical illusions show that the mind is capable of subconsciously emulating top physicists (via instantaneous calculations followed by perceptions), it is also capable of subconsciously emulating top medical doctors (knowing the anatomy and physiology and causing self-created remedies).

What is somewhat surprising is that it takes the placebo effect, therefore, a belief to achieve these results, both for drugs that deliver a physical benefit and for sugar pills. Being aware of the conditions consciously is not enough, there has to be a belief, albeit false, that external intervention is in play to cause the body to act as if it were true and, accordingly, create a real effect from a fabricated cause. **The calming of the body to simply allow enhanced self-healing because of a shift to the parasympathetic nervous system cannot fully explain this because the effects are generally localized and not as a result of some kind of overall boosting of the immune**

system. Furthermore, a calming of the patient alone is ineffective—there needs to be a real belief that a genuinely effective, external intervention is being applied (which makes the belief itself the true force/power/magic). One of the surprising facts about placebo is that it can even work when patients are told what they are taking is a placebo. This would indicate that the "intelligence" of the subconscious is still triggered by the action of taking dummy pills, despite the conscious mind knowing the truth (which is analogous to the conscious mind knowing about optical illusions but the subconscious mind continuing to override what the conscious mind knows).

Placebo has an evil twin known as a nocebo. This means believing a sham agonist cream can worsen a rash or believing that poison ivy is being applied when it is a benign dummy alternative can give outcomes as though the application is real. It also means that the side effects listed for a drug can emerge even when a trial patient is given a placebo because the belief that the pill is real can cause symptoms that are listed as potential side effects for the real pharmaceutical. The effect is clearly driven by fear and expectation after having learned of the potential side effects. In extreme cases, some people that reportedly died from cancer had an autopsy that revealed that the cancer was not as advanced as assumed and nowhere near advanced enough to be the true cause of death. It seems the social context, i.e. levels of care and types of dialogue used by health practitioners, may have created a loss of hope in many cases and it is this, and not the disease, that was the true cause of death. This is why the social context in the health service is as important as the procedures themselves. Also, how much do the warnings and horrific imagery on cigarette packets work as a nocebo (and vision board)?

One of the most profound examples of placebo was when a 15-year-old boy was cured of a disease that would have certainly resulted in an early death, had it not been for the intervention. The boy had a very rare disease that, without full knowledge of the condition, appeared to be an aggressive form of warts over the whole body. His surgeon was disappointed with an attempt he had made to graft some of the rare, unaffected skin which was on his chest, onto his hands. A junior practitioner asked if he had tried hypnosis. The surgeon said "no" quite dismissively but suggested that the junior go ahead and try it. So, he started with just one arm.

A week after the treatment when the boy returned, the arm was clear. The surgeon was astounded. The boy had other sessions which rid of the vast majority of the symptoms. At this point, the surgeon explained that it was not simply warts but a condition that inevitably led to infectious wounds and early death. Hence, the boy's belief (and the junior's intent) was instrumental in causing his own body to systematically rid itself of an incurable condition. Gradually, it all cleared stage by stage, which meant that the effect was **not simply some enhancement to the body's self-healing abilities**, which would have cured the condition in all regions simultaneously. By using this method, the mind was aware of where the treatment focus was in each session, somehow deploying the necessary self-created pharmaceutical type effects in a very targeted way. It seems that although the patient's own belief was key to curing of the condition, the intent of the healer also played a key part in achieving the positive results. This has been further evidenced in recent experiments where rats were "infected" with cancer and healers removed the condition via intent. Healing experience and the feeling that energy was being transferred from the healer were unnecessary in assuring positive outcomes. This seems to indicate that the intent of the healer helps the affected life form to begin generating information that is void of cancer, which is represented as a healthy specimen thereafter in our "flip book" universe.

As mentioned earlier, it has been suggested that the placebo works because the social context and belief stimulate the parasympathetic nervous system and this is what sets the conditions that are necessary for the self-healing properties to be enhanced. I am sure that this is relevant and that, obversely, continuous stress can cause many diseases. Accordingly, the setting and conditions associated with the provision of placebos help to alleviate symptoms by allowing the body to better perform its self-healing abilities. However, when a sham cream is passed off as a local anaesthetic, the belief causes the mind to trigger pain killing chemicals, called opioids, in specific regions of the brain—so it is not some general self-healing property that is made more efficient but a very targeted response, in the same way that the boy's skin condition was cured in a targeted way. This also means that belief causes biochemical and physics-oriented responses and not the other way around. This is the reason why the placebo and nocebo effects are real and yet a "magical force" that is independent of the presently acknowledged fundamental forces of the universe. They help prove there is a mind-body connection.

Moving a PSI wheel (which is a small pyramid-shaped piece of paper balanced on a pin) by using telekinesis causes rotation through the power of the mind is a metaphysical phenomenon that many have reportedly been able to do. I do not believe all the YouTube demonstrations are hoaxes. I have been able to do this myself on many occasions and the fact a third party can request that I stop the wheel and change its rotation on their command illustrates that will (intent) causes the resulting wheel behaviour. Breath is held to eliminate breathing impact. It can be done from a distance, therefore, eliminating the chance of convection, also, although it would be hard to use convection to cause the wheel to stop and alter its rotation at will. I can be seen performing this on my YouTube channels—The Meaning of Life by M. H. Forrest and The Simple Truth by M. H. Forrest.

 https://www.youtube.com/channel/UC2dMaviepWT-naAsYtaa8Ahg

https://www.youtube.com/channel/UCkBfTayGg-h7i3glX8O7zG1Q

Ironically, I would not be disappointed if some other rational (non-metaphysical) explanation ultimately explained what is happening with the PSI wheel experiment. The important thing, for me, is that it forces us to look at all the phenomena we take for granted and look at how everything works in terms of ultimate cause(s). Understanding the anatomy and physiology of what facilitates human movement is one thing, including seeing the results of millions of years of evolution that created this complex engineering feat, but we take the transition from random to nonrandom (the mobility of basic life forms and a will that coexists with all such movement) for granted. In other words, looking at the various classes of metaphysical phenomena forces us to think about how the ultimate cause(s) driving *"normal"* phenomena are equally unexplained but treated as though they are explained, due to hyper-normalization. When consciousness is viewed as fundamental and something which inherently has (and expresses) supreme intelligence, many of the so-called paranormal phenomena seem far less extraordinary. And many of the so-called metaphysical phenomena are merely scientific phenomena awaiting to be recategorized as truths.

Many metaphysical phenomena, that are still deemed impossible by some, have already been shown, using the scientific method, to be real. One example, which has previously been mentioned, is the impact of intent on Random Number Generators. Professor Dean Radin devised an experiment that provided a 50/50 chance of a *"click"* being played and a 50/50 chance of a vocal clip being played on each of 100 runs. The first part of each run commenced with the generation of a "1" or "0" but whatever the outcome was, it led to another level where 80% of the time the outcome would stay the same and 20% of the time it would flip to the opposite outcome. Another level down, and the same thing happened, i.e. 80% of the outcome at that time stayed the same and 20% flipped to the opposite outcome.

With no human mind intervention, the result was 50% clicks and 50% vocal clip plays. The objective of the experiment was for the player to try and get as many of 100 runs to be vocal clips. After

doing the 100-run experiment many times over with many participants, the average vocal clip plays came out at 56%.

This was done in laboratory conditions and the subjects were
not people who claimed special psi powers. The odds of getting 56%
are about 1000 to 1, therefore, it is unlikely that the outcome that
was aligning with intention did so by chance. The experiment was
also repeated numerous times with the same results. What is interesting is that the 100 trials produced roughly 50% "1s" and 50% "0s"
at the level one Random Number Generation (so the initial "1" and "0"
generator was unaffected by the intent), and the tendency towards
the 56% began at the next level, and the effect was amplified at the
final level. Also, the strongest stand against the random outcomes
was mainly quite early on in the 100 runs. This pattern was consistent, therefore, it seems to show that the journey toward the 56%
is nonlinear (and "*pulls*" the experiment outcomes in an ordered but
nonlinear way from the initial intention to the 56% average that we
see at 100 runs). I believe the reason may be the same one that causes
the increasing neuronal activity in the Libet experiment from the
readiness potential point up to the motor action point. It is the intent
outside of linear time preceding, in linear time terms, the augmentation of the effect into our intent-based perceived reality—which
appears as retro causality if the incorrect interpretation is used. In
other words, the intent causes manifestations that are instantaneous
but unfold in a way that is perceived as linear, in accordance with
physical material realm "rules." The reason there is little or no effect
via intent at the 50/50 level one (where "1" or "0" binary outcomes
are generated randomly) is likely to be because the effect of intent
will be strongest when it is closest to what the observer seeks to
influence. Just as the strength of gravity or magnetism correlates
with proximity, it would seem logical that psychic energy influence
is more likely to be strongest at the point just before the outcome
would have settled in its non-influenced way, had it not been for the
application of human intent.

The weakening effect over time witnessed may be partly due to fatigue but is also possibly due to the impact of interacting multiple intents, as linear time progresses. It represents the likelihood that the further into the future we explore, the weaker the intent of a single conscious agent is. The reason is that if you wish to pick up a glass in front of you, for example, the probability for all intents and purposes is one (certain) but if you wish to buy a Ferrari in a year's time there are infinite interacting intents that significantly weaken the probability. Without some individual points of consciousness using the power of intent, outcomes tend towards average (literally). Some *"know,"* in their egoic mind focus of attention state, by instinct or via enlightenment of such power and so influence the manifestations in the various multiverses which contain shared data. The more they know I AM that, I AM the more powerful the intent and effects. Once all points of consciousness become aware that I AM that, I AM the binary world falls away because there are no points of consciousness to buy into the information illusion. In spiritual terms, this is the New Earth. The fact there is an undeniable effect in Dean Radin's experiments is far more important than the distribution of the effect over the 100 outcomes per person and the fact he recorded the effect only in the lower tiers of the switch over system but it is worthwhile considering various interpretations for these also.

Of course, in the world of metaphysics, it can be difficult to separate the potentially feasible, but not as yet accepted by mainstream science, from *"woo-woo."* One example of this is monoatomic gold and other elements (orbitally rearranged). This is purported to be the Philosopher's Stone, which organized religion dismissed as fantasy and fictitious alchemy. Some believe that the stance by organized religion was merely propaganda and that the process was never about gold creation but about its purification.

Monoatomic gold is not simply an allotrope but is a collapsed structure that manifests as a white powder that allegedly has many *"magical"* properties. One of the purported properties is its levitation capability (not just itself but the material that holds it, i.e. containers). Another is superconductor properties with no loss of energy in transmission because it is contactless and, therefore, lacks resistance. It also, allegedly, has inherent intelligence such that faulty cells (cancer) can become self-aware and *"conscious"* of the deviation from its *"intended"* form and self-rectify. ORMUS—based on the same science/pseudoscience claims to have equally magnificent effects.

Another controversial claim is that water can be affected by words and emotions, such that when it turns into ice crystals, the beauty of the crystals reflects this. Here is a short video demonstrating the results of Dr. Masaru Emoto's Water Experiment.

https://youtu.be/Moz82i89JAw

Because I haven't spent decades researching or observing these alleged phenomena, I do not have a strong opinion on which claims will be correct and which are a product of wishful thinking. Of course, advocates of these types of phenomena are absolutely certain that there is a real effect that is at odds with most people's everyday experiences, but being at odds with most people's experiences or beliefs does not mean they should all automatically be dismissed as impossible. My contention is that it is quite difficult to determine what the truth is when it comes to certain alleged phenomena, and this problem is shared with the issue of trying to determine which conspiracy theories are true and which are not. This is looked at separately in a later chapter.

The reason why I am so interested in metaphysics is that the alleged abilities/gifts to sense and/or utilize such phenomena means our reality is far richer than meets the eye and all known senses. And this, in turn, gives a greater insight into the meaning of life (reality) in its broader sense. It also adds weight to the hypothesis that there is a primacy of consciousness because many of the phenomena relate to the potential power of the mind/consciousness. Of course, it also explores the potential for *real magic* to be possible in light of the fact that consciousness itself seems to possess fundamental intelligence (which is already evidenced via the placebo effect, the creation of sense experiences, Random Number Generator influence, laboratory tested psi phenomena, etc.).

Not all scientists turn their back on metaphysics. A controversial biologist, Rupert Sheldrake, has conducted many experiments purportedly showing that some doubted phenomena appear to be real (with *"statistically significant"* results). He has demonstrated that many dogs behave excitedly as their owners begin their journey home. So that the dogs weren't getting excited based on routines that made homecoming times predictable, the owners were assigned random times to set off home. The dogs were filmed all day and there was seemingly a strong correlation, in many cases, where the dog's excited/restless behaviour coincided with the time the owner started their journey home. Other scientists have looked at the statistics, and one sceptic participated in further research to assess the experiment and results. Some sceptics believe that the conditions and/or a misinterpretation of results were responsible for his conclusions. However, Sheldrake maintains that the statistics are much too strikingly correlated to be by chance alone and that he followed good scientific practice to assure that it was not only *"fitting"* statistics that were focused upon. Being a super intelligent individual, he is very aware of the scientific method and I am sure he will, therefore, have accounted for this and operated to the best of his ability. It seems most mainstream scientists are poised to dismiss all of his work without due consideration based purely on the fact that it contradicts their worldview.

Sheldrake also believes (and has studied) a concept he has named *"morphic resonance."* This is a highly controversial concept, which suggests that animals can evolve via information transmission, regardless of apparent space-time barriers. When an animal which is not in the proximity of a group of others of the same species adopts behaviour that is identical to that group, despite separation, it will be deemed as coincidence by the vast majority of western scientists. Sheldrake hypothesizes that this behaviour transmits without direct learning (i.e. the behaviour spreads quite rapidly but without the assumed necessity for visual learning and proximity). Given that *"spooky action at a distance"* is accepted for entangled particles and the double-slit experiment seems to indicate consciousness can also become entangled with coherent particles, it would seem feasible that one point of consciousness can be entangled with another (and that this would be particularly apparent throughout a species that were not long ago derived from a common ancestor). This consciousness entanglement would also explain the pet dog's apparent knowledge of its owner's journey home.

Sheldrake has also researched whether an individual can sense they are being watched. There have been many thousands of studies conducted into this phenomenon/belief and, again, there appear to be statistically significant results showing that there is such an effect. In fact, this sensing of being observed can allegedly be sensed via CCTV cameras too (even many miles away). Many security guards have admitted that they were already familiar with this phenomenon and that they specifically avoid looking directly at a subject when watching them live (because the subject, it seems, can often detect that they are being watched). To mainstream science, this is the stuff of fairy tales. However, as space-time can be transcended by consciousness, as well as quantum particles, it is not so extraordinary. Of course, the space-time containing de-coherent properties (stable illusions) remains, therefore, we effectively have one foot in both realms, although the non-manifest one is only perceived subconsciously, except, perhaps, by those who claim they can fully transcend our conditioned reality at will.

It is worth pointing out that, according to spirituality, all perspectives are simply those of different points of consciousness, focused on a false binary (perceived physical) realm and that ultimately the subconscious resides in true reality, and so what we consider to be *"out there"* is a lie by virtue of the fact we can show linear time and space are illusory.

When one person believes A and another believes B, we feel certain that the only options are that either A is right, B is right, or both are wrong. The idea that both could be right would seem to be $p(x)=0$ (read impossible!). I am not talking about opinion-based issues, such as political beliefs (which, of course, are emotionally based and, almost exclusively, depend on how policies affect the beholder of the beliefs, i.e. highly influenced by the *"selfish gene"* that is inherent in such opinions). Can we really be certain that two diametrically opposing views for seemingly binary only outcomes *both* being true is always $p(x)=0$ (read impossible) though?

For example, if a person visits a Medium and the *"reading"* reveals very specific details, including names and personal information that the Medium cannot have known without hours of detective work (or in some instances, could not have known at all, where the information is *only* known to the person receiving the reading), they may well believe the purported extrasensory perception is real. A sceptic hearing the account would, understandably, look for *"tricks,"* such as the testing of names by the Medium until a reaction is gained. However, although it is blasphemy as far as a materialist scientist is concerned, there is a seemingly impossible chance that both parties are right—and that the closed mind of a sceptic affects what is/can manifest in his or her reality (the difference between *"I will see it when I believe it"* and the usual *"I will believe it when I see it"*). Rational mathematician Alan Turing visited a medium (gypsy) in Blackpool Lancashire and came away from the reading in complete shock. He confessed that certain individuals seemingly knew things that were beyond the explanation of mainstream scientists.

Remember, the *observer* is vital in relativity and in collapsing wave functions (scientists freely acknowledge that the observer affects reality in such cases, and the MIT experiment, referred to earlier, also shows reality can be subjective)—so what if the essence (beliefs) of the observer makes a difference too? This may seem highly speculative but is testable because open-minded scientists could report data that sceptics would have to take seriously.

This is effectively what all the believers in *the "Law of Attraction"* believe. Most scientists will say with absolute certainty that this so-called *"Law"* is a fantastical notion. But many advocates of the *"Law of Attraction"* will claim that they have had many experiences that, when aggregated, go far beyond coincidence.

Many people who purport to be able to perform acts that are paranormal claim that the negative beliefs of observers disrupt their abilities. This may seem to be a philosophy of convenience, but if open-minded scientists and neutral observers can still observe the phenomena under strict conditions, this adds weight both to the assertions of the performers and to the idea that belief itself influences reality.

In the early 1940s, psychologist Gertrude Schmeidler of the City College of New York proposed that people who do not believe in psi subconsciously avoid psi experiences because they do not want to experience them. Alternatively, people who do believe in psi want to see them, so they do. She turned this idea into what she called a *"sheep-goat"* hypothesis, where the sceptics are the stubborn goats and believers are the acquiescent sheep. Questionnaires were used to find out which of the two each person was deemed to be and then psi experiments were done subsequently—and the goats performed as per chance or below and the sheep did better than chance. This effect has been tested for and observed in many experiments since. One person assessed masses of meta-data and the overall result strongly supported the sheep-goat effect, with believers outperforming disbelievers, with odds against chance of over a trillion to one. The person who conducted the analysis, namely psychologist Tony Lawrence of Edinburgh University, concluded that *"the results of this meta-analysis are quite clear—if you believe in the paranormal you will score higher on average in forced-choice ESP tests than someone who does not [believe]."*

Billionaire life coach guru, Anthony Robbins, believes that beliefs affect reality. His intelligence and wealth do not offer assurances to us that he is correct, but as a witness, his credibility is not in doubt.

Although consciousness is an undisputed phenomenon, a more detailed account based on the current understanding of it presently belongs in this chapter because it still remains a mystery to most, if not all, scientists. It is quite ironic because it is the ONLY thing we can be sure of! Our senses are highly unreliable, as we have already seen and, in fact, mean that ultimately, we reside in a 100% mirage, a la "The Matrix." When Descartes wrote the words, "*Cogito, ergo sum*" ("*I think, therefore, I am*")—it should really be "*I am conscious, therefore, I am*" because the actual thought processing can be so misinformed by how evolution (or programming) has developed our perceptions that the only thing that is reliable is this odd state we refer to as consciousness. Better still, it should be, "*I am conscious, therefore, I am. I perceive linear time and space, therefore, I am deceived.*" Descartes was aware that our perceptions are unreliable and even believed that Satan had hijacked our true essence and forced false information ("out there" reality) upon us in order to fully control our experiences. He was ahead of his time in terms of seeing that our sensory perceptions are fallible but was somewhat paranoid when it came to the reasons why this is so.

Matthew Fisher asks, "*Does the brain use quantum mechanics?*" Of course, yes has to be the answer as it is composed of atoms and they follow physics, but he is really asking whether the strange properties of quantum objects—being in two places at once, seemingly able to instantly influence each other over distance and so on—could explain still-perplexing aspects of human cognition. Oxford mathematician, Roger Penrose, proposed than no standard classical model of the brain would ever fully explain how the brain processes thought and conscious experience. That was 1989. Stuart Hameroff, an anaesthetist, suggested a way that quantum effects were perhaps being incorporated into these hard to explain processes. He believes that the protein tubes that make up the neuronal support structure exploit the quantum effects (they exist in *"superpositions,"* as in two different *"shapes"* at once). Each of these *"shapes"* amount to a bit of classical information so this shape-shifting quantum bit or qubit can store twice as much information as its classical counterpart.

Add entanglement to the mix and you get a *"quantum computer"* that can manipulate and store information far more efficiently than any *"classical computer"* (note that some basic quantum computers are now being built). The way that such a computer can arrive at many answers simultaneously, and combine those answers in different ways, would be just the things to explain the brain's peculiar genius.

The idea of protein tubes being the place where the *"magic"* happens has been disputed because the coherent state is so unstable it could not exist long enough in such an environment to be able to behave as consciousness does. Hopefully, it will soon be acknowledged that the consciousness of mind does not reside in the brain but is in a separate realm, and that the brain's constituents and structure (which are ultimately illusory) are primarily focused on space-time information, but also accesses information from the non-manifest realm (e.g. colours). Once science realises that the anatomy of the brain is a perceived phenomenon made from binary information that is quantum information in a perceived collapsed wave function form, then the anatomy and physiology become quite obvious. Every neuron is simply a binary construct with a singularity at its core. Both aspects reside in the quantum realm but the latter cannot be perceived by focused points of attention due to senses honed in on the binary information.

Fisher's personal interest began because a few people close to him had a mental illness. Nobody truly knows how any of the psychiatric pharmaceuticals actually work. This is probably because the drugs aim to modify the human mind (not just the anatomy and physiology of the brain). Fisher's interest began with lithium, an ingredient of many mood-stabilizing drugs.

Fisher has spent $20,000 of his own money filing a patent on treating depression and similar mental conditions with compounds enriched in Lithium-6. He acknowledges that this seems unlikely to be a silver bullet and told me, *"While the Li-isotope experiment remains challenging (probably being inconclusive, when the dust settles) one or two of the other experiments (for example, detecting Posner molecules, nanometer Calcium-phosphate clusters) are looking encouraging. We have funding for another 1.5 years, and are trying to secure 3 years more of funding."* He admits that quantum cognition could be the key to what is currently missing from neuroscience. From my own viewpoint, I envisage a collaboration between advanced software developers and neuroscientists could lead to solutions (using noninvasive Nano-technology). Elon Musk's Neuralink system will be able to do this in a cruder way but it is a highly invasive procedure. In the long term, ways of enhancing belief (placebo) is the solution as, ultimately, there is only a perceived physical world and so the mind can be worked on to repair what is manifest including the symptoms that correlate with anatomy and physiology issues.

Life has had billions of years (in illusory linear time terms) to discover/harness quantum mechanics, as appears to have happened with the Quantum European Robin, discussed earlier. I think atomic nuclei and their associated *"spin"* and how the nucleus *"feels"* electric and magnetic fields is one of the areas where things can go wrong and why some of the drugs that do *"work"* (sometimes, partly) help to cure the problem. It is an identical process to the one that seems to explain the robin's quantum mechanics sensory perception system.

Photosynthesis also uses quantum mechanics. It is said that insufficient photon bombardment exists, and evolution has provided plants with the trick of *"consciously"* manifesting collapsed waveforms at its convenience (by intent) to provide the necessary concentration. When photons reach the plants, they transform into other particles that need to reach the energy centres. There are countless chlorophyll molecules in the way and a *"random walk"* would result in very few getting to the *"target."* Accordingly, the particles maintain a coherent state and take all possible routes in this state, only collapsing when hitting the *"target"*—making the process 99 percent efficient. **If that is not some signature of consciousness and will at a microscopic level, I do not know what is.**

The current methodologies for tackling mood disorders is crude, at best, and results in many unwanted side-effects, as well as partial remission or treatment-resistant depression. For a myriad of reasons, things are being disturbed at a quantum level and this appears to be why these current methodologies are lacking and why the condition is a growing epidemic. When you consider the number of things that could change the background environment of the brain and, therefore, affect it, it is little wonder that this delicate system has gone out of balance in millions, if not billions, of humans.

Regarding the subject of consciousness in general, physicist and writer, Tom Campbell has concluded, as I have done, that consciousness is primary and is the ultimate cause of our reality. In his trilogy, *"My Big T.O.E."* (T.O.E. being theory of everything), which I read many years after the first draft of my first book, he suggests that there were two metaphysical givens. One was pure consciousness and the other was evolution. His theory suggests that pure (benign) consciousness experienced ripples that effectively gave rise to differential states (like binary). This, according to Campbell, led to nonphysical material realms as well as a number of physical material realms (with space-time and rule sets). These rule sets can vary, and the physical material realm we are in has its own arbitrary rule set. He believes that via evolution, consciousness *"aims"* to lower its entropy (which is synonymous with increasing love). In other words, our space-time realm is a computer (Mind) generated illusory state that is a sort of training ground aimed at increasing the order of consciousness (to contribute to an overall system that is doing the same). Unsuccessful realms have been or will be eliminated by the evolutionary process.

The main problem with this hypothesis is that it seems a highly inefficient system. Given the computing power (thus intelligence) required to create and house these multiverses, there would seem to be more efficient methods that would avoid the inclusion of child mortality, mental handicapping, and the vast majority of *"points of consciousness"* (humans and animals) not even understanding this near impossible to decipher *true purpose*, etc. Not only is the system *"cruel,"* keeping the rules hidden from the *"players,"* is completely illogical (as is permitting the emergence of players unable to play). We have also seen how free will can be impacted by phenomena that are outside the control of individuals, e.g. brain tumours. The consequence of this precludes the affected individual agents from being able to contribute to the consciousness entropy reduction programme (and is, therefore, another inefficiency or bug in the system). If consciousness is merely flowering via an experiential space-time (and potentially nonphysical material realms), then these inconvenient birth pangs may make more sense, despite them still being far from ideal when they permit sentient beings to suffer. This alternative is not so different from Campbell's interpretation, but it does make a huge difference in terms of how we view suffering because in his model it is a part of the programming rather than the unfortunate consequence of conscious agents operating in an environment they cannot fully control.

Campbell reports to have encountered many beings from many physical and nonphysical dimensions (using transcendental meditation) so his knowledge will have been enhanced via these entities, as well as gained through deduction. Many disciples of scientism will think he is perhaps deluded and that these encounters are illusory. However, given the evidence in this book that science is far from complete (and instantly denies the possibility of anything deemed metaphysical), I would not be so sure. Reference to *"my big T.O.E."* has been included in the metaphysics chapter because it is certainly far from mainstream science. My two books carry vast amounts of evidence about how reality is actually constructed and this means I am presenting a T.O.E. (theory of everything) that requires no leap of faith.

Given our universe is constructed by, and made up of, consciousness, and the space and time phenomena are contrived to assure individual points of consciousness are fully immersed, there are only two reasons that come to mind as to why this has occurred. One would be as a purification process, whereby deviations from pure consciousness are segregated and placed into an experiential realm as a means to bring it back into line. This would also incorporate religious interpretations and allegories such as the fall from grace and rejection from paradise (Garden of Eden) to the inclusion of a form of pure (Christ) consciousness within the contrived realm to act as a catalyst in the process (dying for the sins of man). The other explanation is that consciousness, set in an infinite realm of no space and no time, would potentially create an experiential realm(s) and devise conditions that allow for creative freedom as well as conditions that allow Universal Consciousness to become self-aware through conscious agents. And that we are a part of the flowering of consciousness within that realm that all become more aware of our intent capabilities in the becoming process.

The proof of space-time being illusory has been mentioned several times as well as the fact it is digital and quantized. Both time and space (distances) have minimum quantities in our realm (known as Planck time and Planck length, respectively, as discussed earlier) which means there is nonexistence between one point and the next nearest one. As such, there is no time between two such points of time and no dimension between two such points in space (which means it is quantized, i.e. forced into one point or the other only). This certainly adds credibility to the idea that consciousness manifests in a computer-like form within our reality, as does the existence of the four-character *digital code in all DNA*. Add to this the fact that our physical reality has only mathematical properties, it becomes difficult to ignore what James Jeans observed, *"The universe begins to look more like a giant thought than a great machine. Mind no longer appears to be an accidental intruder in the realm of matter we ought rather to hail it as a Creator and governor of the realm of matter."*

Metaphysics can essentially be ignored, unless you either have an interest in it or it becomes relevant to your life, because you experience it involuntarily. However, I think it has been of interest to mankind throughout history because it holds the secrets of what is really going on, despite what our unexamined senses would suggest. Given that consciousness seems to be all that there is, what appears to be mysterious suddenly becomes comprehensible. Life after death, for example, is not only real but is the only truth, because the space and time we perceive arises along with illusory life circumstances and this only becomes apparent when we transcend normal mind states or after biological death. All the seemingly odd behaviour in quantum mechanics also becomes comprehensible because there is no real physical separation due to ubiquitous entanglement; and particle journeys do not really take place in space-time, as perceived, which explains the apparently odd delayed choice results in the double-slit experiment. Scientists know that the behaviour they encounter in quantum mechanics is metaphysical and there is even an expression that has arisen because of this: "*Shut up and calculate.*" The fact that these calculations enable scientists to manipulate physical reality quite successfully has led to hyper-normalization, whereby scientists and most of the general public take pattern recognitions to mean understanding. As this book is revealing, base reality is far from how it is portrayed by mainstream scientists.

In defence of those with very sceptical minds, we already saw how easily the mind can create a reality that is contrary to the information that is received by the brain such as in the McGurk effect, for example. In one experiment, boat passengers on Loch Ness witnessed a large stick rising up from the surface of the water and then slowly dropping down again and many of them reported having sighted the Loch Ness Monster. It is likely most of them were genuinely hallucinating rather than lying and it was expectation that fueled how the information was processed. Given that the map is not the territory and nothing in our 3D mind's eye model is a facsimile of the phenomena upon which the mind's eye model is based, it is not surprising that our minds provide fallible interpretations. Even when we believe they are accurate, they cannot be so because they are mind-made interpretations. This does not mean anything goes because there is an agreed upon hallucination we call reality and most of the so-called "out there" information is objective, even though interpretations differ. What post-materialist science is showing though is that even the information, such as the 13.8 billion years' worth that is coming at you from all angles, is a product of consciousness and that space-time is a perceived phenomenon in the same way that colours are. In other words, non-locality is not confined to the quantum realm but is all that there is. Only individual points of consciousness cocreate and experience the physical material realm and the perceived information that forms it (collapsed wavefunctions) and space-time that, in accordance with the agreed upon hallucination, stores information as it expands over illusory linear time.

14

SPIRITUALITY

"Science and Truth are simple phenomenon of nature,
but it is the known that is preventing us from mastering
the unknown."

Chandrakanth Natekar

This subject is really a continuation of the chapter on metaphysics but is so integral to the meaning of life it deserves special attention.

Spirituality, unlike meaning, is not universally felt by unconscious people. But a significant number do get to feel it or, at least, subscribe to it by virtue of their beliefs. Are they deluded or are rationalists the deluded ones? Of course, one of its greatest forms, organized religion, is more likely to be based on geography and family (hand-me-downs) than on a rational choice based on research, personal experiences and introspection. This does not automatically mean there are no "*truths*" within them, but it does automatically mean that fallible human thoughts and practices will have contaminated many potential truths.

People such as Eckhart Tolle, Russell Brand, David Icke, Jim Carrey, and many others are no doubt correct in that there is a spiritual dimension, but nobody can deny that we are in animal form and that our behaviours are primarily driven by the products of evolution.

Spirituality is a difficult subject because, although evidence purportedly exists in favour of it being a fundamental truth, it is, in the main, a faith-based system. There are many reasons why it seems as though it is possibly a part of reality, and there are many reasons to doubt it too (especially the accounts of man passing down through the ages with the errors, biases, and the effects of Chinese Whispers assuring that some corruption of the truth is inevitable, as is the case with organized religion, which has already been highlighted). There are many writings in the scriptures that make the idea of God more terrifying than the idea of no God.

Too many unjustified negative *"God's Dice"* happenings in our reality also call into question a God of the type that organized religions claim is ruling our world. For example, Stephen Fry was asked during an interview with Gay Byrne what he would ask God, given the chance. Specifically, he was asked, *"...And you're confronted by God. What would Stephen Fry say to Him, Her or It?"* and he replied, *"Bone cancer in children... What's that about? How dare you!.... How dare you create a world in which there is such misery that is not our fault. It's not right. It's utterly, utterly evil. Why should I respect a capri-*

cious, mean-minded, stupid God that creates a world that is so full of injustice and pain? That's what I'd say." He was then asked, *"And you think you're going to get in?"* His reply was, *"No, but I wouldn't want to. I wouldn't want to get in on His terms. They are wrong. Now; if I died and it was Pluto/Hades … and if it was the 12 Greek gods, then I would have more truck with it because they didn't pretend not to be human in their appetites and in their capriciousness.... They didn't present themselves as all knowing, all seeing, all kind, all beneficent – because the God that created this universe (if it was created by God) is quite clearly a maniac. Utter maniac. Totally selfish. We have to spend our life on our knees thanking him?... What kind of God would do that? Yes, the world is very splendid, but it also has in it insects whose whole life cycle is to burrow into the eyes of children and make them blind. And eat outwards from the eyes. WHY? Why did you do that to us? We (He/She/It) could easily have made a creation in which that didn't exist. It is simply not acceptable. So, atheism is not only about not believing there is a God – but on the assumption of if there is one; what kind of God is it? It's perfectly apparent that He is monstrous, utterly monstrous and deserves no respect whatsoever. The moment you banish Him, life becomes simpler, purer, cleaner... more worth living in my opinion".* If you have not seen it—the look on Gay's (the interviewer) face is hilarious:

> 🔗 **https://www.youtube.com/watch?v=-suvkwNYSQo**

Of course, this is the tip of the iceberg as there is an endless list of circumstances that can arise that we perceive as horrific. If the cause of certain horrific events lies with nature, as opposed to the act of terrorists, for example, it is no less horrific but somehow has to be accepted; but if there is a God—then both are inexcusable. The philosophy of convenience which a religious leader is bound to adopt: *"It is not for the mind of man to know the (big picture) plans of God"* certainly does not, or should not, pacify us. It is, however, the only way to try to rationalize these situations rather than admit God "*allowed*" it. Hurting victims and those connected to the victims has no justification.

Eckhart Tolle expressed a similar view about the "*justification*" for mental health issues within our reality. He suggested that because the "self" is an optical delusion and everyone and everything is an interconnected part of the flowering of consciousness, there is no "self" to suffer the mental health issues (and other diseases) and it represents a blockage in the overall evolutionary process. He may be right but it is not so consoling for the *points* of consciousness (people or animals) that have been endowed with pain/pleasure sensing capabilities because even if it is an illusory state that only exists in the realm where consciousness arises to "*experience itself*," then this capacity for pain and horror would at least seem to make it amoral. Of course, because there is truly a way to break down the mind-made "*self*" delusion (and override the mind created illusory negative experiences, such as pain), then only the unenlightened suffer. Some believe that the truth is shown to all when we pass from this temporary realm with its inherent perception inhibitors (unconscious behaviour in the case of animals and mind identification in the case of humans).

Of course, there is a distinction between an all-seeing and all-knowing God, and a Universal Consciousness that exists in a more authentic and infinite non-manifest realm, as well as a flowering experiential realm that includes perceived randomness (which is really the result of interacting intents). In the latter case, negative outcomes are neither planned nor preventable, and are only negative to highly conscious beings that happen to emerge and falsely perceive themselves as separate due to having limited minds, therefore, this "*Creator*" cannot be seen as responsible in the same way as God perhaps could. Conscious agents in a waking consciousness state perceive circumstances occurring in linear time, many of these happenings appearing random and highly negative. As mentioned earlier, the fact there is a MASTER intent and infinite SUNSIDIARY intents means there is no randomness at all. However, there is a kind of karma.

Karma is not quite as it is often perceived to be. It is the result of mind duality and the expression of negative emotions in a perceived false, *"out there"* world. How it truly works is known as the Law of Attraction in that what you focus upon emotionally in a world within, manifests in the perceived world without. It then becomes self-fulfilling as the negative outcomes endorse the feelings through confirmation bias. Only the TRUTH can set you free.

If consciousness is within and intelligently governing all that is, it could be seen as synonymous with spirit. Spirit is believed to be infinite, presenting in life form in our realm but belonging to a spaceless and timeless realm in a formless state. This fits with the idea of a primacy of consciousness, which this book evidences, as in the phenomenon that creates our material world from its unmanifest state of infinite possibilities.

I believe biological life experiences on an individual level is a kind of balance sheet, and if the quality of life (joy, happiness, fulfilment, meaning, etc.) is at a zero, or worse, then there seems to be no obvious point to it all. Or, as Victor Frankl said, *"Some worlds are worth living in, some are not."* If it is generally good, then one may as well enjoy this absurd reality, but there is something about the inevitability of death (self and loved ones) that reminds us we are mere gene transfer mechanisms *"designed"* to play the baton passing game of the DNA, and we are little different from bacteria but happen to have evolved a range of senses and self-awareness, providing our egos with ammunition that makes us feel special. Having said that, because the existence of a spiritual dimension is hard to deny, then this experience of life is only a part of some unimaginably complex *"game"* and a kind of illusion, therefore, it would make sense to enjoy this part of the journey while we can, even if the going got really tough. Afterall, whether you believe it or not it is effectively a video game. Furthermore, intent and action can change individual realities.

Most atheists would like religion to be eliminated multilaterally but this is never going to happen. And besides, the key issue is not so much with religion but with human nature. Some of the impressionable young *"religious"* men (usually men) will find opportunities, such as patriotism (*"sugarcoated racism"*) to fuel their predisposition to be violent and kill members of out-groups. Of course, the unshakeable beliefs inherent within religion, combined with the fact that some of the teachings condone and even promote violence, make for a toxic breeding ground. Logic is a blunt instrument to all but a small number of these people, therefore, we have to rely on a morally based legal system to try to prevent their evil behaviours (and punish and rehabilitate where prevention sadly fails). Banning religious teaching in schools would make very little difference. The community and family would still teach it. Ultimately, recognising we are ALL One and bringing about a ubiquitous awakening is the solution. This, of course, is no mean feat.

What if life is multiple personality disorder in the extreme? The only "solution," besides biological death, for every individual point of consciousness (manifest as lifeforms, perhaps including suns and planets as well as sentient beings) would be mass awareness amongst these fragments of Mind that they are all ultimately One Mind. This is what advocates of Solipsism believe but it includes an additional step that involves becoming aware that ultimately there is no YOU rather than concluding there is only YOU. For those who believe Universal Consciousness is having infinite experiences in a process of becoming, where separateness is a kind of optical delusion, the question is a rhetorical one.

In the latter part of *The God Delusion* book, Dawkins is critical of the Amish tradition for stay-at-home education/schooling (a little ironic given that he also says that his wife, who hated schooling, saw it as compulsory whereby he suggested it was only our conditioning that made it so). Their motive may be *"religious"* to some degree but it seems to me to be as much to do with a cultural desire to abstain from modern living. If it could be shown that their life was far more fulfilling overall, is it justifiable to inflict modern culture on them? There is virtually no incidence of depression amongst these people and yet, in the West, we are having an epidemic that is growing exponentially. It is almost certainly their sense of community and problem sharing that is largely responsible for the immunisation. Who are we to *"correct"* their way of life because we perceive ours as the *RIGHT* one? This is little different from the *"Our God is the right God and your God is fictitious"* type arrogance.

Jay Glazerion, known to me via Chris Langan's CMTU Facebook Group, pointed out the following relating to this matter, *"A study [I referenced] looked at happiness in Americans, and correlated that with ancestor origins [per individual] after adjusting for religion/income. They found a correlation between happiness in country of origin and the individual American. In addition, Danish/Dutch DNA had the best genes associated with serotonin uptake. Given the Amish link to Dutch, it is not surprising to see low depression. Although, this could be due to them not letting their sick reproduce."* Regardless of the various factors that influence the happiness and fulfilment of the Amish, if their beliefs and practices are moral and they do not cause harm, they should surely be allowed to believe what they wish and their critics should be more interested in what society as a whole can learn about the factors that immunize them against mood disorder.

Changing society's habit of labelling from *"a Catholic child"* to *"a child brought up as Catholic"* would make no difference either. If the concept of Catholic is offensive, the wording difference is semantics. It is the power of beliefs and the fact that violence is in our nature (and, often, condoned and encouraged) that causes the problem. Changes in beliefs are possible, though, and time will tell how religion(s) will evolve. But, as mentioned earlier, religion is likely to remain as long as humanity does. Nothing short of genetic and nurturing intervention will ever change that.

Human belief variations do not appear to reflect gene fitness. You can believe in all kinds of falsehoods and still function as a survival and reproduction machine. Although innovations in science and technology hold true by incremental changes that in the long term tend to prove their worth, superstitions can live on regardless of the truth. These are neither rigorously tested nor are they detrimental in the survival and reproduction game, so it is not so surprising beliefs vary so much.

Although illusory, there seems to be considerable evidence pointing to a lack of spirituality/truth in religion(s). For example, the ease with which millions of brilliantly *"designed"* humans (that were billions of years in the making) can instantly be annihilated through accident, war, or disease makes it hard to believe that anything other than blind and purposeless evolution is at play. On the other hand, the miraculous unexplained ultimate cause(s) and unreasonable order of our reality (and the existence of phenomena in general) point to the fact there is some kind of Superior Intelligence. Furthermore, the millions of near-death experience accounts, and the fact that many metaphysical phenomena are real, cannot be ignored. The MASTER intent versus the infinite SUBSIDIARY intents discussed a number of times now, create the agreed upon hallucination we call reality.

A sense of spirituality can be induced by the so-called *"God Helmet."* I remember Richard Dawkins being amused by a nun's response to this. She said that it was pleasing that science was able to show there is a capacity for spirituality and how certain regions of the brain were involved in providing a portal. He expected the helmet to be taken as undisputed evidence that the state was imaginary because it can be artificially induced. However, she saw it as a fundamental phenomenon that exists in all (possibly a dormant sense in many) and could be kindled via certain means. Her reasoning is logical. After all, we can move our limbs through a *will* to do so and, yet, if electronically stimulated the same effect can be produced. This does not mean that willed movement itself is not real just because a counterfeit version can be caused through external means.

298

We know that meaning is, in a sense, real, yet can be *"turned off,"* and although senses can be tricked, there seems to be an independent state of spirituality as there is with meaning. In the same way that what is meaningful to some has no meaning to others, it would make sense that what fulfils the sense of spirituality and/or religiosity in some, will not in others (and some will not have any sense of it). There is intrinsic meaning and there is a *"true"* reason why the manifestation of the sense of spirituality/religiosity exist, as their potentiality and actuality gives them a fundamental status within reality. Despite the fact our main senses can be tricked (e.g. mind-altering, drug-induced hallucinations), they only cause the mind (consciousness) to *"mess"* with the existing sense capabilities, giving unusual variations of the experiences we are familiar with. In other words, even if our minds are able to create distortions of *"normal"* reality, the hallucinations are only ever an exaggeration of what is normally created by senses that are fundamental, although ironically there is evidence that brain activity reduces which could support the idea that the brain acts as a filter. In fact, the agreed upon hallucination we call reality is a drop in the ocean subset of the infinite possibilities/manifestations available in experiential form. Accordingly, the experience enhanced hallucinations that we deem to be a false reality are nearer to truth because the limitations of the imprisoning focus of attention are lifted—albeit temporarily.

DMT is a mind-altering substance known as *"The Spirit Molecule,"* and mainstream science would say that DMT *"trips"* are, without doubt, a hallucination. However, some scientists and other reliable witnesses are convinced perception is taken into an alternate dimension and that it is an alternate reality (reportedly, more real than the one we reside in normally). The scientific stance is nothing less than prejudice based on how it perceives reality should be, but quantum physics has already shown us that we can never fully rely upon what is intuitive and we know that our senses are limited and highly fallible too. Much of this book has been dedicated to showing just how much the map differs from the territory in that the mind's eye model may be useful in helping navigate our fully immersive virtual world (dreamworld) but is useless when it comes to understanding the functioning and cause of base reality.

Occam's Razor would suggest that a DMT *"trip"* is a hallucination. But Occam's Razor offers no assurance that the answer with the fewest assumptions is actually right.

A subject that fits equally well in a chapter on metaphysics or one on spirituality is, the *"Law of Attraction"* (made famous by the book and docu-movie, *The Secret*). As already discussed, it suggests that each person has the power within them to manifest what they desire. All it takes is true desire, belief and focus. Advocates of it also suggest that negative events manifest due to thinking also. Therefore, according to them, cancer is self-inflicted. Presumably, all those who die in horrific events, such as 9/11 were lacking positive psychology, as they, too, must have influenced their own fate. It is unlikely that out of a great many people, there will not have been a good proportion who were highly positive along with some who were believers in the Law of Attraction. Having said that, it can still be an effective force but one which comes up against other points of consciousness and their conflicting intent (who are all ultimately YOU anyway). At a deeper level only the life essences are real and all life circumstances are just agreed upon hallucinations and so the horrific deaths are actually a change in binary expression (avatar form) and not a real event, regardless of what our senses scream at us.

The Law of Attraction can seem an unfair phenomenon that prejudices those who are not *"in the know."* What is apparent, though, is that people tend to warm more to people with a positive outlook, consequently success in sales, interviews and dates, etc. is generally enhanced by such a state. This would doubtless provide a level of confirmation bias to the notion of the Law of Attraction because positive results through a more positive attitude could easily be attributed to this more metaphysical concept, when it may just be a result of being positive (although this in of itself is metaphysical but hyper-normalized because it seems so self-evident). The potential viability of the Law of Attraction has already been discussed but the "*sheep-goat*" phenomenon would also suggest that sceptics will see no such "*law*" in view of their beliefs. The fact that human intent can influence Random Number Generators makes the Law of Attraction a real phenomenon even if many people doubt that various anecdotal accounts that indicate it endows practitioners with a kind of super power. The previous clarification of what karma actually seems to be is highly relevant too as karma is synonymous with the Law of Attraction by the definition that was given. It suggests that the polarity of an individual's thoughts and overall energy vibration impacts the experience they have of the "out there" reality. This extends to the phenomenon called synchronicity also, which reportedly features in a person's life more and more as their vibration rises.

To many people, the existence of spirituality is highly debatable. For them, proof may only arise when it is time to depart this realm. Or maybe evidence that they cannot doubt will present itself before such time. However, the plausible idea proposed in this book, that consciousness is fundamental and everything consists of it, would suggest that Einstein's view of God and spirituality was right. He did not spell out that individual points of consciousness are eternal and that we simultaneously exist in the true eternal realm whilst temporarily residing in space-time. However, he did go as far as acknowledging a "*superior Mind,*" the delusion of our separateness and the illusion of past, present, and future.

Many people live their life without much regard to spirituality. However, it does not follow that it has to be illusory. Like the air we breathe, it is simply there whether you are conscious of it or not. Spirituality certainly fits in with the primacy of consciousness hypothesis because individual points of consciousness coexisting in this universe, and the infinite non-manifest realm, are synonymous with spirits in a material world that ultimately belong to the spirit world. Near death experience accounts coincide with what we would predict them to be, based on the idea that our biological form and space-time are illusory experiences that actually *"take place"* within an infinite now in the realm of infinite possibilities. Although the coincidence could be illusory, the huge number of recorded near death experience accounts and the overwhelming evidence within our physical realm that it is a contrived holographic universe consisting of mind-made space-time means that both effectively support each other. Furthermore, the validation of either increases the probability of the other being real, as they are both descriptions of the same thing.

15

MORALITY

*"Our failure to discern a universal good does not record
any lack of insight or ingenuity, but merely demonstrates
that nature contains no moral messages framed in human
terms. Morality is a subject for philosophers, theologians,
students of the humanities, indeed for all thinking people.
The answers will not be read passively from nature;
they do not, and cannot, arise from the data of science. The
factual state of the world does not teach us how we, with
our powers for good and evil, should alter or preserve it in
the most ethical manner."*

Stephen Jay Gould

There is no doubt that altruism and symbiotic behaviour were a vital part of the biological origins of morality. The leading human fitness indicator/desired trait is generosity, including charity (not surprising as it signals support tendencies which are good for potential mates and future shared offspring).

Monkeys have a sense of fairness. When two Capuchin monkeys are fed cucumber pieces in adjacent cages, they eat the treats. Likewise, when they are both given a grape each. However, when one is given a grape and the other is given a piece of cucumber, the monkey given the latter hurls the food out of the cage and shakes the cage in protest. It is illogical, in a sense, because it is tossing a valuable energy source that was perfectly acceptable when the other monkey was also eating this. However, the value of grapes is far greater to them so they display their feelings of unfairness through this behaviour. More advanced primates, such as chimps, will often look to resolve the unfairness through sharing or waiting for the other chimp to receive the same.

When Dawkins discusses morality, he seems unable to note, or at least state, the obvious —that once humans gained high intellect and logic, they could see that organisms have a pain/pleasure axis and could acquire true empathy via cognition. And when human's mental evolution is *"guided"* by logic, it is a powerful tool. It may help when charismatic leaders help emblazon the truth (usually it is not what is said but who says it that counts), but it is logic that tends to be the true winner over time. It is hard to argue a case for black people to be deemed lesser amongst equals (for status, marriage, voting, etc.) when it is understood that they are humans with negligible differences that exist purely due to environmental conditions. Likewise, for women with the minor differences that come with gender. We have explored why racism exists but can and often have risen above innate and emotion-based prejudices by viewing situations with emotional detachment and adopting the use of a rational moral compass.

Recently, it has been discovered through psychology experiments that altruism can be greater towards strangers. When harmless—but quite painful—electric shocks were to be administered to a stranger (maybe someone that could be imagined as old, frail, or have health conditions), the person(s) who effectively determined the number of shocks to be given was more cautious when they did not know the person who was to be shocked. In other words, they generally allowed more shocks to be administered to people they knew than to strangers. This goes against the *"selfish gene"* principle which would predict the opposite. What is clearly apparent is that there is a strong moral compass in humans and even when people deviate from moral behaviour, they sense this as it exerts a force. Once you are able to fully perceive the viewpoint of other people, there is a logic and truth underlying morality.

This would indicate that Stephen Jay Gould's quotation at the start of the chapter is only partially correct. To a greater extent, I think that there is moral behaviour that can be determined through the application of pure logic. As such, it could be determined via algorithms processed by powerful computers and/or AI (and probably be more in line with true morality than Gould's so-called *"all thinking people"* because, as we will see, thinking ability does not assure moral thinking). The main fear expressed about advanced AI is that it may become conscious and given it will be able to outsmart humans by an incomprehensible magnitude, will pose the same potential threat as the kind of alien invasion we often see in science fiction (which according to CE-5 is the opposite of the truth in that advanced alien beings have transcended the egoic mind). A more realistic threat is that, even without consciousness, they will be able to objectively report on moral and immoral practices and the 1 percent that currently owns 99 percent of the world's wealth will have procedures they prefer to keep hidden become transparent (and the injustice of the complete imbalance regarding wealth and legal system will be highlighted by an objective source as well as many illegal practices that got many of them there). This does not mean that wealth and power need to be equally distributed for all of humanity to gain fulfilment but the current imbalance is certainly perverse.

Emotions have evolved (or been *"harnessed"*) due to their usefulness but, in my view, they can stifle progress in the advance of morality. Consequently, I cannot see a time when all humans will become pure moral beings. Notwithstanding that average moral attitudes do seem to shift over time (in the general direction of enlightenment), I do not think intellect and morality are too well correlated. In the same way, there are highly intelligent religious people and highly intelligent atheists, there are intellects with diametrically opposing moral stances and there are people of low intelligence with diametrically opposing moral stances. Accordingly, despite a trend in the direction of improved morality, the idea of a future consisting of pure moral beings is an impossible dream until (if) the whole of humanity awakens.

Although it is an obvious flaw, humans confabulate; they rationalize non-defensible thoughts or actions—they will justify habits like smoking *("John smoked all his life and lived to be 101," "You have to die some way anyway," "I'm a social smoker"*—an oxymoron if ever there was one). People are prejudiced and judges (and lawmakers) are fallible, too, and make judgements and rules they see as morally fair and logical when they are not. It takes time and a form of evolution of its own to make progress towards what is right (incremental changes in both the laws and in the eyes of society). As with racism and crime, where there are people, there are problems—and the goal can only ever be to continually improve the situation because no moral utopia awaits us whilst we remain in the binary realm with the majority bought into the grand illusion.

Vegans are a good example of people adhering to higher moral standards in at least one aspect of their lives. They chose not to see parts of a dead chicken on a plate as indistinguishable from the vegetables. They acknowledge the pain/pleasure axis of other sentient animals and choose a more moral stance by abstaining from eating them. Even though it is contrary to our evolved omnivore status, it is hard to justify the killing now that we have a greater sense of awareness and moral standards. Having said that, I am not a convert to date, although I was for a trial period. I advocate free range products (monitored) and have established a future brand to facilitate the franchising of the practice under strict conditions. This applies to livestock that yield milk, eggs, and wool as well as meat. The technology now exists that will allow vegetable alternatives that will be indistinguishable from meat products as well as meat-based products which were manufactured without anything other than the cell constructs (making them void of any pain potential). Plants have a kind of sentience which is evidenced by their communication systems, the "feeling" capacity of root systems, the sharing of resources via roots, and the capacity to manipulate photons to assure the sun's energy is acquired in the process of photosynthesis in a nonrandom way, but they don't have the capacity for pain in the same way that higher animals do. This will be the same for manufactured meat products also.

I wonder how vegetarians will react to meat that, in the future, is manufactured without the product having lived as a sentient being? I suspect most will avoiding eating it, even though it will be constructed of cells in the same way that vegetables are. In part, this will be due to a belief that meat products aren't as good for us, despite evolutionarily habits persisting for millions of years. The procedures and additives in modern farming means that our present meat products will certainly not be as healthy as they once were, in many cases.

A significant proportion of the world's population probably does not get to contemplate the moral aspects of veganism because they are fighting for every mouthful of meat or rice. For them life is still largely about basic survival so, in the main, they act much like the rest of the animal kingdom. With education and changes in farming practices, it is possible for a transformation. Developing countries such as Thailand already offer a huge range of vegetarian foods and have vegetarian festivals.

Of course, some moral dilemmas are hard to solve by logic alone. For example, is a cure for cancer the Holy Grail for mankind? For a reduction of human suffering, absolutely. But it has its consequential problems—an unsustainable ageing population (a perceived problem, not a real one). This seems to echo Scrooge's "*surplus population*" remark but it is a genuine issue, whilst scarcity is believed, as we head towards the 10 billion population mark (and that is without such a cure). I am not advocating anything other than finding a cure(s), as it is the only humane option. But the highlighted consequences are real in our current paradigm. Even birth control measures would not resolve the problem, as a costly ageing population is already an inevitability and it will prove to be an even greater challenge with a smaller proportion of younger people to provide resources. Of course, once it is known that linear time is illusory and so is space and, therefore, all therein, it becomes a nonissue. At that point, there will be a shift in how the whole world is seen, how scarcity versus abundance is perceived, and how reincarnation works. It truly is a brave new world that is upon us but in an unimaginably good way.

The same situation arises for abortions. Are they moral or immoral? I believe Dawkins' argument that all animals are on an evolutionary continuum, hence, the killing of human embryo is no different/worse than killing a live animal (which vegetarians object to anyway) is a slippery slope. Imagine if we applied that logic to food sources. We forbid the eating of fellow humans (as well as horses and dogs, in most countries). By his logic, we should not be so discerning. I am sure that he would probably refuse the opportunity to eat a dead human embryo and doubtless sees it very differently than eating some other animal. It is odd for a biologist to avoid classifications. They normally thrive on them. Of course, he is mainly referring to the fact that early embryos are not yet self-aware in any sense and, therefore, at this stage are the equivalent to nonhuman animals. It is hard to apply logic alone to these types of situations because they are moral dilemmas where taste and/or religious or spiritual beliefs are unavoidably involved.

Moral dilemmas of this nature will always come down to personal preference until the illusion dies. In the case of rape victim pregnancy (or maybe a child to be born to an abusive lover, drug addict or in dire poverty), it is hard not to justify termination. However, these types of circumstances still form part of the infinite possibilities and experiences.

As already mentioned, there can be no moral utopia, until the "shift" because human nature is fundamentally flawed. We kill for all the reasons other animals do. But we have taken it to a whole new level because we also kill over differing beliefs as described in detail already. This includes different opinions about who created the world or even variations of the same story of who did. How ironic that a system which claims to enhance and enforce moral values is one of the leading causes of murder and other heinous crimes. A stimulated human limbic system can be the worst of all weapons.

Some philosophers suggest that meaning and morality are connected. I think that they are mutually exclusive to some degree. Hitler may have had a life endowed with meaning, yet his beliefs and behaviour were clearly immoral. It is clear that he must have lacked true love, happiness, and fulfilment, though, even if there was some kind of meaning and purpose in his immoral beliefs and acts.

One of the shocking aspects of the human brain, which arises because it is divided into two halves, is the fact that people can have two diametrically opposing beliefs within the same person. However, the dominant belief is what generally manifests. The two minds phenomenon is revealed when brain surgery to alleviate epilepsy is performed which entails severing the connection between the two hemispheres (cutting the corpus callosum). One of the curious side effects can be "alien hand" syndrome—a phenomenon where the hand quite literally has a "mind of its own." For example, a person may select a clothes garment with one hand and the other one grabs it and puts it back. It can even go to strangle a loved one as the non-alien hand is engaged in a loving embrace.

Some psychologists devised a very clever experiment that took account of the fact that the right eye provides information to the left hemisphere of the brain and vice versa for the left eye. The experiment also took into account that speech is usually constructed in the left part of the brain. They played a *"game"* where the *"severed brain"* subject gave verbal answers to questions submitted via the right eye but beforehand gave answers using Scrabble letters where the same questions were given but via the left eye. Because the right brain received information via the left eye and the right brain controls the left hand, the Scrabble pieces that were used to construct the answer were selected and put into position by the left hand. The psychologists were astounded to see that the same subjects were often providing diametrically opposing answers via each method, e.g. religious and atheist beliefs can coexist within the same person.

In another experiment, the subjects were shown an object, such as a banana, via the left eye only and asked to draw what they had seen using their left hand. What was drawn was then seen with both eyes. The subjects were then asked why they had drawn the shape they had. The left part of the brain (that gave the answer) hadn't seen the original object, nor did it communicate with the other side of the brain due to the severing, but it still invariably rationalized why that choice was made, e.g. *"bananas are something quite easy to draw with my left hand."* This has **implications for free will too because it shows how we have evolved to rationalize after subconscious-driven actions**, despite the conscious mind seeing results after the action. Recent research has indicated that overall consciousness is not affected by the split, even though the crosstalk is affected as described. The detailed explanation about how the Libet experiment truly works is highly relevant here too because we know that subconscious INTENT is everything and the fact that the subconscious mind is where many decisions are made does not make individual free will illusory. It just means that the 3D mind's eye model is sometimes the last to discover what the truer self has willed.

How the brain reacts to disgust-provoking imagery is relevant to morality because who a person votes for is highly correlated to this involuntary reaction. This has free-will implications, too, because the way the brain automatically reacts to this type of stimulus determines political leaning and not a rational analysis of policies, as you might expect. It is another example of subconscious behaviour that is subsequently rationalized, giving the illusion of conscious opinion formation.

People who are sensitive to disgusting images (gore, animal remains, bodily waste, etc.) are more likely to vote "right" politically and oppose gay marriage and abortion (due to a bias for bodily and spiritual purity). A learning algorithm compared whole brain responses shown in fMRI scans and compared the response of liberals and conservatives. Despite both reporting similar emotional responses, a pattern of activation differed consistently between the two groups. In other words, there is a neural signature for political leaning. Conservatives not only showed increased activity in brain regions previously implicated in processing disgust, such as the basal ganglia and amygdala, but also in a wide range of regions involved in regulating emotion, attention, and integrating information. In liberals, the brain showed increased activity in different regions but these were just as diverse.

The team from Virginia Tech in Roanoke, who conducted the research, found that these neural signatures of disgust can be used to predict political orientation with striking accuracy.

> "In fact, the responses in the brain are so strong that we can predict with 95 percent accuracy where you'll fall on the liberal-conservative spectrum by showing you just one picture,"

says neuroscientist, Read Montague, the team leader.

There are many other interesting experiments which show how people, in general, react when facing moral dilemmas. In one example, an animated runaway train goods carriage is set to kill a number of track workers, but there is an option in the experiment for the participant to pull a lever which means the carriage will be sent down an alternative piece of track that has only one worker on it. Not surprisingly, the participants pull the level reflexively in order to mitigate the number of deaths. However, in a similar experiment there is a worker on a tower and below is a piece of track that has a similar runaway carriage on it and is likewise heading to a team of workers. This time, pushing the worker from the tower onto the track will bring a stop to the carriage (and save the lives of the group of workers).

Even though the outcome of taking action to prevent the death of the group is the same, the physical pushing of the sacrificial worker makes the act seem very different, and most cannot bring themselves to do this. Clearly, there is a sense of moral wrongdoing when the act is physical rather than mechanical so the behaviour isn't too surprising. One is viewed as proactively causing the death of an individual because of proximity, whereas the other is seen as diverting a disaster towards a bad but better outcome—albeit both outcomes are determined by reflex rather than the result of philosophical analysis. Other experiments have also illustrated the innate drive to divert danger from larger crowds by trying to move the danger (i.e. a gunman) to a place with fewer people. The resistance to push a person over a ledge to their death but willingness to cause a death via mechanical means has implications for modern warfare because remote control actions make the process more mechanical and this seems to diminish the sense of reality.

Although some moral dilemmas cannot easily be solved by cold hard logic alone, I believe that most can, even though emotions generally affect people's ability to make objective/rational judgements. Here are a few controversial examples of modern moral issues:

1. Given that smoking is proven to be bad for the health and kills, should it be banned? Notwithstanding the income

generated through taxes and the implications regarding personal choice—it is a poison and should be treated as such, in my view. It should be treated on a par with a hazardous substance, such as asbestos. Moreover, even with measures in place, secondary inhalation cannot be totally eliminated and so even if some people wish to accept the health risks, despite knowing how serious they are, there is the public health to consider too.

2. Should the tradition of British Royalty be continued? Many of the reasons, such as it boosting the UK economy are not really as portrayed when the matter is looked into more deeply. But should that be a consideration anyway? It is essentially saying that genetics (ironically, not even British descent) is a sufficient reason to bestow "power" and provide huge taxpayer funding upon a privileged few. There is already an issue with 1 percent of the world population owning 99 percent of the wealth as a consequence of the free market economy, compound interest, the fractional reserve banking system and corruption. However, with Royalty, their power status is unearned and not necessarily always desired by them.

    Some Royalists accuse those who desire a Republic of jealousy. This is not so for most, I am sure. The same conclusion arises via a nonemotional moral analysis. Perhaps, if Royalty is happy with the situation and the majority of the country are too—then the tradition should stand, despite the apparent endorsement of class distinction. Ideally, the solution should perhaps come via a referendum. Some believe the passing of the Queen will mark the end of this long-held tradition.

3. Should fox hunting be illegal? Regardless of tradition and the levels of pleasure it may give the participants, it is impossible to justify terrorising a sentient being in this way, resulting in a high likelihood of a vicious death if it does not make a lucky escape. It is barbaric and I cannot imagine there is a viable

argument that would convince anybody that it is moral behaviour.

4. Should Miss World/Universe cease? It is a showing off and judgement of arbitrary gene fitness indicators/beauty. Other than keeping the body in trim and practising speeches, the traits being judged are courtesy of *"God's Dice"* (and the gene fitness of ancestors). Is banning it political correctness going a step too far? Or is the idea of competitions about non-earned "talent" demeaning? Should the celebration of feminine beauty be turned into a circus?

5. Should knife fighting be permitted as a sport? The answer has to be no. But how many would participate for prestige and money, and how many would pay to watch it as a spectator? I suspect the answer would be quite disturbing to those with high moral standards and indicate that human nature is the main reason why there can never be a moral utopia until a shift in consciousness occurs.

6. Should males be objectivized in adverts? If males were replaced by females in some of the British TV adverts that have been aired in recent years, the regulator would have been flooded with complaints. There have been scantily clad ones who are "checked out" at the swimming pool, ones who are being overpowered by a gun-wielding army girl (holding the man down with her stiletto). All the effort that has gone into sexual equality and, yet, what would surely be banned if there were sex role reversals in some adverts seem to be morally acceptable in the era of women's lib.

7. Should soccer stars earn countless millions when there are thousands of families living below the poverty line? I have heard people rationalize the status quo by talking of the "trickle down" effect, where higher taxes are levied and demand for goods is also stimulated by the rich. Apart from the fact the "trickle down" effect has been shown not to

work well at all, if the State used even higher tax revenues efficiently and fairly, it would still permit the wealthy to be well rewarded without such a huge, widening gap. The salaries of some top soccer stars have become so high, it has become a kind of game where fans seem to enjoy seeing new records being broken (forgetting that this not only endorses the widening gap, it has made it a middle-class game from a spectator perspective).

I do not hold strong personal views on all of these issues; they are intended to illustrate that there are nonemotional and logical ways of looking at most, if not all, of these matters based on what is genuinely fair and equitable.

I think there is a case to say that the treatment of most people in the modern world is immoral, although in a way often consented to. It seems many humans have less freedom than wild animals. There needs to be contribution (and some hierarchy is natural and maintains order), but is the current state of society really moral in how it treats its members? There are many ways to make the system fairer but the "*selfish gene*" within the selfish man (usually men) will never let go of the status quo without a fight (read war). Despite the biased opinions of some, it is also far from a level playing field and many homeless, for example, did not have a good start in life or perhaps faced an unfair share of negative "*God's Dice*" (including mental health issues, which have a high prevalence amongst this community). The differing intent levels of all points of consciousness, mentioned several times previously, is the cause, but once people learn of the true power of their intent (inevitability) this all changes.

It is obvious that many humans are predisposed to immoral behaviour and I think the crime and punishment measures in place have little positive effect on society. Deterrents often do not work even if there is a threat of the death penalty. I suspect it is the last thing on the mind of many criminals before an act is committed. They may be aware of it, but in all cases, they will be so emotionally charged it is not really in mind much at all, and the motivation(s) clearly outweigh the potential/likely consequences. It is similar to the pleasure principle experienced by the brain tumour patient, who had immoral compulsions, but the driver in other examples may equally be uncontrollable rage.

It is naïve to believe the current system will ever work fully. There will always be crime. Always, unless there is some mass awakening. Therefore, the only option is to mitigate and, hopefully, a society that is fairer and encourages positive values will have a far greater impact on this than, often useless, punishments. I think if people reflect deeply, they will see that the fairly recent UK riots/looting was a manifestation of social discontent and not, in most cases, an indication of evil for evil's sake.

Many believe that the conditions in prison should be less humane because this will act as a deterrent. However, I do not believe that this is a consideration for a criminal for the reasons stated above. Stiffer sentences for more trivial crimes may have some small overall deterrent effect but it would not alter the behaviour of most. Also, as we have seen, not everyone has the same levels of free will (if it exists at all) so the whole issue is not as those with a strong moral compass would wish for. A *"prevention is better than cure"* approach would definitely be more logical and, in my view, more effective. Crime is very "cause and effect" oriented and evolutionary psychology can certainly explain most, if not all, of the behaviours that present themselves. And deeper thinking is definitely required to make improvements. Sometimes counterintuitive measures such as legalising drugs (i.e. permitting administration under supervision and for personal use levels only) have proven to reverse addiction epidemics, as opposed to the more obvious step of criminalizing the act and implementing useless deterrents.

The handling of crime and punishment is a very complex algorithm and not so relevant to the core meaning of life books/ theory of everything. In fact, it is also complicated by the fact that there are incentives to incarcerate people for petty crimes in order to access vast amounts of tax payer funds, where justice itself features low on the list of what happens to the offenders. However, what morality is and how it works is far more relevant to the meaning of life exploration.

In some Eastern cultures, there is a sense of communal shame as well as guilt. But the *"selfish gene"* is clearly rife in the West and the promotion of *"every man for himself"* (through both politics and culture) means a self-centred society which is unlikely to give rise to some kind of shared responsibility. We seem to have contradictory behaviours when it comes to "justice" and often emotions override logic. Two examples that illustrate this to some degree come to mind. One was the BP oil spillage. The most senior executive faced immeasurable pressure as a result of the event. I cannot imagine the mental toll placed upon him, especially in the wake of the event. Some may say that he is so well remunerated and made fully aware that *"you can delegate authority but not responsibility"* —he should be held responsible. Yet, when you look more closely at the situation, he has so many people in his employ and the firm has so many health and safety issues to contend with, can one individual truly control so many working parts?

He could have acted, in this regard, more prudently than anyone else who may have been directing instead. Yet, sometimes *"God's Dice"* happens, as we have highlighted many times over. If tight procedures were in place and there was clearly no malice aforethought, is this fair? It is like employing 100,000 staff—it is inevitable with such a population size there may well be rapists, partner beaters, and a whole host of other perpetrators of various crimes recruited. It is just impossible to have a zero-risk reality when *"God's Dice"* is at every turn. Acting in a reasonable manner and with a high-level duty of care should really be what is looked at when these things occur. But people like accountability, even if it means blaming the blameless. The leader may be so far removed from an employee who errs, that the blame (if applicable) should surely be directed towards the negligent party(ies).

On the other hand, if you consider the Piers Morgan phone hacking case, he uses as his defence *"I never hacked, I don't know how to hack and I have never asked anyone to hack."* Even if he was genuinely unaware of those in his employ doing such a thing (although **"…and I have never been aware of hacking" is conspicuous in its absence** in his statement), I believe, in this case, there should be responsibility at the top. A clear policy educating his staff that any "unethical activities" are against company policy and quite probably the law would have prevented this horrific situation. If there was any doubt whether an act was likely to be unethical or illegal, a procedure to refer the proposed action to senior management for clarification should have been implemented. This would remove the chance of Piers Morgan and other senior management from using the weak excuse of not knowing what was taking place throughout the company, even though it should be their responsibility to know anyway. It is reasonable to expect a leader in his industry to take such steps given the ethical minefield in which they operate.

It is possible the BP executive did an impeccable job and took every possible step to mitigate risks and assure the best possible procedures but fate conspired to have a disaster happen on his watch. If, on the other hand, he was shown to have fallen short in his duty of care and it had dire consequences, then, obviously he should lose his position and potentially face criminal charges. But the defence provided by Piers Morgan was weak and people should have paid more attention and shown more interest in what steps were in place for people in his employ to refrain from such acts.

One of the worst examples of an overlooked immoral act involved the actions of Donald Trump. During his bid for 2016 presidency campaign, he stood on stage and pointed at all the other candidates and said that he had paid every one of them, which meant that if he ever needed favours he need only pick up the phone. He was rightly showing that there was corruption, in that the acceptance of bribery was morally, if not legally, reprehensible. What most of the viewers seemed to fail to see was that he was also immoral for performing all these acts of bribery. The acceptance of money was wrong but so is the payment and the use of money to gain favours within the political arena. Loyal supporters may argue Donald Trump was bribing to gain favours on an ultimate mission to be a martyr. They believe that it is all part of his mission to *"drain the swamp."* Others just see him as part of the problem.

Justice is a tricky business. Even the timing of application hearings for parole is far more relevant than individual case circumstances. A morning judgement is significantly less likely to result in a positive outcome for the person seeking parole. The act of having recently had lunch and its effect on tolerance and empathy matters much more than facts in the matter. The proportion of those gaining positive outcomes after lunch is so high compared to those before lunch it shows, without doubt, the fallibility of the judges and the system.

The legal system itself is far from perfect. The weight placed on legal procedures is often greater than the apparent desire for justice. As illustrated in the movie, *12 Angry Men*, juries are also far from purely rational, non-prejudicial, nonemotional participants. When a highly qualified expert witness is appointed by one side, you can be fairly assured that an equally qualified expert witness will present diametrically opposing evidence. It is a far from perfect system, but while immoral behaviour exists, so must a legal system. Whilst humans exist so will fallibility in that system. This is to say nothing of the threats and corruption that also exist within the system.

Suzanne Carter, Editor, iDigitalMedium reminds us, as briefly mentioned earlier, that people do not necessarily seek financial equality or a system that lacks a form of hierarchy. She told me, *"One thing that really helped me to come to some logic-based decisions regarding ethics, equality, freedom, and public policy was a paper by Elizabeth Anderson (Chair University of Michigan's Department of Philosophy).*

The problem, she proposed, was that contemporary egalitarian thinkers have grown fixated on distribution: moving resources from lucky-seeming people to unlucky-seeming people, as if trying to spread the luck around. By letting the lucky class go on reaping the market's chancy rewards while asking others to concede inferior status in order to receive a drip-drip-drip of redistributive aid, these egalitarians were actually entrenching people's status as superior or subordinate. Generations of bleeding-heart theorists had been doing the wolf's work in shepherds' dress. In Anderson's view, the way forward was to shift from distributive equality to what she called relational, or democratic, equality: meeting as equals, regardless of where you were coming from or going to.

This was, at heart, an exercise of freedom. To be truly free, in Anderson's assessment, members of a society had to be able to function as human beings (requiring food, shelter, medical care), to participate in production (education, fair-value pay, entrepreneurial opportunity), to execute their role as citizens (freedom to speak and to vote), and to move through civil society (parks, restaurants, workplaces, markets, and all the rest). Egalitarians should focus policy attention on areas where that order had broken down. Being homeless was an un-free condition by all counts; thus, it was incumbent on a free society to remedy that problem. A quadriplegic adult was blocked from civil society if buildings weren't required to have ramps. Anderson's democratic model shifted the remit of egalitarianism from the idea of equalizing wealth to the idea that people should be equally free, regardless of their differences. A society in which everyone had the same material benefits could still be unequal, in this crucial sense; democratic equality, being predicated on equal respect."

This makes sense to some extent, and shows that even with a strong moral compass, the algorithms are so complex that it is nearly impossible for limited human minds to reach optimized fairness. The reference to 'lucky class' is perhaps best seen as a euphemism though, because many of the 1% that own 99% of the global assets didn't get there by chance or hard work, but by cheating the system. Although I would agree that most people do not seek equality or the abolishment of meritocracy, they do expect the abolition of corruption. Although Desmond Tutu was referring to the class distinction and racism in South Africa, I think one of his most noted quotations is highly relevant here: "*I am not interested in picking up crumbs of compassion thrown from the table of someone who considers himself my master. I want the full menu of rights.*"

I still think it is possible for future AI to take into account human needs, fears, and desires, etc. in order to help generate policies that, at least, tend towards optimal morality. However, there are too many powerful people with vested interests to believe things will turn around significantly until there is some mass "*awakening.*"

Morality is an important component that forms a key part of the meaning of life because everyone's behaviour has a direct or indirect influence on others. This is particularly obvious when it comes to mass conflict and wars. I think that the moral compass we often refer to exerts a genuine force that is actually felt at a deeper level than our biological senses. As Eckhart Tolle states: Our life is real but our life circumstances are not, therefore, in a sense none of the moral issues encountered are actually truly encountered. However, it still creates a kind of test and experience in the now, and the "life essence" of moral wrongdoers and their victims is certainly impacted but just not in the way that it seems in this mind conditioned realm where linear time is experienced.

16

CONSPIRACIES

"There's a big overlap between conspiracy theorists, racists, gun nuts, doomsday preppers, fans of the rapture and poor white Republicans. They all have one thing in common: They feel like the oppressed underdogs."

Oliver Markus Malloy

T hanks to the *"selfish gene"* (manifest as selfish behaviour by non-enlightened individuals), most conspiracy theories are feasible, even if the likelihood of any given one being true is probably quite low. Was 9/11 a *"false flag"* operation orchestrated by those who blame others or was it the result of genuine terrorism? There is an absolute truth. However, our reality certainly permits either scenario to be true. We can discount the supernatural situation where *both* realities are true, although this odd behaviour does happen frequently in the quantum world and with Special Relativity. All we can do, really, is know that there is an absolute truth that some people will know for sure and, as people receiving second hand information, allocate percentages to each possible scenario based on the evidence we have to hand. When Oliver Markus Malloy wrote the quote at the beginning of the chapter, conspiracy theorists may well have felt like the oppressed underdogs. However, 2020 has changed all that and now a significant minority see conspiracy theory as conspiracy fact. There has never been a time in history where diametrically opposing views have been so prominent in the world, to such an extent that it practically dominates everybody's life.

Even if someone who considers the chances of a false flag being true as impossible (*"no human could surely act so evil to his own race/community?"*), they have to allocate a small percentage to such chance because it would not be supernatural for it to be true. The subjective allocation of a fraction of a percentage chance to a conspiracy theory being real does not mean it will prove to be false. In light of the predisposition for people to lie and use propaganda, it makes this an identical dilemma to the one seen in the chapter on metaphysics (i.e. which are real phenomena, and which are not?).

Results of investigations, circumstantial evidence, potential confessions/admissions can all help lead to the truth but, often, there is such a complex web that the truth never seems to be assured. In the 9/11 case, an investigation of all those who did not turn up for work on the day of the event may be telling. Some will have had an accident on the way to work, some had prior dental appointments. There are many genuine reasons why they will have not been in work that day without prior knowledge of what was coming. If a significant number of those who did not turn up prove to be related to, or closely connected to, those who stand accused by the believers in the conspiracy, then weight would be added to the conspiracy theory but it would not be conclusive proof. It would be interesting to learn to what extent this has already been considered and reported upon. After some initial research, my suspicions were proven to be well founded as there are quite a few "coincidences" that would seem to indicate the possibility of prior knowledge. Likewise, when there are obvious motives for why those accused by the believers in the conspiracy could potentially act in the manner they are accused of, this cannot be ignored but, again, is not an assurance that the conspiracy theory is true.

This cartoon illustration is not suggesting that religions have been engineered specifically as a means to abuse the human predisposition to be led by their beliefs. However, it reminds us that religious organizations are a form of power and that power inevitably results in corruption. At least when it comes to unconscious ("asleep") human beings.

Often, people believe systems are built around such predispositions when there is merely a correlation, which is convenient and taken advantage of, as opposed to causation. For example, the idea that education is an innovation to assure obedience and slavery (wage dependence) or that the power structures and emergence of authorities were made to look like voluntary systems created by the masses so that the ones in power can maintain their selfish agendas. I am sure those who benefit from the status quo (governments, powerful corporations, the wealthiest 1 percent of the world, etc.) are generally content with the system as it is and recognize the happy coincidence that exists whereby the individual and societal behaviours of mankind suit their goals. Although, I am not so sure that it has been fully designed from the beginning to create and maintain slaves who are unaware that they are slaves, I am sure recent innovations have been. Alexander Warbucks said the following:

> "If you wish to keep slaves, you must have all kinds of guards. The cheapest way to have guards is to have the slaves pay taxes to finance their own guards. To fool the slaves, you tell them that they are not slaves and that they have freedom. You tell them they need law and order to protect them against bad slaves. Then you tell them to elect a government. Give them freedom to vote and they will vote for their own guards and pay their salary. They will then believe they are free persons. Then give them money to earn, count and spend and they will be too busy to notice the slavery they are in."

On the surface, this seems to capture the essence of our society. However, law and order are more a necessity due to the human (and animal) condition as opposed to something contrived as a means to assure powerful positions. Also, although many politicians are doubtless in it for the power, many are genuinely in it to seek positive change. The use of symbiotic behaviour assures societal contribution by the masses, for sure, but the introduction of money did not bring this about. Prior to the invention and use of money, work will have been equally prevalent. There is no doubt that the ability to store potential energy in the form that is money, allows for an abuse of the system and corruption is rife; but the apparent slavery referred to existed in ancestral (or contemporary tribal) communities and has not come about through the advent of a monetary system.

Of course, to maintain a standard of living (pay for shelter, food, entertainment, holidays, etc.) means that most people have to engage in what has been called the "wage slave" cycle/trap. However, this is really just a reflection of how nature works. The unfair aspect is more to do with how some can gain hugely disproportionate amounts of this potential energy (cash) due to the way the free-market economy works (which permits individuals to gain considerably more than their "sweat equity" investment should perhaps justify).

As mentioned, there is also a conspiracy similar to the one about us all being *"designed"* as slaves that relates to the teaching profession. It is often claimed that the education system is an intentional training ground to make the whole population subservient. It does seek to instill obedience and this is useful in the workplace, for sure, and many of the curriculum subjects are based on the enhancement of skills relevant to an industrialized society, rather than the development of creative intelligence. However, the motive is, at least in part, about a civilized and fairly ordered society where everyone benefits from learning more rather than a means to ensure compliance in our division of labour economy. There can be no denying that teaching assures better communication, sharpens logic, and enhances intellect. How it is done is certainly open to criticism and so are the subjects that neither reflect the need to encourage individual strengths nor have much relevance in the information age.

There is a huge amount of psychological child abuse in the past and present education system by virtue of its institutionalized practices. I did not dislike schooling but was very aware of its battery hen programming feel and disliked this intensely. Of course, it is hard to create a sense of freedom and teach effectively at the same time. And I am sure that the status quo is loved by many corporate institutions because it assures its owners and leaders the kind of effectiveness and efficiency that, ultimately, benefits them the most.

Some things that are portrayed as conspiracy are not so much theory but are actual fact. For example, what money really is. It is said that only about one in a thousand people understand what money really is (though, people are becoming more "awake"). Although it used to be backed against real assets (gold), it is now merely fiat money (only given value because of a consensus). Of course, if a starving man in a desert has pots of gold in one direction and food in the other (and he could only choose to collect the gold and die or collect the food and survive), we soon see that even the element we called gold is only of value once basic needs are met. It may have value in terms of its aesthetic appearance, rarity, noncorrosive nature, conductive properties. And even magical value—if the advocates of the alleged properties of monoatomic gold are to be believed but it is not a human essential. Fiat money is another level—mere cash and digital representations of potential energy, highly susceptible to the influence of cheats.

In the same way that we are hyper-normalized when it comes to our natural phenomena, we are also hyper-normalized when it comes to money and very few see it for what it really is. Low-value sweets and toys are purchased using "*tokens*" (cash) as a child and so it is little wonder it becomes something we blindly buy into and earn (via energy) and spend (gain the products of the energy of others). It is clearly a human invention as it is neither used by early ancestors, nor is it an essential system. It is, however, a great concept that allows people to acquire goods or services where they don't have something the seller needs in exchange. In fact, if it were not for the "*selfish gene*" which makes greed and corruption inevitable, it would be one of the world's greatest ever inventions.

According to anthropologists, the invention of money and taxes were not for the reasons that most people think. Money was apparently brought into effect as compensation for personal injury— whereby set amounts of "tokens" (money) was deemed payable by the person causing said injury. Taxation came about because the usual barter system could not work for transient soldiers so taxing people created a means to pay the soldiers (and, of course, the need to raise money to pay taxes meant people offering goods and services would accept money from soldiers). In communities where everybody knew each other, there was no need for money because IOUs were created and repaid via products and services and the use of memory facilitated such system (i.e. who owed who what for previous goods or services supplied).

There are too many conspiracies to mention in the book and most people know about the more popular ones. The more controversial ones claim that the moon landing was faked or that the earth is flat. I think that these are highly improbable and close to zero chance, respectively, although WikiLeaks has recently shown footage of the moon landing (or part of it) being filmed here on earth in keeping with what the *"conspiracy theorists"* have been claiming for years. But as we have discovered in the book our senses, human accounts (history), and seemingly our perception of reality itself are far from infallible.

Besides, all that appears to take place in our space-time reality has to be illusory (perceived but ultimately an agreed upon hallucination) based on the fact that linear time itself is illusory as Einstein had deduced, whereby individual points of consciousness experience what appears to be real but is nothing like base reality (from where perceived space-time arises). Even the fragmentation of Universal Consciousness (Mind) itself, which results in separate minds and egos, has to be a part of the grand illusion because without space-time only a singularity exists. This conclusion about reality makes the idea of conspiracies or otherwise a nonsense because whether the earth is flat or a globe in this "contrived" realm, ultimately, has no ultimate meaning because the realm itself is illusory. This does not mean that there cannot be truths within the illusion because there are clearly laws of nature that are pretty robust within the perceived physical multiverses (universe becoming) we are experiencing. This creates a kind of paradox in that everything experienced is illusory, whilst at the same time there are still universal truths within the illusion. However, this is little different from video games where it is obvious the construct and the rules are contrived but there is still a reality of sorts to all of it.

17

CONCLUSION

"Our Sun is a second- or third-generation star. All of the rocky and metallic material we stand on, the iron in our blood, the calcium in our teeth, the carbon in our genes were produced billions of years ago in the interior of a red giant star. We are made of star-stuff."

Carl Sagan

We have explored all aspects of the meaning of life: The function and purpose of life (including human life), the potential for a sense of meaning or otherwise in humans as well as its broadest definition, which I think is what most people mean when they ask, *"What is the meaning of life?"* (Namely, is there something more to our reality than birth, sickness, ageing, and death, and what lies behind our perception of reality as a whole?).

The answer to the function and purpose of life question is fairly straight forward (it is biological), although how the mechanics and the corresponding *"ingredients"* came about is an equally important and largely overlooked question in science. The function and purpose are complicated by the fact that organisms display more and more complex behaviour as we move higher up the food chain. This is especially so when we are talking about humans, due to the huge brain size (proportional to body size as well as its absolute size). Evolutionary psychology is useful in this case and because behaviours have evolved in the same manner as physical traits, this branch of science is generally very good at explaining our behaviours.

When it comes to a sense of meaning, some philosophers believe that such a sense is illusory because it appears to be a product of evolution (an adaptation to assure certain behaviours). I think this is a short-sighted view because it is just as real (probably more so) as the mind's interpretation of *"solid"* phenomena, which is always a mental model/approximation. It is quite clear that robots, without consciousness, would not be able to sense meaning (or, in fact, see/experience, say, the colour blue [only detect a corresponding wavelength], feel love, feel pain, etc.). There is no doubt that what is felt to be meaningful varies hugely from individual to individual. Biological functions generally result in a **sense of meaning,** too, showing that evolution has *"harnessed"* this fundamental state, if not created it.

Evolution in the illusion of duality is in the business of enhancing gene fitness by utilizing certain phenomena that are in proximity to an evolving organism. But it is incapable of absolute invention, as this would be manifesting a phenomenon from nothing. Think how profound it is that the experience of the colour blue does not exist in nature, therefore, has to be an unquestionable invention of consciousness (mind) itself. Due to hyper-normalization, the colour blue we experience just seems natural/real/*"out there."* How arbitrary and how profound that this experience, which is as distinct as any object, should manifest on the basis of brain stimulation. Meaning is just the same. It, too, is real but is an invention that cannot be explained by mutating DNA alone.

Someone who has completely lost their sense of meaning (e.g. through a mood disorder) will feel that meaninglessness is the true state and that meaning is just a mere illusion. It is impossible to sense meaningfulness and meaninglessness simultaneously and simply knowing what meaningfulness can feel like, based on past experience or the reports of others, does not counter feelings of meaninglessness. Mood and meaning should be viewed like space-time. An inextricably linked continuum. The greater the mood, the more the sense of meaning. One of the key take-home messages from the book, therefore, is that all appears to change when we change by giving value to ourselves and others simultaneously and by receiving value. In other words, much of the meaning of life is about mood and perception and, to a certain degree, these are within our control. In fact, as cocreators that ultimately reach a state which is the equivalent of the Source (Universal Consciousness), the power of intent is far greater than it is often perceived to be.

Mood disorders, such as depression, point the way to how reality works by removing certain consciousness "created" senses. But, in turn, I believe that this shows where the solution(s) for the condition lies also. The causes of the disorder are numerous. These will include a genetic predisposition that is then expressed by virtue of several negative life events, chemical imbalances, chronic stress and negative rumination, loneliness/lack of social cohesion (tribes), brain injury, certain pharmaceuticals (e.g. AIDs treatment), etc. The genes involved will certainly be multifactorial, therefore, neuroscience will likely only uncover all the permutations by utilizing computer programming expertise.

The cause of the symptoms is as much, if not more, to do with the mind rather than solely the brain. There is evidence that the brain disease which results in the symptoms of depression engages the pain-sensing system and also causes a feedback loop to occur. A "pain switch" is triggered and gets stuck. This causes neuronal damage which, in turn, contributes in keeping thinking stuck in negative rumination. This results in a loss of meaning, pleasure, drives, e.g. sex drive and possibly the sense of love in some sufferers too. This all adds to the vicious circle, making recovery difficult and protracted.

There are already many methods that can help alleviate the symptoms (not surprisingly placebo being one of them, because the belief aspect allows the mind itself to begin to repair the damage, which will often have had a proximate cause of thought(s) in the first place). The role of the mind would also explain why the following can help alleviate symptoms: Certain hallucinogenic drugs, pharmaceutical drugs, exercise, mindfulness meditation, talking therapies (altering negative thought patterns), etc. If the hypothesis is correct, then understanding the mind-body connection is the key to future prevention and cure and, in particular, methods of *interacting with both* in more efficient and effective ways.

Stephen S. Ilardi has done extensive research on the causes of depression and believes our current behaviours and the foods we eat are so different from those of our ancestors, it is a small wonder we are facing an epidemic. Humans have behaved in a certain way and eaten certain food types for thousands of years and we have suddenly thrust new habits and foods upon ourselves that our bodies and minds find harmful. Even wild animals, such as lions, have more freedom and relaxation time than we do and this indicates just how imprisoned we have become. This is clearly driven by societal expectations as well as, to a degree, being self-imposed. It is worth looking into his work and I will list this in the recommended reading section in the appendix.

There are many ways to achieve human meaning and many people manage to sustain meaning for a whole lifetime. As Victor Frankl wrote in *Man's Search for Meaning*, "*Everything can be taken from a man but one thing: the last of the human freedoms - to choose one's attitude in any given set of circumstances, to choose one's own way.*" He lived amongst fellow Auschwitz prisoners and saw the difference between those who were resilient and those that gave up the ghost. He realised that when people have a **big enough "why,"** they can face unimaginable challenges.

With the importance of human meaning in mind, Bhutan introduced Gross National Happiness into the political system (GNH being considered more important than GDP). Not only was the country initially laughed at, ironically, by many more advanced countries worldwide but the pursuit of happiness itself has been deemed shallow by some philosophers. The DNA *"game"* is not concerned for its host's happiness or fulfilment either. Unless one is excessively debilitated by the burden of excess unhappiness to such an extent it affects gene fitness, all is about survival and reproduction and anything else just gives the illusion of meaning. But this viewpoint overlooks the fact that meaning and happiness are genuine experiences/states, so who would not prefer to make these a crucial focus in life? Or at least joy, which is potentially more sustainable than fleeting happiness.

China, on the other hand, reportedly seek enhanced IQ amongst their race (via gene manipulation). But what is it to be faster, cleverer. and more efficient without it positively impacting meaning, fulfilment, and happiness? Human progress and efficiency generally just destroys its host, mother earth, more rapidly. Creating a race of efficient but not necessarily happy people is bad enough but creating more environments in which depression will likely continue to be considered an epidemic is morally unjust. Newton and Darwin (and Lincoln, Churchill, Dickens, Tolstoy, etc.) have all had an unimaginable impact on human knowledge and/or progress, but I would, personally, rather they had enjoyed happier lives rather than endured chronic debilitating depression, even if it had meant a lesser contribution by them. Of course, to be gifted as well as happy and fulfilled is better still. High intelligence generally means higher levels of introspection and so the risk of mood disorder has been found to be much higher. With advances in technology, mood disorders will one day be dealt with on a bespoke basis and may eventually become curable (so that treatment-resistant depression will no longer be a problem, and those who normally only enjoy improvement will go into full remission).

Many intellectuals are beginning to believe in the simulation hypothesis mentioned briefly at the beginning of the book. They think we may not be living in base reality. Elon Musk, the genius inventor and innovator, is amongst them. The idea is that in the not-too-distant future humans will have the capacity to create a simulated universe so realistic that the entities created within it will not know they are in a simulation. And if this hypothesis is correct, then some future race could already have created such universe(s) and we are the inhabitants (unaware of the fact we are in such a simulation). In fact, if future humans are likely to behave in this way and create a simulation that is indistinguishable from base reality, it isn't only likely we are in one but almost inevitable. This is because they would doubtless create many such simulations, and we would be statistically far more likely to be in one than be in base reality (whatever that is presumed to be in the hypothesis).

Advocates of a simulated universe tend to believe it is a future human race that is behind the programming but it could, of course, be any entities capable of making simulations, and they could be within a reality so far removed from ours that they are not subject to the same parameters that we are (what we see as self-created laws of nature, usually unquestioned and almost always seen as ordinary due to the hypnotic effect of familiarity). There are definitely hallmarks of programming in nature as discussed at length (DNA; the primacy of mathematics, etc.) and some Japanese mathematicians believe they have proof that we are in a holographic universe.

Whether we are in a simulation or a true reality would make little difference because we have "evolved" into sentient beings either way. But it would mean that the anger Stephen Fry levelled at God in his imaginary interview with Him that was referred to earlier, could equally be levelled at the simulation programmers. With that level of intelligence, they will have known the potential for the emergence of pain/pleasure sensing as a result of their coding and so the horror stories that Fry describes (and worse) would have been foreseeable. This would say a lot about their nature. Of course, given that biological evolution requires linear time and this is shown to be mind-made, the apparent heaven and hell circumstance aspects would also seem to be mind-made.

It could be argued that simulated entities (us) do not really have true pain (i.e. holograms with programmed perceived pain)—but there is still cause to say their actions are/were immoral and not amoral as even perceived pain is pain. Of course, another problem is who/what created our creator(s)? The issue here is that an unexplainable miracle would still be the ultimate cause regardless of the answer. And by the nature of how our reality is supposed to work it *HAS* to breach science's own rules. Accordingly, whether nature or some intelligent energy/force outside of nature created our reality— the process is still a miracle by anyone's standards. But what if it is solely Mind that is creating the heaven and earth via intent?

What I find paradoxical is that Professor Richard Dawkins is willing to consider the possibility of a simulated universe—and yet believes, with 100 percent certainty, that anything deemed paranormal is *impossible*. If we are in a simulated universe, it would be an extremely simple task to include so-called paranormal phenomena into the coding, so by accepting the possibility of one, there has to be an acceptance of the possibility of the other.

Because, it seems, qualia can only exist within consciousness and cannot be made by software models in the same way the wetness of seas or the molecular reality within a hurricane cannot; I believe that the simulation hypothesis is wrong. Or, if it is right, the simulation only provides inputs to our real senses—which means authentic consciousness is being stimulated by controlled/programmed inputs. Given that all our senses are stimulated by inputs that are radically different from what we experience them as (e.g. a wave changes to a colour that is nothing like the wave itself), we are all permanently locked within a hallucination regardless of whether it is the result of programming or some natural phenomenon. Throughout the book, I have evidenced the primacy of consciousness, and consciousness it appears, is both the programmer and the experiencer. The perceived evolutionary growth in brains correlating with a growth in minds, which permits a richer experience of the flowering consciousness/ evolving universe, as well as a means to potentially transcend the mind in order to directly experience pure consciousness that is not contaminated by the incessant thought stream.

Meditation and in particular mindfulness can have an impact on meaning. It has scientifically been shown to alter the brain anatomy and physiology and consequently mood. As one of the key themes of this book is about how meaning is intimately linked to mood, it is interesting to note that meditation practice affects meaning by virtue of it altering mood also. The whole concept of being more present also alters people's relationship with reality and is reported to give a greater sense of meaning.

Presence, The Power of Now, and mindfulness are synonymous. Eckhart Tolle admits in his book that his change of perception arose as a result of a kind of meltdown. He was suicidal and questioned, *"Who is the I that cannot live with myself?"*—and his subconscious seemed to process this and a new reality began. It took him many years to articulate what happened and realised that we are all suffering as a result of too much past and future mind projection. Thoughts, often negative and useless, creating negative emotional arousal. His meltdown, followed by enlightenment, is far from unique and other examples have been written about. One man lost his whole book transcript and subsequently had a bad fall too which resulted in him becoming a paraplegic. This is a real-life example of *"God's Dice"*— and also of how impact bias affects people, too, because after his mind accepted his position he became more at peace and, in fact, happier than in his previous state.

Some people advocate keeping busy, as this also can help to quieten thoughts about the potential for ultimate meaninglessness. They even suggest war is one such distraction (war experience certainly stays with people for life and, understandably, hijacks much of their consciousness for the rest of their lives). How perverse are the minds that wish for our reality to include war as a means of gaining a sense of purpose and as a way to avoid rumination? Likewise, many advocate becoming hardy because being *"soft"* perpetuates emotional suffering. This corrupted way of thinking speaks volumes about the evil of our apparent abject reality. I think being present and grasping a truer sense of reality is the way forward and the distraction method is merely a potential Band-Aid.

I know that beautiful empaths such as George Michael could not bear this illusory physical realm because their focus of attention consisted of a relentless flow of fearful information. Some may say that if empathic people like him had been raised more strictly, they would be a lot more resilient, and they would have more easily accepted the slings and arrows of life. However, it is reality and the perception of reality that needs adjusting not loving upbringing environments. Of course, given the definition of karma discussed earlier, it is clear that empaths, as cocreators, are greatly responsible for the *"out there"* reality (manifestations) they experience but the interactions of billions of subintents mean that full control of life circumstances is impossible.

Having said all of this, actually engaging in the world and not solely philosophising is vital to achieve meaning. Too much introspection and self-talk are the enemies when it comes to meaning, whereas *flow* and *presence* are the saviours.

All but the enlightened suffer Mind Affective Disorder (M.A.D.)—a total identification with the mind. Being present (*"the Watcher"*) helps prove this is so. Emotional pain arises due to a resistance to that which is (i.e. reality differing from expectations). Most, if not all, anger and depression are due to M.A.D. Not only is there a constant bombardment of useless thoughts (mostly negative) that stimulate fear and pain experiences, there is also a false belief that you are your mind-made construct: The job role, past memories, relationships, etc. are given too much gravity—the true *"self"* is much more than this. The true self is conscious awareness. And the solution to emotional problems lies in consistently being focused on the present. This practice is able to transform pain into joy. Reality only exists in the now—as the past and future are merely contemplated in the now (and are, therefore, covering over the now). This does not mean that passive acceptance is the answer as this undermines the fact that intent leads to manifestation in accordance with the intent(s).

Mindful meditation helps to train the mind for this practice but, in essence, it is about becoming aware, then acknowledging with heightened senses the present moment and then appreciating it. Also, feeling a sense of aliveness (e.g. tingling in the hands). The realisation that consciousness is always in the present moment and is the true you, as per the teachings of Eckhart Tolle, allows you to transmute suffering into joy. The so-called problems that seem to arise are external to this true you, as are the momentary times of happiness that arise whilst chasing conventional success.

Although this is a spiritual method to attain meaning, it is a truth that all who are close to death will experience. They will know that all the material gains and past successes mean less than they had thought and realise that the life element is/was what was precious. The real trick in life is to die before you die. Experiencing the infinite present moment also shows that there is no death and that there is only consciousness which transcends the optical delusion of separateness and mortality.

As Eckhart Tolle says, this is not about believing—it is about experiencing it for yourself and realising that the mind may be useful for human progress but is a curse when it comes to peace and joy. Likewise, Tom Campbell says that through transcendental meditation-based techniques, other true realms of reality can be accessed and experienced, including interactions with other beings in other physical and non-physical realms. Minds that are only open to western science's methodological naturalism will instantly dismiss this as impossible, without personal experimentation. Given all the evidence presented throughout the book that metaphysics is as valid as mainstream science and that there is compelling evidence demonstrating the primacy of consciousness, it a display of hubris to reject invitations to take a journey of discovery that costs nothing and purports to offer massive life-enhancing benefits. In fact, once any point of consciousness becomes aware it is equal to the Master intent, it enters the New Earth regardless of whether or not those *"left behind"* understand what this really means.

Eckhart Tolle's genius isn't in question but his teachings are over passive. It is true that it is futile to try and reject the *"isness"* of all that arises (i.e. *"this too shall pass"* is a truism, always), but given we are in the world albeit not of it, every effort should be made to overcome negative manifestations. Acceptance is a last resort. Placebo and other metaphysics should be a part of the non-passive tool box. Intent is everyTHING.

How will this book alter the paths of those who see the meaning of life, and who and what we really are, in a new light? I think the biggest barrier to change is the hyper-normalization effect, whereby there may be a shift in understanding but familiarity with the agreed upon hallucination prevents a full paradigm shift. For example, when I discuss in detail with someone about breasts as a pseudo gene fitness indicator in sexual selection within the realm of evolution-ary psychology (at this point you will have read what they really are in this book), how they ignite sexual arousal and why and how size correlates poorly with milk yield etc. there is no doubt a knowledge transfer. However, even when *"the penny drops"* and there is a result-ing look which often seems to be a combination of astonishment and the recollection of some long-forgotten memory, several minutes later when some rather large breasted lady passes by, I invariably get to witness the jaw of the newly informed person hit the ground as if all the words that had been in a foreign language.

I am, however, sure the book (and T.O.E.) will have a lasting effect once it becomes more widespread. Our perceived reality is like the chequered square shadow illusion…once you know it is an illusion you cannot do anything about it in terms of fully transcending it. It seems more people are recognising that there is something missing in the scientific worldview and that there is an underlying reality that is radically different from what our everyday experiences seem to suggest.

> *"Not everyone is ready for the message, the lessons, or the shift.... all we can do as a collective is to constantly be a conscious co-creator and attract more open-minded people. It is said you can lead a horse to water, but you can't force it to drink. But they will drink, albeit kicking and screaming, as the shift does not need their consent. Even the blind will soon see, literally."*

> *—Kristin Smith and M.H. Forrest*

It is worth pointing out here that a FULL understanding of base reality (The "Hux" Realm) does NOT preclude a person (soul) from enjoying the illusory duality. In other words, pleasures of the flesh. This is about "having your cake and eating it!" The Buddha correctly stated that, "ALL suffering is a result of attachment." What he meant was that if you lose a job, pet, lover, cherished car, the friendship of someone who does not resonate perhaps because they are far from being awake (when you are closer to truth), then when you realise that a) the "video game" never allowed true possession, b) you always deal with spirits in a perceived material world, and c) all that you see as OTHERS is actually YOU wearing another mask, then how can you feel loss? How can you feel division? How can you feel devoid of love? There is ONLY love and it takes enlightenment to know this because it is only punctuated with its opposite in this false world of duality.

Most of life's great secrets are not absorbed through the divulgence of meaning. It only becomes profound and, therefore, makes a difference to life, when a person is ready to absorb its significance within the context of a bigger picture and uses what she or he has learned in everyday life. It is similar to wisdom, which can be gained but, unlike with knowledge, cannot simply be transferred. There is enough scientific and empirical evidence to support the primacy of consciousness assertion in the book. How it is internalized and how it impacts each individual point of consciousness will depend on the quality and readiness of that consciousness. What is apparent is that many people seem to be awakening and science is also being forced to recognize its shortcomings. Most of what is written in the book is already evidenced, despite the beliefs of those who subscribe to methodological naturalism and time (illusory time), will tell whether the mass awakening will be sooner rather than later.

Life seems an odd mix of pseudo-randomness with no apparent goal and the emergence and evolution of consciousness which is goal driven by virtue of its inherent intelligence. It is a kind of energy becoming aware of itself whilst simultaneously experiencing rich senses and emotional states that consciousness in inorganic form is unable to experience in our reality. Yet, each individual point of consciousness in human form can suffer pain, and death comes too easily, not only to the individual but to mass numbers simultaneously through war, terrorism, disease and the like.

Billions of years of evolution to create each life-form and yet it can be shot down in seconds. Perhaps, this is only an issue for the animalistic egocentric self that does not see the delusion of separateness and cannot see that they are a part of a whole field of consciousness. But then, if everyone felt this, there would be no horror of war and terror. The debate over whether consciousness is fundamental or emergent (a consequence of evolution as it forms more complex minds) is irrelevant in this regard. We have potential empathy and strong moral compasses, therefore, there is at least a chance to transcend the amoral behaviour of other life forms, including that of our cousins, the chimpanzee, whose hardwired behaviours have left hard to erase fingerprints on our own nature.

There is a conceptual belief in nearly all scientists in an independent material world—yet, consciousness, like space-time, is both fundamental and has its own intrinsic freedom. **Whilst conscious-**

ness is left out of the equation, the core theory is and will always be incomplete.

Before materialists are quick to dismiss the notion that consciousness permeates and drives everything, they ought to consider the current state of cosmology, 27 percent of matter is said to be *dark matter* (a necessary phenomenon to allow galaxies to form as they have), and when combined with *dark energy*, which constitutes 68 percent (a necessary phenomenon to explain the accelerating expansion of the universe), less than 5 percent of the "stuff" in our universe is what we perceive and can measure as matter. Importantly, as mentioned earlier in the book, neither *dark matter* nor *dark energy* can be observed (or interacted with). However, cosmologists are certain of their existence because the physics simply do not add up without them.

The good news is that my T.O.E. fully explains this as you would expect for a Theory or Everything. It should already be obvious what is going on from the book you have just read. However, I have created five diagrams for book 2 that illustrate this in concise terms.

Consciousness is an invisible phenomenon that only reveals itself through form or influences on form. We cannot deny its existence, though, because it is responsible for our awareness of reality (including our senses, emotional experiences, colour perception, etc.). In the case of Random Number Generator influence, the effects can be scientifically measured. It is just a matter of time before materialism and reductionism are forced into a corner and the primacy of consciousness becomes recognized as the ultimate cause of everything, including the mysterious *dark matter* and *dark energy*.

It has never really been about *"God in the gaps"* but more about "Consciousness in the chasms." Both Universal Consciousness and animal consciousness/minds (especially humans) appear to create order from chaos, and we are likely at the dawn of a new age where science is going to face its most radical paradigm shift ever. There is already overwhelming evidence to help prove the primacy of consciousness, but as technology progresses, I am sure even material scientists are going to have to admit what Einstein said long ago: *"There is a superior Mind that reveals itself in the world of experience."*

Scientists seem to forget that **science is always several steps behind nature, never the other way around.**

Although answers to the meaning of life, in terms of the purpose of life and/or the human capacity to sense meaning are quite straightforward and have been discussed in detail, the challenge has been answering it in its broader sense (i.e. what is the meaning of life in terms of why is reality as it is and where might life fit into the larger scheme?). Based on the thoughts outlined in the book, I say the broader answer can be defined as follows: Reality emerges from Master Intent from the nonmaterial realm of consciousness. The consciousness of individual points of attention (subintents) then influences what appears to be randomness in subtle ways from outside space-time and the emerging order is a signature of the fundamental intelligence of consciousness. Ultimately everything is imagination but is governed by infinite intelligence and intent. Accordingly, when each point of consciousness becomes aware that it is part of I AM that, I AM—it yields the equivalent power of Master intent. However, it seems that it will take all points of consciousness to awaken before a New Earth is ushered in.

The transition from nonorganic to organic strengthens the effect, although, for life at a basic level the intelligence is manifest through the agent unconsciously. Higher up the food chain, the intelligence includes an awareness of the patterns as well as more advanced influence on the environment (and evolution). This extends to the metaphysical, such as the collapsing of a wavefunction prior to what would have been its predestined collapse (based on all the interacting subintents), a measurable effect on randomness and even the transcending of space-time by the minds of some.

Statistically impossible evolutionary manifestations are also the signature of this superior Mind (Universal Consciousness). Although, to the untrained eye, quantum mechanics seems to operate with pure objective randomness, the abstract state of coherence seems to be the perfect target for consciousness to slowly bring about order. Once individual points of consciousness have sufficiently complex minds, they compound the effect.

As there are infinite possibilities in the formless realm, outside the constraints of illusory space-time, the evolutionary change being witnessed here on earth would seem to pale into insignificance when compared to base reality, which is accessed by transcending the mind or passing away.

We all have one foot in space-time and one in the pure consciousness realm. For most people, the presence within the pure consciousness realm is only experienced subconsciously (similar to the vision outside of conscious awareness that controls motor function, as discussed in the book). This means they experience qualia but do not consider its true origins. Likewise, people engaged in the double slit experiment may cause the collapse of a wave-function by gaining information that, at a conscious level, seems to be future information (due to an inability to sense consciously that a part of their consciousness transcends space-time, as does the coherent particle until it is observed). This would mean that the space-time bound consciousness stays focused on the double-slit apparatus and time, whilst non-bound consciousness is entangled with the wave of probability of the particle and causes the space-time bound consciousness to witness an outcome based on which-way information having been observed.

This would also explain phenomena such as colour experience, as well as entanglement and phenomena, like pet dogs sensing when the journey home of an owner is commencing. It would also explain how the PSI wheel can be moved by mind (even at a distance from the wheel) because the distance between consciousness and the object is illusory. The reason that the force is weak is because it has to interact with perceived de-coherent molecules, which in the space-time realm have mass, despite the object moved by mind being quite light. Moving the wheel with our hands is not problematic because the consciousness, driving goal-oriented action creator within us, gets to harness biomechanical systems that are themselves made of matter, i.e. our bodies.

It also explains the existence of evil in the illusion of duality. The experiential realm that consists of mind consciousness in multiple forms has to feature duality for the experience to occur (just as it also requires space and linear time for differentiation to exist). Too much light and objects are not visible. Too much dark and the same is true. So, the blend of two is necessary and the same applies to colour perception which is even more dependent on this contrast. There has to be pain and pleasure, hot and cold, etc. Yin and yang are fundamental in order for the "*system*" to work. In the realm of pure consciousness (The "Hux" Realm) there is no need for space-time or duality, and this is precisely what near-death experiencers' report.

In exploring the meaning of life, the journey has effectively led to a theory of everything. The primacy of consciousness and the idea that space-time is an illusion (on a par with colour experience within our contrived realm) represents an unparalleled paradigm shift. It is not that space and linear time do not have a reality of their own but that they are "*designed*" to create fully immersive experiences for individual points of consciousness we call souls. Just as a video game or great film can take you from one reality to another, where the sense of your physical nature fades to nothing, the flowering of consciousness in illusory space-time hijacks your attention, taking it from the more authentic realm of no space-time into an elaborate holographic flipbook.

This does radical violence to our intuition and destroys the foundation upon which material science stands, namely its self-imposed belief in methodological naturalism. Scientism is as strong as any religious belief and material scientists will fight long and hard to maintain their belief. However, it is becoming clear that we are entering a post materialist paradigm.

The conclusion that this book and you, the reader, reside in an illusory universe, whereby the conscious essence, that is the true you, is part of an eternal now, would appear to be nothing more than fantasy if it were read without having looked at all the compelling evidence. A promise was made at the beginning of the book that the answer to the book title would be revealed. However, the evidence that forms that answer lies in the contents of the book as a whole.

We appear in biological form, which is also consciousness manifest, in a temporary illusory state, whereby, we are so deeply hypnotized by the flowering of consciousness that the true self is largely forgotten. It is only by transcending the illusion that an end to suffering can come about for each point of consciousness represented as sentient beings that temporarily reside in our perceived universe (in one of the infinite multiverses).

This has been worded beautifully by my friend Zanna Gold (The Angelic Ark): *"I've gone beyond ego and the mask. I see the mask as a separate cloning around me that tries to mould to my soul and its expression/psyche. I see the ego as an entity that tries its hardest to hold control over my emotions and views/beliefs, reactions, etc. including my health and well-being. I've broken the veil so see it all very clearly. I AM all love and light; the rest is a surrounding."*

Although the book gives a comprehensive account of *The Meaning of Life*, additional material can be found at my YouTube channels: *The Meaning of Life* by M. H. Forrest and *The Simple Truth* by M. H. Forrest

https://www.youtube.com/channel/UC2dMaviepWT-naAsYtaa8Ahg

https://www.youtube.com/channel/UCkBfTayGg-h7i3glX8O7zG1Q

Now you have completed the book, the following poem by my friend Troy should also hopefully resonate:

All rivers flow to the OCEAN
All raindrops yearn for the SEA
To be wrapped up as one in ITS motion
To lose that rain-droppy feeling of "me"
For a raindrop is part of the water
But the OCEAN is water much more
Its water in stillness and silence
It's the dream of all drops on the shore
Every "rain-droppy" feeling inside you
Each urge to itch, scratch, or drink
Is really the pull of your OCEAN
Though sometimes you feel on the brink
You're part of an ocean eternal
You just feel like a droplet of rain
And whether on desert inferno
Or green pasture you fall, all's the same
For water in droplets will transfer
To water in clouds once again
And water in clouds is the answer
When lit forest's cry out for the rain
So keep with your rain-droppy cycle
Keep thinking how we're all "unique"
While time pulls all raindrops together
To that OCEAN of birth that we seek
By Troy Hallewell

THANK YOU FOR
YOUR REVIEWS

If you enjoyed reading this book, please leave a review. Not only is a review the best gift you can give an author, it genuinely helps other potential readers who value independent feedback.

ACKNOWLEDGEMENTS

I AM truly grateful for all the help that has been given by my cousin, Richard Hughes. He has spent countless hours over many months debating with me some of the key issues in the book. We agreed on most issues in most cases, however, his method of diplomatically challenging me to force me to go even deeper has resulted in a far richer book. I truly believe that no book has been able to challenge scientific dogma (scientism) to the same extent this one has and if it was not for his tireless discussions, there may have been knowledge gaps.

Likewise, his sister, Rosamund Young, another much loved cousin, has helped in a similar way. She had reached similar conclusions to the book independently and it has been rewarding sharing our knowledge and understandings. A big thanks also to Kathryn Waldrom, who has inspired me to create some of the many Off Grid Entrepreneur/The Meaning of Life photo-quotes (memes) as well as being there as a remote spiritual guide on the book writing journey. Thanks also to my chief PA, Nuttapong Siriprom, for all the help with the book, whilst also supporting a number of the MHF Holdings organizations (including www.ITZA.Global). There are very few people able to manage so many processes over so many business sectors, let alone helping get a series of books (THE MEANING OF LIFE) to market in addition.

M. H. Forrest

BOOK RECOMMENDATIONS

The first recommendation is my upcoming book *The Meaning of Life – Up the Rabbit Hole*, which is book 2 in the series.

When I am not decoding the meaning of life, I am an inventor, visionary entrepreneur, and successful exec music producer (and last but certainly not least, a traveller). Accordingly, another upcoming book, which is part of the *The Meaning of Life* series, is mainly about business. The book introduction (audio) can be seen/heard on the Facebook Page of the same name: **"Off Grid Entrepreneur."**

Not surprisingly, evolutionary psychology (which is a key part of the *Meaning of Life* books) also underpins business behaviour. All business, without exception, is about meeting human needs that arise due to pain avoidance and pleasure-seeking drives. If you have an interest in entrepreneurialism (and matters such as intellectual property), then I hope you will check out this other upcoming book.

Off Grid Entrepreneur is book number 4 of 9 in the *MEANING OF LIFE* series. Book 1 is, *When the Black Dog Is Barking Up the Right Tree*. Book 3 is *The Simple Truth* (a simplified version of book number one and two, that delivers the same imagery and messages but in a less scientific way). Book 2, mentioned above, is *Up the Rabbit Hole*. Most people refer to taking a trip down the rabbit hole but this book is based on the premise that we enter the physical material realm from the truer realm (the rabbit hole). The second book continues on from book 1 by providing the additional scientific proofs like the ones contained in book 1 and focuses on the provision of greater detail.

Other forthcoming books by Off Grid Entrepreneur include *Complain! Get what you Deserve* (a way through the "by design" anti-justice tactics that persist in consumer goods and services and have strengthened in recent years), and *Manifest! Get what you*

Deserve (a course in manifestation techniques and Law of Attraction mastery).

The other recommendations are by authors that have contemporary views on "the black dog" (depression), spirituality, happiness, and positive psychology. The list is as follows:

The Positive Psychology of Synchronicity
by Chris Mackey

The Mindful Way Through Depression: Freeing Yourself from Chronic Unhappiness (includes Guided Meditation Practices CD)
by Mark Williams, John Teasdale, et al.

Happiness: A Guide to Developing Life's Most Important Skill
by Matthieu Ricard

The Power of Now: A Guide to Spiritual Enlightenment
by Eckhart Tolle

The Depression Cure: The Six-Step Programme to Beat Depression Without Drugs
by Dr. Steve Ilardi

Printed in Great Britain
by Amazon

79875354R00210